MAKING SPACE IN POST-WAR FRANCE
THE DREAMS, REALITIES AND AFTERMATH OF STATE PLANNING

LEGENDA

LEGENDA is the Modern Humanities Research Association's book imprint for new research in the Humanities. Founded in 1995 by Malcolm Bowie and others within the University of Oxford, Legenda has always been a collaborative publishing enterprise, directly governed by scholars. The Modern Humanities Research Association (MHRA) joined this collaboration in 1998, became half-owner in 2004, in partnership with Maney Publishing and then Routledge, and has since 2016 been sole owner. Titles range from medieval texts to contemporary cinema and form a widely comparative view of the modern humanities, including works on Arabic, Catalan, English, French, German, Greek, Italian, Portuguese, Russian, Spanish, and Yiddish literature. Editorial boards and committees of more than 60 leading academic specialists work in collaboration with bodies such as the Society for French Studies, the British Comparative Literature Association and the Association of Hispanists of Great Britain & Ireland.

The MHRA encourages and promotes advanced study and research in the field of the modern humanities, especially modern European languages and literature, including English, and also cinema. It aims to break down the barriers between scholars working in different disciplines and to maintain the unity of humanistic scholarship. The Association fulfils this purpose through the publication of journals, bibliographies, monographs, critical editions, and the MHRA Style Guide, and by making grants in support of research. Membership is open to all who work in the Humanities, whether independent or in a University post, and the participation of younger colleagues entering the field is especially welcomed.

ALSO PUBLISHED BY THE ASSOCIATION

Critical Texts
Tudor and Stuart Translations • *New Translations* • *European Translations*
MHRA Library of Medieval Welsh Literature

MHRA Bibliographies
Publications of the Modern Humanities Research Association

The Annual Bibliography of English Language & Literature
Austrian Studies
Modern Language Review
Portuguese Studies
The Slavonic and East European Review
Working Papers in the Humanities
The Yearbook of English Studies

www.mhra.org.uk
www.legendabooks.com

RESEARCH MONOGRAPHS IN FRENCH STUDIES

The *Research Monographs in French Studies* (RMFS) are selected, edited and supported by the Society for French Studies. The series seeks to publish the best new work in all areas of the literature, language, thought, history, politics, culture and film of the French-speaking world and to cover the full chronological range from the medieval period to the present day. Proposals are accepted for monographs of up to 85,000 words, while proposals for 'short' monographs (50,000–60,000 words), a traditional strength of the series, are still welcomed.

❖

PUBLISHED IN THIS SERIES

www.rmfs.mhra.org.uk

Making Space in Post-War France

The Dreams, Realities and Aftermath of State Planning

❖

Edward Welch

l

LEGENDA

Research Monographs in French Studies 69
Modern Humanities Research Association
2023

Published by Legenda
an imprint of the Modern Humanities Research Association
Salisbury House, Station Road, Cambridge CB1 2LA

ISBN 978-1-839541-81-0 (HB)
ISBN 978-1-83954-182-7 (PB)

First published 2023

Copy-Editor: Charlotte Wathey

CONTENTS

❖

ACKNOWLEDGEMENTS

❖

Making Space in Post-war France has been a long time in the making. The germ of the idea emerged when a French friend gave me a copy of François Maspero's *Les Passagers du Roissy-Express* before I headed for the Eurostar back to the UK. It was in the early days of the service when the train would flash through northern France to the tunnel before making more sedate progress towards Waterloo once out the other side. Reading Maspero's account of a journey of exploration along the RER B rail line while overtaking its distinctively tricoloured trains on the way out of the Gare du Nord, cruising past Roissy-Charles-de-Gaulle airport and running alongside the A1 motorway gave a sense of how the structures, systems and locations of French modernization during the post-war years had shaped French life and space, and of how they were predicated on accelerated movement as the route to civilizational advance.

The project's foundations were laid during my time as a Laming Junior Fellow at The Queen's College, Oxford, at the turn of the millennium, which supported a sustained period of archival research in Paris. Grants at different points over subsequent years from the British Academy, the Carnegie Trust for the Universities of Scotland and the Fondation Maison des sciences de l'homme enabled me to return to the archives as I investigated the rich and extensive array of material generated by the planners in the course of their work. Staff at the Archives départementales du Val-d'Oise in Cergy-Pontoise, the Archives nationales in Pierrefitte and the Institut Paris Région in Paris (formally the Institut d'aménagement et d'urbanisme de la Région parisienne, established in the 1960s to facilitate the development of the Paris region) have always been helpful and generous with their time during my visits.

My thinking about post-war spatial planning has been enriched over many years through conversations and collaborations in and on French space with a number of people, including Ari Blatt, Ruth Cruickshank, Lisa Downing, Alison Fell, Russell Goulbourne, Fiona Handyside, Michael Hawcroft, Jean-Pierre Le Bourhis, Chris Lloyd, Jonathan Long, John Perivolaris, Douglas Smith and the much missed Andrea Noble. Ari Blatt and Douglas Smith read chapter drafts with perceptive eyes, and I am grateful too for incisive input from Diana Knight and the RFMS Editorial Board. Graham Nelson was a pleasure to work with as the Managing Editor of Legenda, as was Charlotte Wathey, the copy editor. The book is dedicated to Sophie, for her love and companionship, and to Orla, who supervised.

E.W., Aberdeen, November 2022

ABBREVIATIONS

❖

CERFI	Centre d'études, de recherches et de formation institutionnelles
CGP	Commissariat général du Plan
CIAT	Comité interministériel permanent pour les problèmes d'action régionale et d'aménagement du territoire
CNDSQ	Commission nationale pour le développement social des quartiers
CNRS	Centre national de la recherche scientifique
DATAR	Délégation à l'aménagement du territoire et à l'action régionale
DGEN	Délégation générale à l'équipement national
DSQ	Développement social des quartiers
ENA	École nationale d'administration
ENPC	École nationale des ponts et chaussées
EPA	Établissement public d'aménagement
GCVN	Groupe central des villes nouvelles
HVS	Habitat et vie sociale
IAURP	Institut d'aménagement et d'urbanisme de la Région parisienne
INSEE	Institut national de la statistique et des études économiques
PADOG	Plan d'aménagement et d'orientation générale de la région parisienne
PARP	Plan d'aménagement de la région parisienne
RER	Réseau express régional
SARP	Service d'aménagement de la région parisienne
ZAC	Zone d'aménagement concerté
ZAD	Zone d'aménagement différé
ZUP	Zone à urbaniser par priorité
ZUS	Zone urbaine sensible

ILLUSTRATIONS

❖

INTRODUCTION

❖

A Space Odyssey

Suddenly, at the turn of the 1990s, it seemed that everyone was exploring and writing about French space. In May 1989, during the bicentenary year of the French Revolution, Anaïk Frantz and François Maspero arrived at Roissy-Charles-de-Gaulle (Roissy-CDG) airport. From there, they began a journey south along the length of the RER B rail line, alighting at every station along the way except those in central Paris. Their account of the trip, *Les Passagers du Roissy-Express* (in English, *Roissy Express: A Journey Through the Paris Suburbs*), was published a year later. At the same time, Annie Ernaux was accumulating the diary entries that would appear in *Journal du dehors* [Exteriors] (1993), which depicted her experience of life as an inhabitant of the new town of Cergy-Pontoise and a commuter circulating round the transport systems of the Paris region. She pursued the theme in *La Vie extérieure* [Outside Life] in 2000.

In 1995, Jean Rolin published *Zones*, placing his text under a title whose meaning oscillates between the prosaic demarcation of space for administrative reasons and the poetic evocation of marginal and non-conformist existence. It features a narrator who undertakes three trips round greater Paris for obscure and unspecified reasons. Circulating via the RER and the Métro through La Défense and other nodes in the network, he then sets out on foot to scrutinize the shifting forms, configurations and frontiers of the contemporary urban landscape, and the fortunes of people making their lives there. Rolin carried that mode of traversal investigation through a series of texts in the 2000s, expanding the scope of his narrators' explorations to include France's maritime borders and other points in the territory which reveal the complex set of economic and geopolitical forces at work on French space.

Meanwhile, a couple of years after Frantz and Maspero set out from Roissy-CDG, the airport appeared again in the prologue to *Non-lieux* (1992), anthropologist Marc Augé's influential essay about the peculiar proliferation of 'non-places' that were homogenized, corporatized, anonymized and otherwise evacuated of markers of identity and history. Augé imagines a corporate executive's journey from his home, via the cashpoint of his bank and the motorway network, to the airport's main terminal and a long-haul flight. The executive's seamless integration with different sorts of infrastructure reveals a form of 'supermodernity' that overlays yet is disconcertingly dislocated from the life in which it is embedded. Its bland reproducibility appears intent on eradicating heterogeneity in the relentless pursuit of efficiency, at least for those with the necessary PINs and other credentials.

The realities facing those less fortunate were finding expression on film in particular. In 1994, Malik Chibane released his first film, *Hexagone*, set in the unassuming suburban town of Goussainville lying under the flight path to Roissy-CDG. As the soundtrack captures the planes passing over on their approach to the runway, the film portrays the challenges faced by those stuck in the *grands ensembles* (housing estates) of the suburbs, especially the younger generations of Maghrebi heritage, and the ruses they must deploy as they negotiate their place in French society. In its gravitation towards the peripheral housing estate as the locus of social exclusion and alienation, *Hexagone* shared common ground with a number of other films, marking the emergence of what the French film press, following the high-profile success of Mathieu Kassovitz's *La Haine* the following year, began to call 'cinéma de banlieue' (Jousse 1995, Tobin 1995).

How to account for this shared reckoning with space over the course of a few years? In her defining study of French modernization during the 1950s and 60s, Kristin Ross argues that the unrest of May 1968 can be interpreted as a 'confirming afterthought, the event that certified the massive social upheaval and land grab of the decade that preceded it' (1995: 3). Similarly, the urban unrest that broke out in peripheral housing estates during the 1980s confirmed the radical transformation of French space during the post-war period, not least by revealing how social problems of exclusion, marginalization and discrimination had taken on a distinctively spatial form. The growing political recognition of France's socio-spatial problem was reflected in the Mitterrand government's Développement social des quartiers [Social development of neighbourhoods] programme (DSQ), which ran alongside architect and *soixtante-huitard* Roland Castro's Banlieues 89 renovation scheme, and its subsequent creation of a ministry for cities in 1991. Then as the 1990s progressed, under successive right-wing governments, France's problems of space were increasingly framed and treated as a problem of national security (Dikeç 2007, Tissot 2007). At the same time, the spatial uncertainties of the period found expression in the proliferating number of texts and films concerned with the look, feel and implications of urban change and modernization. In their common preoccupation with spatial forms and urban life, we can read a form of collective negotiation with the nature of modernized French space.

Certainly, this is how Ernaux accounts for the writing of *Journal du dehors*. Her ability to start writing about Cergy-Pontoise, albeit through a fragmentary mode, was the sign that she had achieved a sort of psychological adaptation to life there; that she had emerged from the psychical shock — the 'schizophrenia', to use her term — into which she had been plunged by the new town (1996: 7). Nevertheless, the fact that her text adopts a fragmentary form itself bears witness to the transformational nature of that adaptation. Fragmentation, it seems, is the form best suited to the nature and experience of life in Cergy. Moreover, as the focus and settings of *Journal du dehors* indicate, our cluster of texts and films from the early 1990s have some more specific ground in common. They bear the imprint of the systematic spatial planning (*aménagement du territoire*) that flourished especially during the presidency of Charles de Gaulle (1958–69).

Aménagement du territoire represented a concerted attempt to create the conditions for French modernity through spatial organization and development. In the words of Olivier Guichard, a close political ally of de Gaulle and first director of the Délégation à l'aménagement du territoire et à l'action régionale [Delegation for spatial planning and regional action] (DATAR), it made manifest 'la volonté précise d'une collectivité qui pense son organisation générale en fonction de ses ressources territoriales' [the precise will of a collectivity that reflects on its overall development in the light of the territorial resources at its disposal] (Guichard 1965: 14).[1] The DATAR had been established by presidential decree in 1963 to coordinate spatial planning and regional development across the national territory. Its brief included the development of the country's physical infrastructure, from motorways, port zones and hydroelectric dams to new tourist resorts on the Atlantic and Mediterranean coasts. In a sign of the strategic and political importance of *aménagement du territoire* for de Gaulle's government, Guichard reported directly to the prime minister.

Meanwhile, 1965 brought the publication, by the Délégation générale au District de la région de Paris (DGRP), of the *Schéma directeur d'aménagement et d'urbanisme de la région de Paris* [Master plan for spatial development and urbanism in the Paris region]. The *Schéma directeur* was overseen by Paul Delouvrier, the man at the centre of the decision-making action on the cover of this book. A senior civil servant who had spent two years as the government's representative in Algeria between 1958 and 1960 (the first civilian holder of a post until then occupied by the military), Delouvrier was appointed *délégué général* for the Paris region in 1961. Like Guichard at the DATAR, he reported directly to the prime minister. Taking the year 2000 as its horizon, Delouvrier's *Schéma directeur* mapped out a new airport at Roissy to the north of the city, a ring of new towns to divert population growth away from the city centre, one of which was Cergy-Pontoise, and the RER rapid rail network to connect them all.

Gaullist spatial planning was modernization as megastructure. In its desire to spread modernity across the country, it envisioned circulation and flow through a complex system of nodes and networks whose material forms as airports, motorways, rapid transit rail lines and new towns would create the landscapes depicted subsequently by Maspero, Ernaux, Augé and others. Yet as the work of these writers suggests, the monumentality of Gaullist spatial planning meant that it was almost too big to see. Such was its reach across the territory that it framed everyday experience to the point where the system became lost from view. More obvious instead to those navigating it on the ground were its constituent parts: the RER station, the train carriage, the bus stop, the flyover, the airport terminal. Often as well, we get a feel for the phenomenological distinctiveness of life in France's modern spatial systems, whether it be the smooth glide of the RER train into the underground amphitheatre of Charles-de-Gaulle-Étoile station, the disorienting turns of a shuttle bus round the curving service roads of the airport terminal, or the panoramic view that opens up as the car crests a rise on the motorway.

1   All translations are my own unless otherwise indicated.

From that point of view, perhaps the most provocative gesture made by Anaïk and François in *Les Passagers du Roissy-Express* was to use the RER system otherwise from how it was intended. They disrupt the imperative to circulate efficiently by getting off at every stop, having a walk around, telling and hearing stories about what they find.[2] Indeed, stepping beyond the system soon revealed the extent to which the project of French modernization remained unfinished, uneven and, in a number of respects, almost unhinged in its scale and ambition. As Jean Rolin's narrators also show, movement on foot brings to light what modernization leaves out and what it leaves behind, its afterthoughts and leftovers, the things which resist its transformative power.

Anaïk and François discover that exploring the vicinity of Roissy-CDG airport means navigating from the sleek supermodernity of its main terminal, via the endless loading bays of the Garonor logistics hub, to a network of informal footpaths crossing open land nearby taken by people pursuing their own inscrutable itineraries. 'Il existe comme cela aux confins du monde des contrées apparemment inhabitées où l'on voit parfois surgir sur les routes des gens qui cheminent vers d'improbables destinations' [often at the ends of the earth, in apparently uninhabited regions, one encounters people on the road travelling to unlikely destinations] (Maspero 1990: 45). In Aulnay-sous-Bois, a couple of stops to the south, they meet residents of a housing estate built in 1970 for a Citroën car factory whose anticipated levels of employment never fully materialized (1990: 49–50).[3] Marooned away from the rest of the town on the other side of a motorway, the residents struggle with problems of long-term unemployment, delinquency and drug abuse. In the RER B, whose schedule is determined by a carefully calibrated system of train movements, the uncontrollability of the world nevertheless asserts itself. To their dismay, the network's engineers cannot understand why the tunnels and platforms around Châtelet-Les Halles are pervaded by the smell of rotting vegetation (1990: 8), as if the ghost of the food market that once stood there was coming back to haunt them.

Maspero's text, along with the others, is about living with, interpreting and interrogating the outcomes and consequences of decisions taken by the *aménageurs* over the preceding three decades or so, fuelled as they were by the sustained period of growth that came to an abrupt end with the global oil crises of the 1970s. Those decisions, in producing complex new built environments on a monumental scale, would shape and influence how millions of people went about their lives for decades to come. They were technical and administrative, but driven too by a striking political, ideological and moral investment in the idea that civilizational advance could be achieved through the organization and physical transformation of space; that done properly, spatial planning had the power to make dreams of the future a present reality.

2   On the modalities and ethics of travel in *Les Passagers du Roissy-Express*, as well as their ambiguities, see Silverman 1999, Ridon 2000, Forsdick 2005a and Milne 2006.
3   Between its opening in 1973 and 1989, Aulnay produced Citroën's technologically advanced DS and CX models, whose status as emblems of French modernity we will encounter at various points. Production at Aulnay ended in 2013 and the plant closed in 2014.

Much has been written in France about *aménagement du territoire* as an area of public policy or a set of aims and outcomes. From that point of view, it frequently emerges as a domain of rational territorial management in which the French state sets out to exercise its command over the space of the nation for the collective good.[4] Yet far less attention has been paid to the distinctive philosophy of time, progress and futurity that informed its Gaullist iterations in particular, and at times seemed redolent of science fiction. Meanwhile, work outside France has adopted a more distanced and critical perspective on spatial planning, alert to the dynamics of power in which it is bound up, and its disciplinary functions as a mode of government (Busbea 2007, Newsome 2009, Cupers 2014, Paskins 2016, Wakeman 2016). But some key protagonists get only passing attention, such as Paul Delouvrier, whose command of the *Schéma directeur* for Paris on his return from Algeria illuminates the continuities between French colonialism and modernization. Likewise, the philosopher Gaston Berger, whose curious notion of *la prospective* influenced people like Pierre Massé, head of the French national plan and as such in charge of directing France's search for modernity through economic and spatial development.

Here lies the extraordinary drama of France's post-war modernization, one that *Making Space in Post-war France* sets out to explore. How was it that a relatively small group of individuals could produce epic transformations that still frame and inflect the daily lives of millions, for better or for worse? How did they conceive, envision and express their ideas? What do their activities reveal about the relationship between space, state and power in France, and what do they tell us about the (over-determined) role of space in the French political imaginary? At the same time, the book turns to the sphere of cultural production as a place where those transformations have been captured, registered and displayed. It considers how literary and visual cultural forms have evoked, portrayed and digested France's modernized environments and the experiential changes they bring with them. Sometimes they do so directly, but oftentimes they do so obliquely or unconsciously, through the settings they depict or the characters they deploy.

In examining the nature of post-war spatial development, its effects and its representation, my book pursues the analysis of French modernization begun by Paul Rabinow (1989) and Kristin Ross (1995).[5] More accurately, it pursues their interrogation of the *project* of French modernity, one rooted philosophically and politically, as Max Silverman reminds us, in the Enlightenment and the French Revolution (Silverman 1999: 1–4). In *French Modern*, Rabinow demonstrates how

---

4   Many such accounts, which often have authority as academic textbooks or overviews for the general reader, have been written by actors in the field or closely aligned with it. Jérôme Monod, Olivier Guichard's successor at the DATAR, was the original author of the volume on *aménagement du territoire* for PUF's *Que sais-je?* series, currently in its eighteenth edition (Monod & Castelbajac 2021). Pierre Merlin, who combined roles as an urban planner in state administration with an academic career at the Sorbonne and other Parisian universities, has written one of the standard textbooks on the subject (Merlin 2002). Olivier Guichard wrote the preface for a history of *aménagement* by Desportes & Picon 1997. Both are graduates of the École nationale des ponts et chaussées, France's national engineering academy, where a number of those involved in post-war spatial planning were trained.

5   With all due modesty, bearing in mind the huge influence of both works.

France in the nineteenth and twentieth centuries was shaped by an investment in urbanism and spatial planning as privileged realms for rational action on the world. With the implementation of an array of techniques and practices in related fields (hygiene, statistics, demography, architecture, engineering) came the possibility of producing and maintaining 'a healthy, efficient, and productive social order' (1989: 11). As such, the regulated cities birthed by urbanism 'can be seen as one of the most complete examples of modernity' (1989: 12).

A crucial factor as well is the centrality of space and territory in the political imaginary of the French nation state, enshrined as the principle of the 'one and indivisible Republic' in the first article of the Revolutionary constitution of 1791. The physical development of the national territory would become one of the most tangible ways of asserting and consolidating that political principle over the course of successive French republics. It is thus no surprise to find Guichard describing *aménagement du territoire* as a 'symbole par excellence de l'unité nationale' [one of the most powerful symbols of national unity] (1965: 246). Nor indeed that *aménagement* became such a focus of attention for the Gaullist Fifth Republic as it navigated its way through the territorial reconfigurations required by decolonization and worked its way back into the hexagonal frontiers of metropolitan France.

Yet in many ways, the Gaullist preoccupation with space was more fundamentally about time. If French modernity was conceived as a project, then it was in the literal sense of projecting the country forward in time. The route to futurity lay through the physical development of space. And those spatial forms would in turn help shape the feel of the future. The book homes in on Gaullist spatial planning's preoccupation with the future, the ideas which informed it, and the unexpected way in which a domain seemingly governed by technical expertise and rational thinking gave itself the freedom (and power) to dream. The planners went boldly into the future as they imagined how life would look in 1985 or 2000, then set out to bring their imaginings to life in the present, with more or less success. Certainly, they were not alone in doing so. Larry Busbea (2007) has shown that French experimental architecture during the 1960s and 70s positioned itself as a radical alternative to the state's spatial planning programmes; but *Making Space in Post-war France* draws out how the state's own planners were themselves fuelled by visions of the future, and moreover, had the resources to bring them into being.

Kristin Ross underlined one obvious explanation for the French preoccupation with the future in *Fast Cars, Clean Bodies* (though we will also see that others are in play). In the midst of France's painful and protracted departure from Algeria, it reflected a desire (avowed or otherwise) to untangle decolonization and modernization, and assert a sequential relationship between them (Ross 1995: 6). Colonialism could be left behind as a 'dusty archaism' (1995: 9), while the loss of imperial power and influence was converted into the gain of becoming an advanced European nation whose status was expressed through technological sophistication. Berger's notion of *la prospective* provided philosophical sanction for the relegation of the past and a resolute focus on the future. Meanwhile the increasingly frequent turn to the hexagon as a figure of speech for the nation during the 1960s smoothed

France's post-colonial transition through its associations with geometric precision and its demarcation of a clearly defined territorial domain.

Gabrielle Hecht (1998) has demonstrated how France's investment in nuclear energy, necessitated in part by losing access to the Algerian oil and gas fields, can be understood in terms of swapping the figurative *rayonnement* of colonial expansion and the 'civilizing mission' for the rather more literally radiating power of the atom. *Aménagement du territoire*, conceived as a way of engineering the future into the present, became freighted with similar political significance. By improving efficiency and speed of circulation, infrastructural developments like the RER and the motorways became both means and symbol of the country's acceleration into the future and away from the past.

Yet modernization and decolonization remained stubbornly, persistently and inevitably entangled. Their very real continuities were embodied in figures like Paul Delouvrier, whose role overseeing the Plan de Constantine, France's last-ditch attempt to promote economic growth and maintain colonial authority in Algeria through urban planning and development, foreshadowed his involvement in the *Schéma directeur*; or Bernard Hirsch, a graduate of the École nationale des ponts et chaussées [National academy of bridges and roads] (ENPC) who made his career as director of public works in Mali and Mauritania before he returned to France, taking on responsibility for the construction of Cergy-Pontoise in 1965. Indeed, when we turn to the creation of the new town, we will see that Hirsch drew quite freely on his colonial experience to discuss Cergy's development and the life it could offer.

Marxist spatial theorist Henri Lefebvre was quick to point out that modernization and spatial planning could disguise a form of internal colonization by the state (Lefebvre 1970), down to the recurrence of shared discursive tropes like 'under-development'. If spatial planning displayed colonial reflexes, it was because they were both fundamentally concerned with the management and control of territory, populations and resources. Though in fact, as Rabinow makes clear in his account of General Lyautey's urban planning experiments in colonial Morocco in the first decades of the twentieth century (1989: 277–319), those reflexes were already part and parcel of the broader project of French modernity and its conceptual, discursive and practical forms. Their return home with France's engineers and administrators after decolonization marked the end of a long odyssey. Going out via the colonies had honed them further and left them ready to enable the great leap forward of post-colonial France.

Simultaneously, much of the transformative *labour* of French modernization during the 1950s, 60s and 70s — the hard graft of construction, manufacturing or road building — was undertaken by immigrant workers, particularly from Algeria and the other (former) North African colonies.[6] Their children, French

---

6   On the role of immigrant workers in the French construction industry during the post-war period, see Paskins (2016: 65–71). Paskins notes that by 1967, nearly half of those employed in public works were of immigrant origin (2016: 66). The largest constituencies were from southern Europe (Italy, Portugal, Spain), North Africa (Algeria, Morocco, Tunisia) and West Africa (Mali, Mauritania, Senegal). While formal caps on arrivals from Algeria were introduced after independence in 1962, it

citizens by birth right, would struggle to lay claim to a place in the post-colonial Republic during the 1980s and 90s and on into the 2000s. Instead, they would find their politically and socially marginal status in French society reflected in their relegation to peripheral locations in the metropolitan territory. In many respects, as Todd Shepard (2006) has argued, their situation could trace its roots back to the hurried political, legislative and administrative efforts to enact France's separation from Algeria in 1962. Its mobilization of definitions of French identity based on race and ethnicity ('Europeans' versus 'North Africans') would continue to haunt what Shepard terms 'post-Algerian' France (2006: 15). For all that Gaullist spatial planning aspired to ensure national unity through an even development that would neutralize conflict based on class, the legacies of France's colonial project had resulted in a much more complex demographic, social, cultural and ethnic reality that the country was failing to recognize and assume (Hargreaves 1995).

The tensions of that reality were captured in Malik Chibane's appropriation of the hexagon for the title of his first film, motivated by a desire to assert France's post-colonial populations as constitutive of the contemporary French republic: 'voilà pourquoi *Hexagone* était un titre provocant: je ne prenais que des Beurs et disais l'Hexagone, c'est ça' [that's why *Hexagone* was a provocative title: I was showing only Beurs on screen and saying, that's what the Hexagon's about] (Marchais 1995). They would reach something of a logical conclusion in the autumn of 2005, when the right-wing government of Dominique de Villepin, seemingly now willing to revisit at least some aspects of France's colonial history, reactivated legislation drafted during the Algerian War in order to declare a state of emergency during the riots that broke out across the nation's deprived suburbs.

In *Making Space in Post-war France*, then, I set out to investigate the production of space in post-war France: how it happens, what its mechanisms are, where the power to make it happen resides, as well as its longer-term consequences, intended or otherwise. I begin in the 1950s and 60s, when economic expansion made it easy to dream about the future and Charles de Gaulle, freshly returned to power in 1958, found in *aménagement du territoire* a means of giving material form to his sense of France's grandeur. The 1970s and 80s are a time when modernized forms and backdrops surface regularly in literary and visual culture; but they are also the period when economic recession, deindustrialization and economic globalization displace dreams of the future with a mood of crisis. Between them, globalization and the socio-spatial problems created by modernization provoke challenges of territorial integrity for the state that persisted into the 1990s and on into the new millennium. Rather than an impression of space in time, oriented towards the future and shaped for movement and circulation, came a sense that space had somehow stalled. The emphasis falls on boundaries, frontiers and territorial divisions, signalled by the appearance of figures of speech like 'zones' and 'fractures' in administrative and political discourse.

was estimated that by 1965, some 300,000 Algerians were working in France formally or informally (2016: 67). As Paskins goes on to discuss (2016: 90–123), many immigrant workers lived in *bidonvilles* (shanty towns) whose peripheral locations marked out the terrain of the *grands ensembles* that would gradually displace them.

In Chapter 1, I consider the political, ideological and philosophical foundations of *aménagement du territoire* as it took shape in the context of post-war reconstruction, exploring the development of the French national plan in the 1950s and 60s and its relationship to Gaston Berger's notion of *la prospective* as a form of anticipatory planning. In Chapters 2 and 3, I turn to Delouvrier's *Schéma directeur* and the building of Cergy-Pontoise in the 1960s and 70s in order to think about spatial planning as a form of power, its mobilization of discursive and other representational forms, and the curious way in which it resides between the discursive and empirical domains. I am interested in how planners use texts, images, maps and models to imagine new worlds and bring them into being, creating new empirical realities in the form of built environments and spatial organizations. I am interested as well in the stories they tell about the aims of spatial planning, and what those stories reveal about the philosophies and ideologies that inform their work.

At first glance, this might look like quite well-mapped terrain, located as it is at a nexus of disciplines including urban geography, urban planning and architectural history; but coming to it with a background in literary and cultural studies reveals some important lacunae. For example, several recent histories of post-war French urban planning and architecture (Busbea 2007, Cupers 2014, Vadelorge 2014, Wakeman 2016) are certainly alive to the diversity and volume of representational material generated by the planning process, and put it on display in their accounts. Similarly, the past two decades or so have seen a growing recognition of the centrality of narrative and other representational practices in spatial planning amongst planning practitioners and theorists (for example, Throgmorton 1996, Debarbieux & Lardon 2003, Sandercock 2003). Yet with the notable exception of Kory Olson's *Cartographic Capital* (2018), on the emergence of a cartographic regime of planning in relation to Paris, there still remains very little in the way of close critical analysis of what we might call the discursive apparatus of spatial planning, and how discourse and representation are mobilized in the production of space.

Here is where the critical methods of literary, visual and cultural studies can be useful, attentive as they are to the workings of language, image and other semiotic forms, and the centrality of discourse and representation in articulating our perception of the world. Drawing on these methods, I consider the terms in which the planners envision the future; the ways in which they express their understanding of how a territory and its population can be organized and governed; and what happens when ideas about time and futurity begin to shape territorial organization and spatial production. I bring that material into dialogue at various points with French cultural production. In Chapter 4 especially, I examine how the manufactured landscapes of French modernity begin to surface in cultural forms during the 1970s and 80s, and how they evoke the nature of modernized space as it frames and moulds everyday life. In Chapter 5, I home in on the zone as a key term in French spatial discourse. I explore its striking migration across a range of discursive fields, from the military to the poetic via the administrative and the . political, and how its ambiguities capture the tensions and anxieties inhabiting attitudes to space in France.

As my lines of enquiry would suggest, unpicking the dynamics at play in spatial planning involves reaching for some key French thinkers on space, territory and government, including Henri Lefebvre, Michel de Certeau, Michel Foucault, Gilles Deleuze, Félix Guattari and Paul Virilio. If I do so, it is because crucially, as Verena Andermatt Conley also observes (2012: 4), their ideas were forming in relation and in response to developments in France at the time. On a number of occasions, in fact, they serve as a direct commentary on them. Kristin Ross points out that 'theoretical categories are not free-floating devices, innocent of historical content' (1995: 5). Ross was reflecting on the emergence of everyday life as a critical concept during the 1950s and 60s. But the same can be said of the growing concern with space, territory, state power and practices of government in the later 1960s and 70s, one sharpened most recently by the events of May 1968: first through the transgressive appropriation of public space by the protestors when, as Virilio puts it, 'inhabiting became an offensive revolutionary act' (1976: 84); and second through the subsequent and inevitable repression of that act by means of police violence.

Such is the collective influence of French thinking about space on the humanities and social sciences over the past few decades, and so varied the contexts in which it has been deployed, that it is easy to lose sight of the extent to which its origins lay in the specific situation of post-war French modernization, whether it be Foucault's work with Deleuze and Guattari on infrastructure as a technique of government, or de Certeau's analysis of practices of daily life as forms of resistance to spatial planning (both projects, incidentally, funded via government research contracts during the 1970s as the state sought to plan its way beyond the societal antagonisms laid bare in 1968).[7] French spatial theory, along with work it has inspired in urban geography, planning studies and related fields, opens the way for a critical understanding of *aménagement du territoire* as a regulatory practice of government, an expression of state violence, a (persistently fraught) negotiation between state and capital, and a gendered realm of predominantly male action. Tellingly expressed by our cover image of Delouvrier in committee with his prefectural colleagues, all of these themes surface throughout the book, and in Chapter 2 especially. At the same time, I set out to keep in play the ambiguities and tensions inhabiting spatial planning as an enterprise, and not least the fact that it can be a manifestation of state violence *at the same time as* it is an expression of hopes fuelled, in the *Schéma directeur*'s own terms, by a desire to create the conditions for a happy life (DGRP 1965: 27). In short, I explore planning as a human adventure, carried out by historically-situated people filled with their own imaginings, dreams and desires.

As such, *Making Space in Post-war France* joins work in urban and architectural history by Kenny Cupers (2014) and others (Newsome 2009, Vadelorge 2014, Wakeman 2016) in seeking to navigate past the hermeneutics of suspicion that often

---

7   The 'spatial turn' in the humanities and social sciences originates in the work of geographers such as Edward Soja (1989) and David Harvey (1985, 1989) who pioneered Anglophone engagement with the spatial thinking of Lefebvre and Foucault. Indeed, one of the spatial turn's curiosities is that its profoundest influence has been on geography, that most spatial of disciplines. The arrival of French theory seemed truly revelatory, as if it afforded a sudden vantage point on the discipline that allowed geographers finally to see what it was all about.

informs spatial theory and sees *aménagement du territoire* above all as an oppressive or disciplinary form of state action. Thus, Lefebvre's monolithic view of the state as an all-powerful actor in *La Production de l'espace* [The Production of Space] (1974) (reinforced by the capitalization of the term: the state is always 'l'État') occludes human agency, and the fact that the state is constituted by a host of bodies both individual and corporate who interpret and enact spatial planning according to their own perceptions, education, shared practices and competing interests. Meanwhile in *L'Invention du quotidien* [The Practice of Everyday Life] (1990), Certeau champions the plucky agency of the displaced individual faced with the structures imposed by state-led planning, while taking for granted the imposition of those structures by 'la Raison technicienne', as the cover blurb has it, a remote and faceless technocracy similarly granted force through capitalization.

That is not to say that the outcomes and material forms of post-war French spatial planning have not been alienating or socially detrimental. On the contrary, in fact. At various points in the book, I explore ways in which they are portrayed as such, and how a sense of alienation is captured in literary and visual culture. But I also want to understand how they might nevertheless be conceived with other effects and affects in mind, as enabling of liberty, community, fulfilment or self-expression. Equally, if I resist a mode of analysis grounded solely in a hermeneutics of suspicion, neither do I set out merely to recuperate planning action, nor to narrate French spatial planning, as a straightforwardly heroic and progressive domain of activity — the sort of narrative told by Peter Hall (1988) in his classic (and classically patrician) history of urban planning, or indeed by many of the (male) French planners themselves.[8] Doing so would in any case be misconceived in the wake of feminist critiques of planning as a domain of male desire and power by Barbara Hooper (1992, 1998), Leonie Sandercock (1998) and others.

In other words, *Making Space in Post-war France* seeks to maintain a more interesting sense of the complexity of French spatial planning and production in the journey from the heady confidence of prospective thinking in the 1960s to the confused and uncertain attempts to piece space back together again in the 1980s and 90s as the legacies of that confidence were confronted. What emerges, in effect, is a form of excavation of the unconscious of the French state and its imaginary relationship to the territory under its dominion. At stake is its preoccupation with creating territorial order and system (or, to borrow terms from Deleuze and Guattari, with processes of spatial striation and territorialization); how that order is conceived and what material forms it takes; why *zones désertiques*, empty quarters, *terrains vagues* and other 'unproductive' areas become points of fixation; or how, when challenged by the economic forces of globalization in the 1980s and 90s, the state displaces its energies on to transforming ragtag bands of youths in the *banlieues* into a threat to national security, one it eventually seeks to contain by deploying neo-colonial measures of territorial management.

The social and spatial crisis of the suburbs became the most apparent outcome of French modernization towards the end of the twentieth century. It also brings us

8   On such narratives, see Gaïti 2002, Vadelorge 2005 and Welch 2018.

to a second, more figurative sense of making space in post-war France, or perhaps more accurately, the failure to do so successfully. To make space is to make a gesture of accommodation. In a literal sense, that gesture was about 'housing post-war France', to draw on the subtitle of Cupers' book, as the most urgent task of reconstruction and modernization after the Second World War. But making space is also about giving room, about finding a place for all those who constitute the population assembled within a given territory. It is primarily France's failures of accommodation, both literal and figurative, that have crystallized over the decades since the project of French modernity enjoyed a last burst of energy. They find their most telling expression in the fact that a (policed and dislocated) place on its spatial and social margins represented the extent of the hospitality France seemed willing to extend to its post-colonial populations.

If the *problème des banlieues* has dominated discussion of space across French cultural and social studies over the last two decades or so, it is because of the fundamental questions it raises about the French project. A republican ideology forging a singular national identity on a unified national territory has demonstrably struggled to accommodate the consequences of its own history, something manifested in the plural realities of a globalized and postcolonial France, tense negotiations over belonging, integration, hospitality and marginalization, and a significant body of scholarship investigating those consequences.[9] *Making Space in Post-war France* does not set out to make a direct contribution to that work: it is not another book about the *banlieue* and its representation per se. Rather, its aim is to fold the specific spatial forms of the *banlieue* — the *grand ensemble*, the *quartier*, the RER station — back into the broader context of spatial production in post-war France, a context sometimes lost from view because of the extent to which the deprived urban periphery dominates the horizon of debate as much as it does the visible horizon.

In doing so, the book proposes a more nuanced sense of the intricacy of post-war French space, the different pressures at work upon it, and how those pressures manifest themselves in co-existing yet often conflicting spatial forms. Hence its investigation into the shifting uses of the zone as a trope of territorial management, and the ways it structures suburban and other spaces discursively, administratively and politically; or how the presence of Roissy-CDG airport in depictions of peripheral urban life serves to bring different moments of spatial production and modes of contemporary existence into dialogue. And we will see how French culture captures the reach of modernized space across the territory, from the urban to the rural via the strange hybridity of the peri-urban and the speed space of the

9   The literature on France's urban peripheries is vast, bound up as they are with broader cultural, social and political questions. On the *banlieue* in literature and film, as well as the intersection of space, ethnicity, gender, marginalization and integration, see Carpenter & Horvath 2015, Dobson 2017, Durmelat & Swamy 2011, Hargreaves 1995, 1997, 2011, Levine 2008 and Tarr 2005 among many others, along with references in Chapter 5. Rosello 2001 explores portrayals of immigration from the perspective of hospitality, its limits and failures. Met & Schilling 2018 offer a historical perspective on cinematic portrayals of the *banlieue* which underscores the diversity of suburban space.

motorway.[10] Modernized space is revealed to be often unobtrusive in its presence, but subtly significant in how it shapes our understanding of life and its possibilities.

By way of conclusion, I consider where French space finds itself as the twenty-first century advances. With Nicolas Sarkozy's Grand Paris project unfolding as a neoliberal reprise of Delouvrier's *Schéma directeur* (Enright 2016), environmental activists transformed the planned location of a controversial airport at Notre-Dame-des-Landes near Nantes into a *zone à défendre* [zone to defend], achieving an astonishing victory in 2018 when the project was abandoned. Later that year meanwhile, the so-called *gilet jaune* (hi-viz vest) protests, driven by anger over rising fuel prices among rural, provincial and peri-urban populations, made eye-catching moves to occupy roundabouts, recognizing their strategic significance as nodes of transport infrastructure. Both movements bring into focus new understandings of peripheral and marginal territories in France, and the sorts of tactical incursions that can be deployed as forms of protest.

The odyssey of space and spatial planning is one of post-war France's defining narratives. It has shaped the country in a real and material sense, and its legacies continue to play themselves out politically, socially and culturally. *Making Space in Post-war France* seeks to capture something of the epic scale of Gaullist modernization, but also what historian Vincent Guigueno calls its 'strangeness' (2003: 41). We will encounter the planners' startling faith in the possibility that ideas for the present can be brought back from the future, and how manifestations of France's future-in-the-present end up resembling memories of a dream of the future from the past. Our story brings back into the frame some actors often lost from sight, yet whose ideas and actions had a profoundly transformative effect on how French space is perceived and lived. It unpicks the material and discursive forms taken by planning ideas, how those forms produce space and territory, and how in doing so, they engender socio-spatial tensions. It reflects on how literary and visual culture can help us grasp the transformation of space in post-war France and its impact on life. To begin, it explores how the vision of modernization takes shape, and the sometimes quixotic ideas that lie behind it.

---

10   On modernity and modernization in rural France see also Levine 2019 and Farmer 2020.

CHAPTER 1

❖

The Prospective View:
Space, Time and Planning

Between Space and Time in Post-war France

Writing about visions of mass utopia in the liberal democratic West and communist East during the twentieth century, Susan Buck-Morss argues that 'space has absolute priority in the political imaginary of nation states' (2000: 22). Time, on the other hand, is the fundamental concern of revolutionary movements. Nation states think and imagine themselves spatially: their concern is to establish, maintain, develop and defend, not to say extend, a territory and the population it contains. Revolution (and specifically class-based revolution, for Buck-Morss), 'is a historical event understood as an advance in time'. What counts above all in moments of revolution is 'historical progress rather than territorial gain' (2000: 23).

The history of republican France offers an intriguing illustration of Buck-Morss's argument. Having secured epochal change through class revolution in 1789, and attempted to reset time by means of the revolutionary calendar, the Jacobin republic proceeded to define itself legally and constitutionally in spatial terms as 'one and indivisible'. This emphasis on the republic as a corporate entity blended the popular collective as singular revolutionary agent with the territorial domain they shared. It was a domain they would be called upon to defend through the revolutionary wars beginning in 1792, as the political and military logic of the republic as nation state rather than revolutionary moment took hold.

At the same time, asserting the link between territorial unity and national identity gave space and territory an over-determined role in the French social and political imaginary, and meant that subsequent moments of national crisis would be figured and articulated in spatial terms above all. This was particularly the case in the circumstance where France had to reposition and reimagine itself geopolitically after decolonization, defined by the symbolic caesura of Algerian independence in 1962, a revolutionary moment to equal that of 1789.

The conclusion of the Algerian War, after eight years of revolutionary struggle (from the Algerian perspective), or attempts to defend the nation's territorial integrity (from the French point of view), saw France on the losing side of history, insofar as the desired outcome of revolution is historical progress. A sense of Algerian independence as a rupture with the past can be found in Kristin Ross's description of France 'having decisively slammed shut the door to the Algerian episode' (1995: 9). Its increasingly troublesome colonial activities could be consigned to history as it pulled back within its metropolitan borders. Ross makes telling use of a spatial figure (door as barrier or barricade) to describe the temporal break that defines the emergence of post-imperial, post-colonial France. For an immediate consequence of the epochal change marked by Algerian independence, as in the Revolutionary period, was an emphasis on space and territory as the primary means through which a strong national identity could be articulated and (re)asserted.

The need to reimagine the country within its metropolitan frontiers was signalled, as Eugen Weber observes, by the growing use of the figure of the hexagon in political and public discourse during the 1960s (Weber 1997). Indeed, in a contemporary article on its use and history, Nathaniel Smith noted how the Gaullist UNR party deployed a logo incorporating the hexagon for its campaign posters during the 1967 legislative elections. That it did so suggested that political capital could be mined from the connotations carried by the figure: 'of schematic regularity, its three maritime borders blue, its three land borders red, it symbolized the national strength, prosperity, and unity promised by the UNR' (Smith 1969: 150). It was as if the necessary historical reckoning of decolonization had at least enabled a means of figuring France that could mask the reality of territorial retreat through an image of geometric precision and sleek newness. Indeed, the intricate connection between the two things is captured neatly in the title of André Trintignac's *Aménager l'hexagone*, published in 1964, which makes explicit how the project of spatial development (*aménagement*) had as its aim the shaping and definition of a new territorial entity (hexagonal France).[1]

The UNR's desire to mobilize the hexagon for a message of national strength through territorial unity reflected the fact that *aménagement du territoire* had become one of de Gaulle's key political strategies following his return to power in 1958. Paul Delouvrier had been appointed *délégué général* of the new Paris District in 1961 and gained prefectural status in 1966 to coincide with the implementation of the *Schéma directeur*. Olivier Guichard had become the inaugural director of the DATAR in 1963. The creation of these roles, as well as their elevated position within the government hierarchy (each reporting directly to the prime minister) confirmed the strategic importance of *aménagement du territoire* for the Gaullist regime and its steady integration into the broader apparatus of French planning.

State planning was a cornerstone of post-war governance in France. The Commissariat général du Plan [General Commission for Planning] (CGP) was established by de Gaulle's provisional government in January 1946. De Gaulle appointed Jean Monnet, who would go on to be a key architect of the European Community, as its first *commissaire*. The declared function of the CGP, as defined in its founding government decree, was to organize 'la modernisation et l'équipement

---

1   Trintignac's text makes no attempt to explore or explain the figurative reference in its title, from which we could draw one of two conclusions: either that it was so common a trope of public discourse that it needed no clarification; or (more likely at that stage) that to do so would mean evoking the recent geopolitical crisis from which the hexagonal France had emerged. I return to the figure of the hexagon and its implications in Chapter 5.

économique de la métropole et des territoires d'outre-mer' [the modernization and economic infrastructure of the mainland and overseas territories] (*Journal officiel*, 4 January 1946, cit. in Bauchet 1966: 341). It would do so via a series of multi-year plans, the first of which (le Plan Monnet) was published later in 1946.

Ideas about *aménagement du territoire* were developing in parallel. Like the impetus behind the CGP, they in fact had their roots in initiatives developed during the wartime Vichy regime. For, notwithstanding the radical political divide separating the Vichy regime under Marshall Pétain from the post-war Fourth and Fifth Republics, there were important conceptual and ideological continuities between them in terms of asserting the need for a rational and efficient organization of the national territory. As Paul Rabinow notes, the defeat of 1940 and the demands of the German occupiers were the catalyst for plans to better 'equip' the territory with different forms of infrastructure as part of a programme of national renewal (1989: 1–2). The Délégation générale à l'équipement national [General Delegation for National Infrastructure] (DGEN) was established in 1941, and published a Plan d'Équipement National the following year.[2] As Rabinow also observes, the development of the plan marked the point at which a 'technical elite' began to play 'an enduring structural role in the French state' (1989: 2), one that would become increasingly significant during the post-war decades.

In broad terms, while *équipement* can be understood as the building of physical infrastructure in all its forms, *aménagement* implies the systematic organization and distribution of those structural elements as a part of a strategy of territorial and thereby national development. The notion gained wide public exposure in 1950 with the publication of *Pour un plan national d'aménagement du territoire* [For a national plan of territorial development] by Eugène Claudius-Petit, minister for Reconstruction and Urbanism. His *brochure verte* [green paper] represented the first attempt within government to set out the principles of a national strategy for territorial development, and established him as a pioneer of the subject in France.[3] Claudius-Petit also set about reorganizing the ministry to create a new Direction de l'aménagement du territoire, making national spatial planning (as opposed to mere infrastructural 'equipment') an explicit focus of government action for the first time.

The need for a strategic approach to the country's development and modernization had been articulated vividly a few years earlier by geographer Jean-François Gravier in what would become a famous essay. *Paris et le désert français* [Paris and the French desert], published in 1947, had been commissioned by the first minister for Reconstruction and Urbanism, Raoul Dautry. Its eye-catching and provocative title captured the essence of Gravier's argument, that France suffered from a fundamental imbalance between Paris and the provinces. The capital city had been allowed to grow too much and too chaotically, while the rest of the country was

2   On the DGEN and the Plan d'Équipement National, see Kuisel (1981: 146–56).
3   The document's canonical status is signalled (and further reinforced) by its inclusion in a compendium of *Les Grands Textes de l'aménagement du territoire et de la décentralisation*, published by the DATAR (by then renamed the DIACT) in 2003 to mark its fortieth anniversary (Alvergne & Musso 2003: 127–34).

left in a state of economic, technical, demographic and social under-development. The key aim of reconstruction and modernization should be decentralization, stimulating industrial and economic activity across the whole country, and through that, enabling a more balanced population distribution, at once easing the pressure on Paris and promoting the growth and development of the provincial areas.

Claudius-Petit in turn felt that reconstruction represented an opportunity for what he termed, addressing the National Assembly in 1950, 'une orientation intelligente des activités nationales en vue de satisfaire les besoins réels du pays' [the intelligent organization of the nation's activities in order to satisfy its real needs] (*Journal officiel*, 13 June 1950: 4696). His concern was that the opportunity was being missed. Claudius-Petit had come to his ministerial role by an unorthodox route. Born in 1907, he had no formal training in architecture or urban planning, starting out as a cabinet maker before qualifying as a drawing teacher. Like many others who held high political and administrative office in the post-war period, he was active in the French Resistance, and joined de Gaulle's provisional government in Algiers in 1943. There, he participated in discussions about questions of post-war reconstruction and planning, and secured an appointment to a new Centre d'études et de recherches en urbanisme [Centre for study and research into urban planning] established by the national research council, the CNRS (Pouvreau 2003: 44–45). Having initially been overlooked for the new Ministry of Reconstruction and Urbanism in favour of Raoul Dautry (ultimately better qualified, as an engineer and minister in pre-war governments), he was finally called to the role in 1948. Nevertheless, there was a sense that his lack of formal training or expertise in the domain would often count against him. As he remarked in 1944, 'je ne suis pas assez chevronné aux yeux d'un certain nombre de personnes' [I am not suitably qualified in the eyes of certain people] (Pouvreau 2003: 46).

Claudius-Petit positioned *aménagement du territoire* conceptually (and inevitably, therefore, politically) in opposition to the CGP's approach in its first plan. The immediate aims of the Plan Monnet were to re-establish France's industrial and economic base, returning to and then surpassing pre-war levels of production as quickly as possible. One consequence was the focus on sectorial modernization and 'équipement économique' expressed in its founding decree (particularly in relation to the coal and steel industries), rather than an overall strategy of territorial development (Girardon 2006: 34). In contrast, Claudius-Petit argued in *Pour un plan national d'aménagement du territoire* that the focus should switch from questions of rebuilding the economy and modernizing industrial production to the strategic development of the territory as a whole.

Claudius-Petit defined *aménagement du territoire* as 'la recherche dans le cadre géographique de la France, d'une meilleure répartition des hommes, en fonction des ressources naturelles et des activités économiques' [the search within the geographic framework of France for a better distribution of people, determined by natural resources and economic activity] (Claudius-Petit 2003: 131). He then went further: the aim of national territorial planning should not simply be to ensure strong economic development, but to attend to and foster the wellbeing of the country's citizens:

> Cette recherche est faite dans la constante préoccupation de donner aux hommes de meilleures conditions d'habitat, de travail, de plus grandes facilités de loisirs et de culture. Cette recherche n'est donc faite à des fonds strictement économiques, mais bien davantage pour le bien-être et l'épanouissement de la population. (2003: 131–32)

> [The constant aim of that search is to give people better living and working conditions and better facilities for leisure and culture. It is not done purely for economic reasons, but for the population's well-being and development.]

There was no benefit to economic development if the consequence was 'un cadre de vie médiocre' [a mediocre quality of life] (2003: 131).

However, Claudius-Petit struggled to impose his vision of a coordinated approach to national spatial planning during his time at the ministry. Moreover, as Benoît Pouvreau notes, his policy agenda was quietly shelved once he had left his post in 1952 (Pouvreau 2003: 43). A glimpse of Claudius-Petit's difficulties is afforded by the parliamentary debate on his ministry's budget at the National Assembly on 13 June 1950. While the *Journal officiel* recorded that his account of the principles and aims of *aménagement du territoire* was met with 'applause on numerous benches' (*Journal officiel*, 13 June 1950: 4696), the immediate concerns of the deputies taking part in the debate were more with the continued practicalities of reconstruction, and in particular the post-war housing crisis (*la crise du logement*), than with Claudius-Petit's grander strategic ambitions.

Indeed, when the deputy Jean-Paul Palewski invited Claudius-Petit to outline his conception of *aménagement*, he remarked that 'il serait intéressant pour l'Assemblée de connaître votre position à cet égard *tant sur le plan de l'urbanisme qu'en matière d'habitation*' [the Assembly would be interested to hear your position on the matter *in relation both to urban planning and housing*] (*Journal officiel*, 13 June 1950: 4695, my emphasis). Like several other deputies who intervened that day, and notwithstanding his evident sympathy for Claudius-Petit's idea, Palewski was translating it back into more established and recognizable categories (*urbanisme* and *habitation*). The themes and terms of the debate suggested that the political, discursive and administrative conditions were not yet in place for Claudius-Petit's more expansive sense of territorial planning and development to gain the necessary traction.

Attempts were made to include regional development as part of the second Plan (1952–57). But while eight regional plans were published, only three had been approved by 1957. It was finally the fourth Plan (1961–65), under the direction of economist and engineer Pierre Massé, that incorporated territorial planning more explicitly, in the form of a concerted emphasis on regional as well as sectorial development, and an acknowledgement of the need to expand the purview of planning as coordinated action across the territory as a whole. The shift in thinking was confirmed by the creation in 1963 of both the DATAR and the Commission nationale de l'aménagement du territoire [National commission for territorial development], which undertook more long-term strategic planning as part of the CGP. Indeed, the simple fact that the term was enshrined in the name of these new administrative bodies was itself a demonstration of the central place it had now acquired within government, thirteen years after Claudius-Petit had published his *brochure verte*.

The increasing emphasis on *aménagement du territoire* within planning activity was in many ways entirely logical. The development and production of space across the territory (as new infrastructure, new urban centres, or other forms of built environment) would be the most visible manifestation of planning as a concerted effort of organization in the name of the nation's modernization, progress and renewal. It was also where the planners' sense of *aménagement* as a form of what Massé, addressing the National Assembly during a debate on the fourth Plan, termed 'prospective geography' could achieve its fullest expression. By identifying key trends in the present and using them as the basis for long-term projections — as far ahead as 1980 or even 1985, suggested Massé — it was possible to orient, gear and drive the country towards its future (*Journal officiel*, 29 May 1962: 1359).

Furthermore, the political stakes of *aménagement du territoire*, or perhaps more accurately, the possibility that spatial planning could fulfil political ends, were also becoming clear. If policy initiatives need the right political conditions in which to develop (and conversely, politics gravitates towards particular ideas at specific historical moments), then it was during France's Gaullist decade, and the first half of the 1960s especially, when a set of economic, political, intellectual and ideological circumstances converged to give *aménagement du territoire* the political traction it had not previously managed to acquire. Guichard signalled as much in his 1965 essay, *Aménager la France*, when he described *aménagement du territoire* as a 'symbol' of national unity (1965: 246), spelling out the relationship between territorial development and national identity.

Moreover, if territorial unity was the key to securing the country's political unity (best served implicitly, from Guichard's perspective, by the Gaullist status quo), it was because spatial development, by enabling better distribution of the national wealth, could help neutralize class antagonisms. As Guichard puts it, making explicit reference to two key social categories, 'l'ambition de l'aménagement du territoire est de faire que la richesse nationale soit mieux répartie, que l'expansion profite autant au citadin qu'au rural, à l'ouvrier qu'au paysan, aux habitants d'une région à ceux d'une autre' [the goal of spatial planning is to ensure that national wealth is more evenly distributed, that growth benefits those in the city as much as those in the country, workers as much as farmers, the inhabitants of one region as much as another] (1965: 245). The best defence against the epochal disruptions of revolutionary time lay in consolidating space: strengthening the structural fabric of the national territory (what Trintignac nicely describes as its 'armature'), and producing the spatial equilibrium which would produce social equilibrium in turn.

Now, it is certainly the case that space is to the fore in reflections on French modernization, a sense given visual and discursive consistency through tropes like the hexagon, or the use of maps and cartographic diagrams in an array of different publications. Punctuating the text of Guichard's *Aménager la France*, for example, are outline maps of the metropolitan territory (showing departmental boundaries, but not always Corsica, and never France's remaining overseas territories), with data visualizations of population density, the regional influence of different cities, or population flows between Paris and the provinces. Their repetition helps to establish hexagonal France as the theatre of action, while also creating the visual impression of a contained space whose defined form implies a controllable environment.

Yet lurking not far beneath the surface in Guichard's text is a persistent concern with time as much as space, and in particular with the time of the future. Guichard puts it eye-catchingly, in a moment of brio that presents spatial planning as something approaching the essence of futurity: 'l'aménagement ne vit pas dans l'époque présent: il doit toujours la devancer, projeter sur l'avenir' (1965: 26). One step ahead of the present, spatial planning could glean insights from the future and use them to shape the country's direction of travel. As such, spatial planners were positioned at the vanguard of efforts to modernize France and orient the country resolutely towards an ever-brighter horizon.

In foregrounding spatial planning as a discipline of and about the future, Guichard joins Massé in echoing a recurrent theme amongst post-war French planners, who are preoccupied to a striking degree with questions of time, temporality and progress. In particular, Guichard's evocation of planning as a step beyond the present reveals the influence of the philosopher Gaston Berger, and his notion of *la prospective* as a form of future-oriented thinking. Berger coined the idea in the 1950s, and it rapidly gained currency amongst those at the heart of the enterprise of French state planning (Durance 2007). The fact that the concept of prospective thinking had become an established part of political discourse by the mid-1960s, mobilized not just by Guichard, but also by figures such as Georges Pompidou as prime minister and Valérie Giscard d'Estaing as finance minister, signalled the extent to which it had gained consensus and become part of the governing orthodoxy. Its reach also meant that it could have a profound influence on how planning activity took shape, and how the nation's fresh start would be enacted and produced.

The enthusiasm for prospective thinking that developed amongst the planners in the 1950s and 60s was certainly intellectual, but also had a significant political and sociological dimension as part of a broader modernizing agenda. Those involved in state planning were among a new generation of post-war civil servants, many of whom, like Claudius-Petit, had spent time in the French Resistance during the Second World War. This had given them a strong sense of public duty, but also an impatience with established ways of working, as well as a frustration with the political and economic status quo as an impediment to France's reconstruction and modernization.

The creation of new state institutions like the CGP (in 1946) and the École nationale d'administration [National academy for administration] (ENA) (in 1945), where a number of those involved in planning would either study or teach, created opportunities for them to position themselves as innovators and disrupters in the field, and establish what Brigitte Gaïti describes as 'la figure du nouveau fonctionnaire audacieux, indépendant, parfois héroïque, visionnaire' [the figure of the new civil servant, audacious and independent, sometimes heroic and visionary]

(2002: 301). Indeed, the advantage of a new organization like the CGP, which had no history in terms of established hierarchies or ways of working, combined with the fact that its new recruits had a diverse range of professional backgrounds, was precisely that it enabled more unorthodox approaches or professional practices. It provided those who moved there the opportunity to develop (and equally significantly, be *seen* to develop) what Gaïti terms 'new models of professional excellence' (2002: 299), models which they could subsequently impose as the most legitimate forms of administrative practice.

Moreover, as Delphine Dulong has demonstrated, the civil servants engaged in developing the French state plans were part of a wider coalition of actors, including politicians, industrialists, intellectuals and journalists, who were lobbying for the country's political and economic modernization during the 1950s, and shared 'un intérêt commun à proclamer l'avènement des temps nouveaux' [a common interest in proclaiming the coming of new times] (1997: 10). For them, the political opportunity for change would come with the constitutional crisis provoked by the Algerian conflict in May 1958: the collapse of the government of Pierre Pflimlin, the return of Charles de Gaulle, and the drafting of a new constitution to replace the Fourth with the Fifth Republic. The moment was properly revolutionary insofar as it seemed like anything could happen. As Dulong observes, 'les acteurs ont soudain le sentiment que les conventions sur les formes de justification et de rationalisation de l'action dans l'espace public sont en pleine recomposition, que désormais tout semble possible, même le plus improbable' [those involved suddenly had the impression that established ways of justifying and rationalizing action in the public sphere were undergoing profound transformation, that henceforth everything seemed possible, including the most improbable things] (1997: 177). De Gaulle's new constitution shifted the balance of power decisively from the legislative to the executive, and the relative sidelining of the French parliament facilitated the modernizers' concomitant, less obvious, but no less significant attempt to define political legitimacy in terms of technical competence and expertise rather than parliamentary deliberation.

In many respects, therefore, the moment of rupture in 1962 that created post-colonial France served to reinforce an existing direction of travel for those in a position to influence the country's future. The clean break it enabled was enacted both through the sustained focus on the future in political and public discourse, as well as through the more obscure and determined way in which, as Todd Shepard (2006) has shown, the division from Algeria and the process of decolonization was encoded through a series of legal and administrative protocols. Thus, by 1965, Guichard was able to make the audacious claim that France's rate of growth in the post-war period was like those of a number of 'developing countries' (1965: 30); and that 'l'évolution récente nous a donné à nouveau les dimensions d'un pays neuf' [recent changes have once again given us the dimensions of a new country] (1965: 27). It is hard not to hear in Guichard's mention of the country's 'évolution récente' a careful allusion not simply to the Second World War, but to a more recent conflict of decolonization, with its inevitable and literal consequences for the country's 'dimensions'.

As Dulong suggests with her choice of verb, the modernizers' desire to 'proclaim' the coming of new times certainly had a performative dimension. It was one of the most obvious ways in which they could position themselves as the modernizing avant-garde in relation to the status quo. However, this would be to underestimate the extent to which the rhetorical pronouncement of new times, as well as being straightforwardly political, was also married to an epistemological foundation, a particular way of conceptualizing time, agency and historical progress. In turn, it is not just that the political claim of 'new times' coincided with philosophical reflection on planning and modernization, specifically in terms of *la prospective* as a future-oriented method. Rather, the political claim could find parallels in (and derive legitimacy from) the philosophical reflection, which provided an epistemological framework for the new political time it accompanied, and a rationale for the actions developed as part of the new politics.

That is to say, notwithstanding planning's apparent foregrounding of space as a means of articulating French modernity, identity and unity, what in fact seemed to be at stake was the navigation of another sustained revolutionary moment, one reflected in the planners' preoccupation with time and newness, and in their simultaneous attempts to help engineer a profound realignment, or modernization, of French politics. In short, what looks to be about space is actually as much about time. The envisioning of a modernized national territory through the figure of the hexagon was really only the most noticeable form through which a certain understanding of French progress (that held by the country's modernizing elite) could find expression. Using the terms of Buck-Morss's analysis, it would be through the remodelling of French space that the revolutionary impulse contained within the planners' understanding of time, history and progress would find its most tangible expression. The remainder of this chapter sets out to explore the philosophical undercurrents of post-war French planning, the nature of the prospective view, and the influence they had on thinking about spatial planning and the production of space.

Planning or Death

By 1966, Pierre Bauchet, director of studies at the ENA and former member of the CGP, could assert that the fundamental business of government was planning as *prévision*: 'l'adage "gouverner c'est prévoir" indique que cette nécessité n'est pas nouvelle. Mais elle est aujourd'hui générale et impérieuse' [the adage 'to govern is to foresee' indicates that this need is not new. But it is now widespread and urgent] (Bauchet 1966: 26). Bauchet argued that the requirement to plan lay especially in the need to keep pace with technical advance, which also had the happy benefit of producing tools useful for the planner: 'la technique rend la prévision nécessaire en même temps qu'elle lui fournit des instruments' [technical innovation makes planning necessary at the same time as giving it tools to do the job] (1966: 25). Here, a phrase that at first glance appears to be a declarative statement of fact ('la technique rend la prévision nécessaire') is in reality doing a substantial amount of rhetorical and political heavy lifting, insofar as it positions planning as a necessary process, and therefore one that any serious government would be negligent to ignore.

Bauchet's comment unobtrusively freights planning with a moral imperative, one that Georges Pompidou had expressed with greater drama the previous year, when he told the French parliament that progress meant planning, and that without planning there would be decline and death: 'nous sommes engagés dans une évolution qui nous contraint, *sous peine de décadence, et même de mort*, de progresser. Mais nous voulons progresser les yeux ouverts, c'est-à-dire prévoir' [We are undergoing an evolution which commits us to progress, and without progress, *decline and even death await us*. But we want to progress with our eyes open, and that means planning] (*Journal officiel*, 13 June 1965: 2252, my emphasis).

As we have seen, planning was engaged throughout the 1950s in a battle to consolidate itself as a legitimate form of action in the public sphere, in particular by challenging the established authority of the legislature. Both Bauchet's claim and Pompidou's more florid assertions before parliament illustrate the extent to which the planners had succeeded in establishing their vision as the dominant mode of governance by the mid-1960s. The expertise marshalled by the planners became a primary locus of authority, but was given democratic sheen through mechanisms of parliamentary reporting, debate and approval. That the planners were nevertheless aware of concerns over their power, and the need to sustain the democratic credentials of planning, is signalled by the space devoted in Bauchet's account to the relationship between planning and democracy, which is the title of the first part of his book.

Indeed, the degree of soul searching in Bauchet's reflection on political oversight of the Plan, in terms of the need to balance administrative 'efficiency' with the 'primacy' of politics (1966: 158), acknowledges the suspicions in which the planners were held as representatives of a technocratic regime that could easily evade democratic oversight and control. While the French parliament was not consulted over the third Plan in 1959, Bauchet notes approvingly its renewed engagement over the fourth Plan in 1962, as well as the passing into law as part of that Plan the requirement for parliament to be consulted prior to the preparation of subsequent Plans (1966: 162). Even so, that parliamentary scrutiny and input took place in a context where the balance of power under the Gaullist constitution had swung definitively away from the legislature to the executive.

Bauchet's analysis comes in a book described by the journal *Critique* in 1965 as a 'work of reference' on planning (Devaud 1965: 283). First published in 1958, *La Planification française* was updated after each iteration of the Plan. It was one of a proliferating collection of publications on French planning by a range of actors, most notably the planners themselves, including Pierre Massé and the economist Jean Fourastié, as well as politicians such as Olivier Guichard, and figures from industry and business such as Louis Armand and Philippe Lamour. Many were designed to reach a wide audience, published as cheap paperbacks in Gallimard's *Idées* series (for example Massé's *Le Plan, ou l'anti-hasard* in 1965) or the *Que sais-je?* collection by Presses universitaires de France (François Perroux's *La quatrième*

Plan française from 1962), which offered the general reader condensed accounts of important topics by experts in the field.

At the same time, analysis both of planning and its literature featured regularly in periodicals like *Critique*, *Esprit* and *Les Temps modernes* which, in the way they set out to provide commentary across the spectrum of cultural, political and societal issues, played a central role in structuring the terms of intellectual debate in post-war France, and ensuring its visibility.[4] The debates happening in their pages had a more restricted audience, but a disproportionately influential one (highly educated and occupying positions of influence in the fields of cultural production, knowledge and power). This was the case especially of *Esprit*, under the editorship of Jean-Marie Domenach. The journal's non-conformist, progressive Catholicism was closely aligned with many of those involved in French planning, such as civil servant François Bloch-Lainé, who held various senior government roles, and made a number of contributions to the journal on the topic. Even when the tone of engagement with planning was sceptical or critical (like Devaud's piece for *Critique* in 1965), the effect was to lend the planning project a sense of intellectual significance through the very act of glossing and interpreting its premises and principles.

The accumulating literature on planning during the 1950s and 60s is one of the most striking things about the enterprise in post-war France. In part, the planners' desire to communicate about their activity had a political dimension to it. As Dulong argues (1997: 193), it can be understood in the context of their battle to position themselves as legitimate voices in the public sphere, establishing the authority of planning as a domain of action. The planners' publications were at once demonstrations of expertise, and accounts of how that expertise was decisive in addressing the task of France's modernization and development. As such, their role was to help establish the legitimacy of the planners' credentials and their vision within the political field, as well as to assert planning as an integral part of the democratic process (in turn modernizing the democratic process by demonstrating how technical expertise should be integral to it).

Yet notwithstanding the political function of their interventions, the fact remains that the planners devoted a considerable amount of energy to establishing what amounts to a veritable philosophy of planning and its theoretical foundations. Planning emerges not simply as an area of technical competence and administrative activity, but one guided by a coherent set of ideas and beliefs, whose texts reveal particular ways of seeing the world, understanding its direction of travel and acting on it. In particular, it signalled and enacted a more profound epistemological shift amongst those involved, a moment of rupture or break with the past that translated into a concerted orientation towards the future.

Planning is unavoidably inhabited by thoughts about the future. At an immediate and practical level, futurity is inherent within the activity of planning as *prévision*, or projection forward over a given period of time. (That *prévision* also implicitly

---

4   On the role played by periodicals in structuring the intellectual field in post-war France, see the classic account of Sartre and *Les Temps modernes* by Anna Boschetti (1985).

foregrounds the role of looking and the visual is something to which we return in due course.) The first Plan, concerned above all with reconstruction and economic recovery after the war, confined itself to a round of annual programmes focusing on production, reconstruction, investment and import-export activity (*Journal officiel*, 17 January 1947: 590). But the ambitions for the second Plan, established by government decree in December 1951, were already more far reaching, and made clear that there was more at stake with planning than short-term target-setting. The decree spelled out the CGP's role in taking 'une vue d'ensemble sur l'évolution à long terme de l'économie française' [an overview of the long-term evolution of the French economy] (*Journal officiel*, 12 December 1951: 12227). By the time Pompidou was addressing the French parliament in 1965, planning was a matter not just of the economy, but of the future of French civilization. Far beyond output targets, in play now was nothing less than, in Bauchet's words, 'une action consciente, collective, orientée vers un avenir en progrès' [conscious and collective action oriented towards a future in progress] (1966: 25).

In Bauchet's terms here, we can see an outline of the ideas that had been shaping French planning since the 1950s. Rather than a bureaucratic process, planning emerges as a theory of action in the context of a dynamic and evolving world. Our attention should be fixed on the future as the most important horizon. But given that progress means the future is always advancing, action on our part is essential if we are to keep it in sight. Or, to return to Pompidou's more brutal assessment, failure to progress means the death of civilizations.

If Bauchet highlights planning as agency in the world, poised between the present and the future, Pierre Massé's writing develops further what this means and what its implications are. As *Commissaire général du Plan* between 1959 and 1966, Massé was France's chief planner. He was also one of its most prolific theorists and philosophers. In his book *Le Plan, ou l'anti-hasard* [The Plan, or Against Chance], Massé injects a sense of intellectual and existential daring into the planning enterprise. Human agency is key to Massé's understanding of history, which is driven by figureheads, *figures de proue*, who recognize that 'l'homme est contraint à l'action' [mankind is compelled to act] (Massé 1965: 10). History is made by those who take action, and do so because they recognize that action is an unavoidable response to man's situation in the world. Yet as well as being an obligation (we return below to the moral weight lurking in that idea), action for Massé is also an adventure. It opens up an unpredictable combination of opportunities and risks, and a concomitant rush of hopes and fears (1965: 10). In order to maximize the opportunities and mitigate the risks, action should be a calculated adventure, 'une aventure calculée', and this is the title he gives to the book's opening chapter.

In a striking first paragraph, Massé highlights those *figures de proue* who demonstrate the twin attributes of imaginative audacity and rational acuity: Socrates, Alexander the Great, Caesar, Christopher Columbus, Galileo, Martin Luther, Michelangelo (1965: 9). An immediate implication of Massé's roll call is to position French planning against a backdrop of other heroic and epochal moments of history; not least, perhaps, in order to convey the scale and ambition of the enterprise. Noteworthy too is how his selection of (exclusively male) figures covers the spectrum of military, political, philosophical, scientific and artistic activity, as if to suggest both the breadth of abilities planning might require, and its uniqueness as an endeavour in manifesting the qualities of each. Massé is also quick to introduce the note of moral gravity which pervades the planning perspective, triangulating adventure and calculation as the paragraph concludes by quoting Pascal's wager: 'Il faut parier. Cela n'est pas volontaire. Vous êtes embarqués' [You must gamble. You have no choice. You are embarked] (1965: 10). Planning is at once a heady leap of the imagination, and a leap of faith. In a world where action is necessary and unavoidable, it is also the most appropriate, indeed the only viable, form of response.

If planning's time has come, Massé suggests, it is due especially to the moral and existential uncertainties that haunt the post-war world, and stem from the technological progress which otherwise defines it (the dark power of the atom being his first and most predictable example). Man may well be 'embarked' on a journey, but its destination is unclear. Massé refers approvingly to Gaston Berger's suggestion that 'l'incertitude et l'hésitation prennent la place des valeurs qui semblaient les mieux assurés' [uncertainty and hesitation replace what seemed to be the most assured of values] (1965: 16). Rather than be naively optimistic about the inevitability of progress, we need to recognize that 'l'ambiguïté fondamentale de l'avenir est apparue et ne disparaîtra plus de l'horizon' [the fundamental ambiguity of the future has appeared and will not disappear from the horizon] (1965: 16). However, argues Massé, room for manoeuvre lies in this uncertainty because it provides scope for human agency: 'elle laisse espérer que quelque chose dépend de nous' [it lets us hope that something depends on us] (1965: 16). The anxieties of the present can be neutralized if we are prepared to embrace the possibilities afforded by 'the risks and chances' of adventure (1965: 16). Planning provides the best answer to the existential and moral challenges of the age because man's agency can be channelled through the act of planning itself, and a sense of certainty can be regained. What counts above all is one's approach or attitude to the future.

That Massé concurs with Berger's diagnosis of the contemporary mood is unsurprising. It signals Berger's influence not just on Massé, but on the philosophy and politics of French planning as a whole. Berger's ideas, and in particular his notion of *la prospective*, surface repeatedly in the discourse of the practitioners and politicians whose role it is to communicate and persuade about the aims and benefits of French planning. More than that, what emerges from Berger's thinking, and finds its way into the writing of people like Bauchet, Massé and Guichard, is a sense of planning as a state of mind or, to use one of Berger's favourite terms, an *attitude*. It is the attitude, as he puts it is, 'de ceux qui se tournent vers ce qui va être et non pas ce qui a été' [of those who turn towards what will be and not what has been] (1964: 238). Moral force resides with those whose eyes are fixed resolutely on the future. The question remains how that future is to be enacted and achieved.

Planning and the Prospective Attitude

The influence of Berger and his ideas is an obscure but revealing story. Prospective thinking formed an important element of what, in an article published in 1976, Pierre Bourdieu and Luc Boltanski termed the 'dominant ideology' of France's post-war period (though Berger himself does not feature in their discussion, overshadowed by more well-known protagonists such as the economist Jean Fourastié). The fortunes of *la prospective* also illustrate Bourdieu and Boltanski's analysis of ideology not as a body of ideas existing in abstraction, but as a way of seeing the world (a *schéma de perception*) produced and maintained through a set of social, cultural, institutional, material and discursive practices.

The means by which the tenets of prospective thinking were absorbed and mobilized by a range of actors holding positions of influence shows how ideology as a common sense or shared understanding of the world gains consistency: first, through the circulation and relaying of discourse (terms and ideas recycled, quoted or paraphrased from one text, speech or publication to another); and second, through the range of networks, organizations and institutional structures (committees, think tanks, political clubs, higher education institutions, periodicals) which serve as points of intersection between the intellectual field and the field of power. Here, when 'enlightened leaders meet enlightening intellectuals', as Bourdieu and Boltanski put it, is where 'la parole devient pouvoir' [words become power] (1976: 6). It is where certain ideas gain traction and are transformed into guiding principles for political action. That prospective thinking quickly found favour amongst the country's highest levels of decision-making is important because of how it informed decisions about the future which were translated into concrete outcomes, particularly in terms of the production and development of space.

'Gaston Berger,' observes Jenny Andersson, 'was not your ordinary French philosopher' (Andersson 2018: 66). Like Claudius-Petit and others who positioned themselves at the vanguard of French planning, his career trajectory was unconventional. Born in 1896, he fought in the First World War before working in industry. He came late to the academic world, completing a degree in philosophy in the 1920s, and founding what would become one of the major French academic journals of philosophy, *Études philosophiques*, in 1928. He pursued his academic interests while continuing to work in industry, becoming a specialist in Husserl, phenomenology and consciousness and completing research degrees shortly after the start of the Second World War.

In 1953, he was appointed Director of Higher Education at the French Ministry of Education, where he supported the development of France's research infrastructure in the social sciences. He encouraged the creation of the École des hautes études en sciences sociales [Academy for advanced study in the social sciences] as the famous 'sixth section' of the École pratique des hautes études [Practical academy for advanced study] under Lucien Febvre, and worked with Lebvre's fellow *Annales* historian, Fernand Braudel, on what would become the Maison des Sciences de l'homme (Andersson 2018: 66). Berger died in a car crash on a motorway south of Paris in November 1960, shortly before he was due to take up a professorship in 'prospective anthropology' at the École pratique des hautes études. In an appreciation published in *Annales*, Braudel noted the irony of Berger dying 'dans un paysage ultra-moderne, pareil à ceux dont il s'acharnait à découvrir le visage' [in an ultra-modern landscape like those whose contours he worked hard to reveal] (Braudel 1961: 210).[5]

A decisive moment for what Philippe Durance calls the 'institutionalization' of prospective thinking (2007: 2) came in 1955, when Berger was invited by André Gros to address members of the French employers' federation. Gros led the Conseillers de synthèse, a group of management consultants with interests in theories of organization, progress and human adaptability (Gros 1957; Andersson 2018: 67). Gros's background was in fact in medicine. He had developed a successful career as a surgeon and occupational health specialist before the Second World War, with an interest in eugenics and social hygiene. But while Berger and many other key figures of the period participated in the French Resistance, Gros tacked more closely to the Vichy regime, during which he played a leading role in the implementation of occupational health (Clarke 2011: 144–45). Consequently, he was suspected but ultimately cleared of collaboration after the Liberation, and his association with Vichy meant he was obliged, as Vincent Guiader rather delicately puts it, 'à demeurer en marge du champ scientifique' [to remain on the margins of the scientific field] (Guiader 2008: 29). He found an opening in management consultancy, and developed close links with the French employers' federation.

Discussions following Berger's lecture set in train the creation of the Centre international de prospective in May 1957, with Berger as president and Gros as general secretary. Signalling the political momentum behind the Centre, its board included a number of influential figures from industry, government and higher education, such as François Bloch-Lainé (at that time the director of the state investment bank, the Caisse des dépôts et consignations), Louis Armand (head of the French state railways) and Pierre Racine (co-founder of the ENA, who in 1963 would be appointed to oversee the development of a string of tourist resorts along the Languedoc-Roussillon coast as part of the work of the DATAR). The Centre is a nice example of what Bourdieu and Boltanski term 'lieux neutres' (1976: 59–60), the network of organizations which enable different actors within the field of power to assemble on what appears to be neutral territory in order to engage in discussion and reflection. The staged confrontation of different ideas, perspectives and 'points

---

5   Death by car crash gathered significant cultural momentum during the 1950s and 60s, as Kristin Ross (1995) has explored, aided by high-profile victims such as Albert Camus (also in 1960). Greater numbers of car accidents were an inevitable by-product of expanding car ownership, faster cars and faster roads, and were covered by the popular press with a mixture of horror and fascination. They made manifest the rapid modernization and acceleration of post-war French society, as well as the latent violence of the energy that modernization at once mobilized and required. Indeed, Berger uses automotive technology to find a chillingly prescient analogy for the role of prospective thinking in his foundational essay, 'L'Attitude prospective' (1959), writing that 'notre civilisation est comparable à une voiture qui roule de plus en plus vite sur une route inconnue lorsque la nuit est tombée. Il faut que ses phares portent de plus en plus loin si l'on veut éviter la catastrophe. La prospective est ainsi essentiellement l'étude de l'avenir lointain' [our civilization is like a car going faster and faster along an unknown road once night has fallen. Its headlights need to project further and further forward if catastrophe is to be avoided. Likewise, the prospective approach is fundamentally about studying the far future] (Berger 1964: 271).

of view' parallel to the formal structures and locations of decision-making allows an emerging consensus to take shape which can coalesce into the 'common sense' or axiomatic principles informing policy and political action. Even if their purpose and effect is to draw together groups whose interests are in fact in broad alignment, and for whom collaboration is mutually beneficial, they perform the production of orthodoxy as an enlightened process of debate and synthesis.

In 1957, the Centre created the journal *Prospective*, the first issue of which appeared in 1958. As I noted earlier, journals and periodicals played a central role in structuring the field of intellectual debate in post-war France. Consequently, it is no surprise that the Centre established a journal as a way of staking out its position and promoting its ideas. Journals offer a material form of visibility in the field of debate, and a similarly tangible means of putting ideas in circulation. From a Bourdieusian perspective, they are an effective means of accumulating and distributing different forms of political and symbolic capital. By attracting and displaying contributions from influential figures, they at once acquire legitimacy themselves, and can use that legitimacy to further influence the shape of the discussion. Indeed, that *Prospective* was published by Presses universitaires de France, the country's most prestigious academic press, was itself a sign of the symbolic capital already in the Centre's possession.

A regular contributor to *Prospective* was Pierre Massé, who joined the Centre's board after Berger's death in 1960, underscoring its role as a meeting-place for the country's modernizing elite. Thanks not just to his position as head of the CGP, but also to his writing, Massé would perhaps do most to maintain the principles of prospective thinking in circulation, and use them as a framework for shaping government policy. At the same time, the fact that Berger's terms and ideas resurfaced across a range of forums and texts during the 1960s, from Bauchet's monograph on French planning to Pompidou's speeches in the National Assembly and Guichard's popularizing account of *aménagement*, demonstrates the extent to which the notion of *la prospective* had become axiomatic amongst those in positions of power, structuring their vision of the world and the possibilities for action within it.

If *la prospective* was an attitude or a state of mind, it was not simply a matter of looking towards the future and not the past. It was also about understanding the relationship between the present and the future, and more specifically, grasping how the future could be shaped. This in turn was predicated on the crucial assumption that the power to do so is within our means, a power Massé went on to foreground in his case for French planning, as we have seen. In an article on time for the *Encyclopédie française*, subsequently reprinted in *Prospective*, Berger mobilizes Henri Bergson's critique of temporal causality in arguing for the need to challenge the perception that the future arises mechanically from present states and actions. Space for human agency opens up once we recognize that we have the capacity to intervene in the present in order to determine the future: 'l'avenir n'est plus ce qui doit inévitablement se produire, [...] il est ce que l'ensemble du monde va faire' [the future is no longer a matter of what must inevitably come about, [...] it is about what the whole world will do] (Berger 1964: 210). In decoupling present and future, cause and effect, the future becomes of the domain of the possible and the as-yet-conceived: 'si rien n'est garanti, rien du moins n'est fatal ou inexorable' [if nothing is guaranteed, at least nothing is inevitable or inexorable] (1964: 211). As Berger makes clear, agency also implies and demands creativity. Above all, the future is a work of the imagination.

Elsewhere, Berger ups the stakes still further. Writing on *la prospective* for the *Revue des deux mondes* in 1957, he argues that action and invention are required more than ever at a time in history when 'des forces nouvelles sont à l'œuvre' (Berger 1964: 221). Developing the theme of progress as (moral) imperative that will appeal to Pompidou, Berger argues that, 'pour faire face à des situations originales, nous sommes condamnés à un effort d'invention qui ne saurait se suspendre' [in order to confront novel situations, we are condemned to a perpetual effort of invention] (1964: 221). One of the most fundamental forces at work is acceleration, with which Berger is especially preoccupied, and which emerges in his thinking as the defining quality of modern life. It is not simply that we are living in a period of accelerating change, he suggests, but that 'l'accélération est devenue immédiatement perceptible' (1964: 221). It has emerged as a force with a tangible impact on our lives, both physically and phenomenologically.

The key thing for humanity is to recognize this fact and embrace its consequences, the first of which is to acknowledge that humanity in turn is evolving at an accelerating rate. Not only is the future opening up in a multiplicity of different ways, but we have to find new ways of responding to those changes. The accelerating change that derives from our increased inventiveness will enrich and strengthen humanity by concentrating and organizing human energy ever more effectively. In turn, we can fend off the forces of entropy otherwise at work in the universe. It is by adopting the prospective attitude that we can harness the momentum of change, channel our inventive energies and bend the future to our will; or, as Berger puts it, 'infléchir, dans le sens qui nous paraît désirable, le cours des événements' [inflect the course of events in the direction that suits us best] (1964: 230).

At this point, Berger's thinking acquires what appears to be a curious edge of science fiction. The acceleration of progress and our increasing creativity, he suggests in an article on 'The idea of the future' in *Les Annales* in 1960, are signs that as it heads into the future, humanity is getting younger not older: 'nous allons vers notre jeunesse' [we are heading towards our youth] (1964: 236). If ageing is a form of entropy, then the ever-burgeoning energy, ingenuity and creativity on display in the contemporary moment must imply the opposite; that 'loin de vieillir, l'humanité devient progressivement de plus en plus jeune' [far from getting old, humanity is getting progressively younger] (1964: 235). While we might be startled by what Berger terms this 'temporal inversion', we must capitalize on it rather than be disconcerted by it. Indeed, argues Berger, a phenomenology of acceleration can provide us with the basis of a metaphysics of hope (1964: 237).

In developing his arguments about acceleration and progress, Berger draws in another thinker whose ideas were in play amongst the broader cadre of France's modernizing elite. He returns to the notion of humanity's accelerating evolution in a lecture in May 1960 on Pierre Teilhard de Chardin, who had died a few years earlier. Indeed, Berger begins the lecture by positioning Teilhard de Chardin as a theorist of the prospective attitude *avant la lettre*:

> Ce qu'il a écrit sur l'avenir et sur ce qu'il faut bien appeler l'attitude prospective, c'est-à-dire l'attitude de ceux qui se tournent vers ce qui va être et non pas vers ce qui a été, me paraît revêtir une importance considérable. (1964: 238)

> [What he has written about the future and on what should be termed the prospective attitude, that is to say, the attitude of those who turn towards what will be and not what has been, seems to me to be of considerable importance.]

Teilhard de Chardin (1881–1955) was a Jesuit theologian, palaeontologist and geologist who set out to reconcile the apparently conflicting positions of faith and science through a theory of spiritual evolution. What emerges from his work, in effect, is a form of modernized Christianity better adapted to the age of scientific reason. Or, put another way, a Christianity intent on co-opting the scientific theory that had done most to challenge its worldly authority.

Teilhard takes the optimistic view of history as progress, with evolution as its motive force, and humanity as the highest form of evolution. In evolutionary terms, progress is above all a process of gradually increasing intelligence and consciousness, which reaches its most heightened and concentrated form with the birth of thought in mankind. The collective power of human thought in turn generates a skin or web encompassing the planet, a 'thinking substance' he terms the 'noosphère' (Teilhard de Chardin 1959: 203). Teilhard is also insistent on humanity's youth. If humanity is the highest form of evolution, then its potential for advancement remains considerable. Moreover (and this is where God can re-enter the equation) the ultimate consequence of progress is ascension and convergence towards the so-called Omega Point of supreme consciousness, which for Teilhard is the Godhead (Teilhard de Chardin 1955: 259).

If Berger was happy to find affinities between prospective thinking and Teilhard's evolutionary theology, it is undoubtedly because they shared the same sense of humanity as bound to progress, and progress as a journey of moral and spiritual enlightenment. It was also an acknowledgement of Teilhard's popularity amongst those involved in French planning. Teilhard's synthesis of science and spirituality offered a variant of the progressive French Catholicism associated with Marc Sangnier's Sillon movement at the start of the century, as well as the *mouvement personnaliste* of Emmanuel Mounier and his fellow travellers at the journal *Esprit*, which Mounier had established in 1932 (Bourdieu & Boltanski 1976: 33–34). Teilhard's status as a heterodox thinker within Catholicism (he was sanctioned by Rome for his views on evolution and authorization to publish his theological writings was withdrawn) was equally significant. Not only did his theology chime with the sense of planning as a spiritually enlightened and socially progressive project, but its contested status resonated with the planners' self-styled position as heterodox and disruptive actors in the field of power.[6]

6   Paul Delouvrier tells of encountering Teilhard's writings while at the École des Cadres d'Uriage during the war (Chenu 1994: 153). Teilhard's work circulated clandestinely until his death in 1955. The École d'Uriage was another important location for the transmission of ideas that would

A theory of progress through action also had the useful corollary of translating into secular as much as religious terms. As Berger observes:

> L'humaniste et le spirituel peuvent faire un bon morceau de chemin ensemble et cette idée sans doute aurait séduit le P. Teilhard de Chardin, lui qui désirait, dans le concret, et pas seulement dans l'abstrait, la convergence et la collaboration des hommes les plus différents. (Berger 1964: 254)

> [The humanist and the spiritual teacher can travel a good distance together and this idea would undoubtedly have appealed to the Rev. Teilhard de Chardin, who sought not just in abstract but in concrete terms the convergence and collaboration of very different men.]

Through their shared emphasis on technical and intellectual advancement as at once a moral necessity, a source of spiritual fulfilment and a means of enlightened action on the world, Berger and Teilhard between them provided a powerful moral and philosophical foundation for what might otherwise have appeared simply to be a technical and administrative activity. In the notion of accelerating evolution, we can find the source of Pompidou's stern warning to the National Assembly that only planning lies between France and terminal decline, as well as Guichard's rather more upbeat and audacious claim that post-war France was like a developing country, regaining lost youth (or lost time) through concerted action into the future. Hence too Guichard's proposal that spatial planning works ahead of time, scouting out the future so it can be brought to bear in the present.

The most consistent advocate of prospective thinking after Berger's death was Pierre Massé, and this is not inconsequential given his role as France's chief planner. Whether in articles for *Prospective*, or in his book, *Le Plan, ou l'anti-hasard*, Massé mobilizes Berger repeatedly, as he seeks to give planning a level of conceptual, philosophical and societal ambition. This becomes clear most obviously when he draws on Berger to theorize the difference between planning as *prévision* on the one hand, and *prospective* on the other. Like Berger, he sees them as complementary activities; but as a form of projection, *prévision* has feet of clay. Operating in the short term, it is bound by its nature to see the future as an extrapolation of the past and 'suppose ce qui sera dans le prolongement de ce qui a été' [sees what will be in terms of the prolongation of what has been] (Massé 1967a: 108).

To think prospectively, on the other hand, requires a creative leap and a radical change of mind. As Massé puts it with some force, mobilizing a key term from Berger's lexicon, '*l'apport de la prospective est une mutation plus complète de notre attitude*' [*the prospective approach represents a more radical change in our attitude*] (1967b: 337). Shifting from the short term to the long term, following Berger's injunction to 'regarder au loin' [look afar] (1964: 271), prospective thinking assumes that the

shape the planning worldview after the war. Funded by the Vichy regime to train an elite corps of administrators, its teachers included Hubert Beuve-Méry (founding editor of *Le Monde*), Emmanuel Mounier and the sociologist Paul-Henry Chombart de Lauwe. As Bourdieu and Boltanski note, its emphasis on personal asceticism and competence, but also on discussion and negotiation, would be a defining feature of the attitudes, style and ethos of France's governing elite after the war (1976: 35). On Uriage, see Josse 1966, Bitoun 1988 and Hellman 1993. On the role of Catholic networks and progressive Christianity in post-war French urban planning, see Newsome 2009 and Tellier 2014.

future has nothing to learn from the past, that 'aucune projection du passé ne peut constituer un avenir' [no projection from the past can constitute a future] (Massé 1967a: 108). Instead of extrapolating the future from the present, prospective thinkers set out to imagine and explore possible futures with which the present could be aligned: 'la logique de la recherche prospective est ainsi d'inverser le cheminement traditionnel et de partir de l'*exploration de l'avenir* — non pas d'un avenir déduit, mais d'une pluralité d'avenirs imaginés' [the logic of prospective research is this, to invert the established approach and to take as its starting-point the *exploration of the future* — not a future deduced, but a plurality of imagined futures] (Massé 1965: 33). In doing so, they must free themselves from what Massé terms 'la soumission aux apparences observées' [subjection to observed appearances] (1967a: 109), so as to seek out the deeper trends at work and uncover the signs of the future (1967a: 113). Conceived in prospective terms, planning becomes a startling alchemy of administration, divination and imagination. The vision and creativity of the prospective attitude enables a paradigm shift that goes far beyond the technical (how to do better planning) to become societal or even, to recall Berger's aspiration, metaphysical (how to build a better world).

While the prospective attitude is about looking to the future, it is also, and in a very conscious way, about forgetting the past. Massé could not be clearer: the past has nothing to teach us about the future. What counts is the relationship between present and future, and more specifically, what the present can glean from the future through the prospective view. Rhetorically and philosophically, the past is bracketed off. Indeed, there is something over-determined about such a resolute insistence on the future. It is as if the prospective attitude provides the philosophical sanction for an ultimately political decision to focus on the future and eclipse the past from sight. Here more than anywhere, to return to Ross's metaphor, we can hear the door being slammed shut on the country's recent past, while before us opens up the prospect of a bright new future that, with the right attitude, is waiting to be shaped.

Far Horizons: Prospecting the Future

The appeal of *la prospective* for France's modernizers lay in the fact that it was at once a promise about the future, and a solution to the problem of how humanity might get there. From Massé's point of view — that, we should not forget, of one of France's most senior administrators, responsible for charting an economically and socially viable course for the country — the prospective method offered the reassuring possibility of command over the future. More accurately, perhaps, it allowed command over the present from the perspective of the future. Indeed, his gently oxymoronic description of planning as a 'calculated adventure' captures the prudent mix of cautious excitement one might expect of someone occupying his position.

The title of Massé's book, *Le Plan ou l'anti-hasard*, makes clear that planning is a matter of neutralizing or mitigating chance and risk. Neutralizing chance is in turn about disarming the threat posed by entropy. Massé picks up Berger's argument that decision, invention and action drive progress, and that progress is the motor society needs to avoid the terminal dangers of entropy and decline. Without planning (in other words, without a recognition of our ability to make decisions and take actions, and a recognition of the need to control and work with time) there is only contingency, disorder and decay: 'si l'écoulement du temps se présente, au niveau des éléments, comme un choix contingent entre les possibles, rien ne peut prévaloir, au niveau global, contre la montée de l'entropie, l'accroissement du désordre, l'acheminement vers l'équilibre thermodynamique final' [if the flow of time presents itself, at the level of component elements, as a contingent choice between possible options, nothing can prevent, at a global level, the rise of entropy, increasing disorder, and movement towards ultimate thermodynamic equilibrium] (Massé 1965: 30).

In economic terms, planning for Massé makes the difference between a static and a dynamic economy. Here is where Massé's economic and philosophical reflections on planning become a politics of planning. Prospective planning was the key to moving beyond the 'static economy' that had dogged France until that point, an economy understood in terms of (class) conflict which becomes a zero sum game of opposing interests (1965: 18). Through collective action based on technical expertise, argued Massé, dynamic economies create a 'surplus' of value that can be redistributed. That surplus might still be the subject of a struggle, he suggests, but more important is the fact that the surplus is produced, and that it derives not from 'situations of conflict', but through 'concerted action' (1965: 18).

It was through the concerted growth of a managed economy, what Richard Kuisel describes as 'a system of permanent collaboration among the administration, business and labour' (1981: 251), that France could on the one hand neutralize the ideological threat posed by communism, and on the other, corral the *laissez-faire* economic liberalism that had resulted in France's uneven development and the uneven distribution of opportunity. The *économie concertée* was a solution typical of the synthetic, 'third way' thinking, 'ni de droite ni de gauche', that characterized France's modernizing, neo-liberal avant-garde. Moreover, it could present itself as lying beyond ideology, derived not from political *parti pris* but from the empirical realm of rational decision-making (Bourdieu & Boltanski 1976: 47–48).

At the heart of prospective planning lay human agency, the will and ability to act on the possibilities it opened up. As Massé put it, 'l'homme des années soixante veut être sujet actif de son destin' [the man of the 1960s wants to be the active subject of his destiny] (1965: 17). Yet that destiny was inchoate without a setting and a form in which to express itself. To help their thinking take shape, the planners gave themselves some ambitious temporal horizons. In 1962, Massé established the Groupe 1985 as part of the preparations for the fifth Plan (1966–70). Its membership, a *Who's Who* of French modernizers, included Eugène Claudius-Petit, Jean Fourastié and Philippe Lamour. The group produced its report, *Réflexions pour 1985*, two years later.

The year 1985 was the group's preferred horizon for two reasons. First, it marked a change in generations, as those born in 1964 entered active life. Second, it gave the modernizers of the current generation the time they needed to undertake the transformational changes demanded by the future, and to engineer a radical shift in 'les manières d'appréhender et de traiter les problèmes' [the way in which problems are perceived and resolved] (Groupe 1985 1964: 10). It would not be an exaggeration, suggested Massé in 1966, to say that the fifth Plan was established as much by working back from 1985 as by working forward from 1965 (Massé 1967b: 342).

Meanwhile, Paul Delouvrier gave himself the even more ambitious horizon of the year 2000 in planning the future of Paris, having established projections for the capital that indicated an increase in population from around 8.4 million in 1965 to 14 million by the new millennium. At stake was more than just managing numbers as the urban population expanded. In the terms of the *Schéma directeur*, the task of the *aménageur* was to anticipate changing desires — not just those of the inhabitants of the day, but those from one generation to the next, from father to son and grandson (DGRP 1965: 29).

At the same time, the view to the horizon had to be mapped out, its contours articulated and envisioned. By definition, the prospective view is an uncertain one. Whatever the strength of one's will, observes Massé, 'nous sommes dans l'attente d'un futur à plusieurs visages dont certains sont mal discernables' [we are awaiting a future with multiple faces, some of which are difficult to discern] (1967a: 106). For Guichard, prospective thinking requires 'audacious thinking' (1965: 31). For Massé, its essential quality, indeed its 'cardinal virtue', is imagination (1967a: 106). In turn, the planners' imagined futures found expression through an array of discursive and iconographic forms. Maps, plans, charts, scale models, photographs, artists' impressions, brochures, media stories: a vast machine of representation emerged whose role was to give shape and form to the future; but also, as we shall see in later chapters, to help bring that future into being in the present.

What this material also tells us, whether it be images of infrastructure, or television footage of urban planners with scale models of new towns, is how *aménagement du territoire* was a privileged domain of prospective planning. As Pompidou observed, making clear the link during a debate on *aménagement* at the National Assembly in 1963:

> Il s'agit de composer le futur visage de notre patrie. Il s'agit aussi, au jour le jour, dans nos actes et dans nos réalisations, de choisir, en fonction de nos moyens, les entreprises qui permettront de préparer le modelage d'un pays plus homogène. Un tel choix, croyez-le, est difficile. Il suppose d'abord de larges vues d'avenir, des vues prospectives, comme on dit maintenant. (*Journal officiel*, 26 November 1963: 7412)

> [It is about shaping the future face of our nation. It is also about choosing, on a day-to-day basis, in our actions and our outcomes, and in relation to our means, the undertakings that will enable us to help shape a more unified country. Such choices, believe me, are difficult. First and foremost, they imply a long-range view of the future, a prospective view, as we say these days.]

Indeed, *aménagement* was the domain in which the philosophy and activity of prospective planning could find its most obvious expression. Pompidou makes this explicit in the terms he uses: spatial planning is about the country's visible appearance, its look and feel. It is about the shape the country wants to take. The development of national territory through the creation of infrastructure and other forms of built environment made the concerted effort of modernization real and tangible. Put another way, remodelling space from a prospective point of view could produce what we might term 'chronoscapes' of futurity, materializing in built form the revolutionary time of la prospective as a future-in-the-present.

As planning's key theorist, Massé understood this point well. It is captured in the title of an essay from 1964, 'L'Aménagement du territoire: projection géographique de la société de l'avenir' [Spatial planning: geographical projection of the society of the future] (reproduced as the fourth chapter of Le Plan, ou l'anti-hasard). That is to say, the outcome of spatial planning should be to anticipate in physical form, and thereby bring into being, the social and economic frameworks France will need in the future. It is a future, Massé understands, defined by the steady shift from primary and secondary to tertiary industry, a more balanced distribution of opportunities and facilities across the territory (Pompidou's 'modelage d'un pays plus homogène'), greater physical (and therefore, implicitly social) mobility, and more efficient modes of circulation through better infrastructure.

But the title of Massé's essay also underlines that the planning and production of space necessarily implies the creation of a new society and new citizens. Likewise, Guichard spells out the transformative effects of aménagement not simply in terms of new physical infrastructure or built environments, but of everyday life and lived experience. More precisely, the transformation of one will require and produce the transformation of the other. By 1985, he suggests, mobilizing the preferred horizon of prospective planning, 'une mutation sensible se sera produite dans les mentalités. Un nouveau cadre de vie, de nouvelles manières de penser et de réagir seront nés' [there will have been a noticeable shift in mentality. A new way of life will have emerged, new ways of thinking and reacting] (Guichard 1965: 34). Guichard takes mobility as his prime example, predicting that it will be the defining characteristic of life in 1985. The challenge for the aménageurs was that unlike the Americans, driven by the frontier spirit and always on the move, 'le Français est un être stable, attaché à la terre, vivant et travaillant au lieu de sa naissance' [the French are stable beings, attached to the earth, living and working where they are born]. If the French were to adapt to 'changes made necessary by technical evolution' (1965: 35), then stability would have to give way to mobility.

An unsurprisingly similar theme emerged in the text presenting Delouvrier's Schéma directeur when it was published in 1965. The physical transformation of the region, argued the introduction, should ensure the wellbeing and happiness of the population by creating the 'conditions matérielles d'une vie heureuse' [material conditions for a happy life] (DGRP 1965: 25). However, that promise came with an expectation. In a pamphlet two years later, Delouvrier argued that in daring to 'think prospectively about happiness', the Schéma directeur could 'permettre à ceux qui jouent le jeu de la ville d'inscrire leurs choix dans un contexte évolutif' [allow those who play the game of city living to make their choices in an evolving context] (Delouvrier 1967: 30).

The name of that game was again mobility. To Delouvrier's concern, though, it was one that the general population seemed reluctant to play: without a 'radical change' in habits of thought and behaviour, mobility would not properly take hold in the region (1967: 30). Delouvrier's frustration signals one of the most obvious risks of prospective planning, namely the failure of the present (or more specifically, its unresponsive and unwilling inhabitants) to align itself with the opportunities found in the future. It also reveals the logic of the self-fulfilling prophecy that Luc Boltanski (1982: 245–46) diagnoses as symptomatic of the prospective view: a future is imagined in which certain behaviours are presumed; those in the present are then expected to adopt such behaviours in anticipation of the future being predicted.

More than anything, perhaps, the combination of expectation and frustration expressed by two of the chief architects of French modernization draws out the project's moral, ideological and political complexities. What Dulong terms the 'collective adventure' of planning (1997: 11) is one of the defining stories of post-war France. For the groups who coalesced to form the country's modernizing avant-garde, it was a time when anything seemed possible, thanks to a heady combination of technical expertise, imagination and collective will. But they also understood planning's adventure into the future in part to be a moral quest. Massé for one was sensitive to the weight of responsibility they felt: 'le développement n'est pas seulement la marche vers l'abondance, c'est plus encore, sans doute, la construction d'une société' [development is not just about a march towards abundance. It is undoubtedly more about the construction of a society] (1965: 54). If modernization was a social as much as economic project, then it also had moral and ethical implications for our understanding of the common good and the social contract. It was about 'les valeurs que nous entendons respecter, les fins que nous désirons poursuivre' [the values we want to respect, the ends that we want to pursue] (1965: 54).

Some of these were explored in an essay by philosopher Paul Ricœur, writing in a special issue of *Esprit* on 'Prospective et utopie' in 1966. Among the other contributors was François Bloch-Lainé, reflecting the journal's status as one of the philosophical homes of French modernization. Ricœur draws attention to an important tension within planning. On the one hand, it offers a way to overcome problems of chaos, contingency and inequality, and to do so on behalf of (or indeed as) the social collective. On the other, if planning is predicated on bringing order to chaos, then implicit within it is the narrowing down of choice as one of the defining principles of liberal society. Aligning himself with the prospective view, Ricœur makes the contrary case. Rather than seeing a threat to liberty through planning, we should recognize that planning will frame and open up different choices:

> Nous avons donc à rectifier notre compréhension de la liberté et à découvrir les formes nouvelles du choix offertes par une société de la prévision et de la décision rationnelle, au lieu de penser avec nostalgie à ces formes anciennes de la liberté. (Ricœur 1966: 181)

> [We need to revise our understanding of liberty and uncover the new forms of choice offered by a society of projection and rational decision-making, instead of harking back nostalgically to the old forms of freedom.]

As such, Ricœur makes a bracing call for a form of moral and ethical modernization that parallels the economic and political modernization being realized by prospective planning.

In doing so, however, he is also highlighting the fundamental question that planning raises about the nature and reach of power in a liberal democracy. For if planning was indeed a collective adventure, it was one in which the whole nation was embarked, willingly or knowingly or not. This sense of the planners acting for, or on behalf of, the nation's citizens is one of the basic political challenges of France's planning enterprise. In political terms, the debate about planning coalesced quickly around the critique of an unelected, technocratic elite arrogating to itself the right and ability to make decisions about the future, and having the administrative and political means to implement those decisions.[7] Indeed, for all the careful thought and philosophical reflection behind it, or the enthusiastic investment in *la prospective* as a way to the future, there is no escaping the disciplinary qualities of prospective planning. Lurking in the future tense of the prospective view was an imperative mood: the trends it foresaw, and the adaptations they required, exemplified the kind of governmental practices of population management that would capture Michel Foucault's attention in the mid-1970s.

The critique became a persuasive and influential one, not least in terms of drawing out the nature of state power, and the frequently problematic implications of decisions taken by a few for the lived experience of millions, and we will return to it at various points. But the denunciatory mode of critique (the mode adopted, for example, by Henri Lefebvre, or by Bourdieu and Boltanski, and returning as a motif across French culture) needs nevertheless to be accompanied by careful attention to how spatial planning produced its new realities, as well as to the limits it encountered, and the complexity of the motivations that lay behind it. After all, if planning was a collective adventure, it was also a human one, fired by the imagination and driven by a range of passions, ideas and emotions. To overlook the human dimension of planning action — that it is something done by individuals bound up in particular situations at particular moments — is to forget that ideology and power are embodied, and not abstract, forces. They shape ways of seeing the world, talking about it and thereby acting upon it; and one of the most effective ways they do so is through the performative power of discourse and representation.

Spatial planning offers one of the most dramatic examples of that power, in terms of the ability of language, text and image, when in certain hands, to produce what Bourdieu and Boltanski term 'realised ideology' (1976: 55); in other words, ideology rendered concrete in new material forms and lived realities. One of the central concerns in the remainder of the book is the movement from and between the symbolic domain of representation and the real terrain of construction and development, or as Guichard puts it, between conception and action. How, asks Guichard, do we move from one to the other? What is at stake in 'la mise en œuvre des textes' (1965: 109), in putting texts to work? How do modernized landscapes take shape? But also, we might ask, what do they start to look and feel

---

7   On the politics of technocracy, see Hecht (1998: 28–39) and Thœnig 1987.

like? What forms does life start to take in a modernized France? And where does French modernization reach its limits? What does life look like when the planners' temporal horizons have arrived?

By the time those horizons had been reached (whether they were 1985 or 2000), it was perhaps inevitable that French modernization looked partial and unfinished; inevitable in large part because it could not escape the effects of time. As Guichard, for one, was well aware, 'l'aménagement du territoire dialogue constamment avec le temps', spatial planning is in constant negotiation with time (1965: 26). In Guichard's mind, it was a question of how planning might outwit time and anticipate the future. Once the diggers and builders move in though, it is more a question of how planning becomes *overtaken* by time.

Massé sensed the temporal complexities lurking within spatial planning, not the least of which is the length of time it involves: 'l'aménagement du territoire a sa spécificité: c'est qu'il implique une action de longue haleine dont les résultats sont visibles, durables, inscrits dans le sol' [the specificity of spatial planning is that it implies long-term action whose results are visible, durable and inscribed on the ground] (1965: 106). Not only do its activities unfold over a substantial period of time, but its outcomes, and particularly the physical environments it produces, persist in the landscape and give shape to lived experience long after the vision and ideology which produced them have been eclipsed.

Spatial planning's modernized landscapes would become increasingly complex temporal objects, like fossils or relics of an imagined future from the past. In the new towns of the Paris region, or the infrastructure shaping the national territory, prospective planning succeeded in bringing the future into the present. Yet it could not prevent its future-in-the-present also becoming a future-from-the-past.

CHAPTER 2

❖

Man Made:
Planning, Power and Desire

Critique and Interpretation

With the whole territory under its purview, spatial planning in post-war France had a totalizing scale and ambition, and left a concomitant imprint on French life. Its legacy is woven throughout French society and culture, not simply as backdrop or setting but as structuring principle. It gives shape to how life is lived, perceived and portrayed. An example would be the modernized landscapes embedded within Agnès Varda's film *Sans toit ni loi* (1985) (in English, *Vagabond*), to which I return in Chapter 4. The drama of French spatial planning lies as well in the fact that its motive force lay in a relatively small group of individuals, apparently unaccountable to their fellow citizens, who nevertheless had the will, power and administrative ability to initiate transformations affecting millions of people.

At best, given such an unequal distribution of power and agency, spatial planning risked being a project whose ambition slid into hubris. Rosemary Wakeman implies as much when she describes Paul Delouvrier's *Schéma directeur* for the Paris region as 'one of the most grandiose regional land-use programs ever attempted' (2016: 220). At worst, if a state maintains power through 'violence exercised on space', in Henri Lefebvre's words (1974: 323), then spatial planning was a particularly visible manifestation of state violence against its citizens because of the way in which it cut into the fabric of everyday life, doing so literally once the diggers and bulldozers moved in to rip things up and start again.

Yet simultaneously, as we saw in Chapter 1, the planners were a group whose professed motivation was to enable better lives for their compatriots, and who brought their hopes and dreams of the future to bear in their work. Speaking in 1975, Delouvrier argued that the planners developing the new towns around Paris 'se battent pour des choses nouvelles, pour que les hommes vivent autrement' [fight for new things, so that people can live differently] (Murard & Fourquet 2004: 246). Looking back in 1984, Jean Millier, who had joined Delouvrier at the District de Paris after fifteen years as director of planning and public works in Côte d'Ivoire, suggested that the planning enterprise was driven above all by a spirit of liberal humanism, underpinned by the moral sense of public service which grounded the planners' corporate ethos:

On a parlé technique, finance, mais je crois que nous étions animés par le désir très humain de faire mieux vivre les gens qui vivaient dans cette agglomération. Je crois que c'est ça qui nous animait au premier chef. On se sentait responsable de l'amélioration du sort des citoyens de l'agglomération parisienne. (Hirsch 2003: 187)

[We've talked about technical matters and about finance, but we were also driven by the very human desire to make life better for the people who lived in the region. That is what I think motivated us first and foremost. We felt responsible for improving the lives of the citizens of the Paris region.]

When Delouvrier published the *Schéma directeur* in June 1965, freedom and opportunity were central themes of the commentary that accompanied the 1:100,000-scale map showing the master plan. The concluding pages amplified them further, with the claim that the *Schéma directeur*'s fundamental goal was to create a world offering 'davantage de liberté, davantage de beauté' [more freedom and more beauty], as well as 'la commodité qui permet à chacun de jouir et de la liberté et de la beauté' [the means for everyone to enjoy freedom and beauty] (DGRP 1965: 245).

Delouvrier's team conceived of the Paris region as an interconnected system, with a polycentric network of new towns around Paris structuring urban development west and east along the two axes of the Seine and Marne river valleys. The new towns would be connected to Paris and each other by motorways and rapid transit rail lines (the RER) designed to speed up the flow of people and goods. To conjure and project their visions of the future, the planners mobilized a whole machinery of symbolic, iconographic and discursive forms. Texts, images, sketches, drawings, maps, plans and scale models all helped to make the planned world more tangible. Not the least of these was the map of the *Schéma directeur* itself, in many ways the foundation and catalyst for the imaginative efforts that would go on to shape space and life in the Paris region.

Put another way, spatial planning was a complex and mercurial combination of power, imagination and desire. On the one hand, it was one of the most striking and consequential manifestations in post-war France of the ways power works, what it looks like, who enacts it and how. On the other, images of the planners in action or accounts of what they set out to achieve are reminders that, notwithstanding the magnitude of its consequences, planning was not the product of state power as a singular, monolithic and abstract force, but the collective work of human beings; that is to say, subjects situated in specific historical contexts, with their own biographies, trajectories, relationships and affiliations. As people, they were constituted consciously and unconsciously by ideas, beliefs, perceptions and assumptions, and by emotions, feelings, passions and desires. It seems unavoidable, therefore, that their work as planners would reflect those perceptions, emotions, feelings and desires. In addition, if the stakes of what they dreamt and imagined were so high, it is because of the scale on which their imaginings could play themselves out.

But here lies another aspect of post-war spatial planning's complexity as a social and political intervention. For, as my discussion so far suggests, and much of the archival and historical material makes clear, it was also to a large extent a realm of *male* power, action and imagination (Fig. 2.1). The environments and landscapes

FIG. 2.1. Men at work. Meeting in 1967 chaired by Paul Delouvrier (prefect of the Paris region) in the centre, with Maurice Doublet (prefect of Paris) and Jean Verdier (prefect of Seine-et-Marne) on the left and Maurice Grimaud (prefect of police) and the prefect of Seine-et-Oise on the right. Collection of the Institut Paris Région, rights reserved.

of modernized France, in other words, emerge as man-made in more senses than one. French planning is far from unusual in this respect, but the gendered nature of the discipline carries a number of significant implications, as feminist historians of planning such as Leonie Sandercock and Barbara Hooper have underlined. Not only is planning historically a largely male domain, but its history is frequently narrated and established by the actors themselves. At stake are the unseen or unacknowledged assumptions that come freighted with planning as a discipline which sees the world through male eyes (eyes that are usually also white and middle-class).

What Sandercock calls the 'official story' of planning is told as a heroic and progressive enterprise, working for the greater good, 'always on the side of the angels' (Sandercock 1998: 4). It is the narrative articulated (in good faith, we can assume) by Pierre Massé as he develops his philosophy of prospective planning, by Millier and Delouvrier as they reflect on their motivations, or by the commentary setting out the ambitions of the *Schéma directeur*. But what is celebrated as a progressive enterprise is also (or in fact) about implementing a disciplinary and regulatory regime. As Hooper puts it, planning 'came to function not simply as the emancipatory practice it theorized but as a participant in new forms of social control' (1998: 229), forms whose impact would be disproportionately felt by women and other subordinated groups within society.

From a planning perspective, progressiveness meant bringing order to chaos. From a feminist perspective, the worlds made by planning reflect, articulate or express, consciously or not, the desires, fantasies and anxieties of the (largely male) planners who produce them. In Hooper's words, planning becomes 'the poem of male desires' (1998: 227). For her, the desire to install order 'must be understood, at least in part, as a masculinist fantasy of control, a fantasy that reverberates from planning's inception into the present' (1998: 248).

In many ways, there is no better illustration of Hooper's critique than the *Schéma directeur*. Its origins lie in de Gaulle's (in)famous injunction to Delouvrier on his appointment as *délégué général* of the District de Paris in August 1961: 'la région parisienne c'est le bordel, mettez-moi de l'ordre dans tout cela' [the Paris region is a mess, sort it out for me] (Saint-Pierre 2002: 17). De Gaulle's remark has entered into the mythology of post-war spatial planning in France, and while it has various reported forms, some phrased more loftily than others, their general tenor remains the same. Moreover, it is the earthier version we have here that has stayed in circulation, and which Delouvrier himself tended to relate.[1]

De Gaulle's reference to the Paris region as a *bordel* in need of 'sorting out' at one level reflects common colloquial usage in French, equivalent in meaning to 'shambles' or 'mess' in British English. The abruptness of his command further reinforces the sense of *aménagement du territoire* as something approaching a military operation to restore discipline (parallels manifested visually on occasion, as we shall see later). But the term's literal meaning (brothel/bordello) imports some revealing metaphorical resonances. It figures the area as a feminized space on which the imposition of a masculinist order will bring necessary improvement — moral as much as technical, seemed to be the message, the one achieved through the other. As Delouvrier put it in 1984, echoing de Gaulle's words, 'il s'agissait de remettre du rationnel dans le réel, par nature désordonné' [it was a question of putting some rationality back into reality, which is disordered by nature] (Hirsch 2003: 45).

Whether about power or desire, spatial planning emerges from feminist and Marxist critiques as compromised politically and morally, and expressive of fundamental tensions within society. If Lefebvre sees the state-led production of space as inherently violent, it is because of the structural distortions it imposes, the imbalances of power it sustains, and the alienating effects of the environments it creates. Planned space is the 'dominant' form of space in society (Lefebvre 1974: 48), not necessarily because it is the most prevalent, but because it most acutely asserts

---

1   On the life, forms and functions of de Gaulle's command, see Welch 2018. Some historians of French planning, notably Loïc Vadelorge (2005, 2014), have expressed frustration with the traction gained by the story, and argue that its mythologizing emphasis on planning as the realm of providential men obscures a fuller picture of the political, administrative and historical context in which it unfolded. But stories like these are important *precisely as* foundational myths, because of how they reveal, often inadvertently, the assumptions, prejudices and ideologies in play. Such things are all the more important to understand given the consequences of the decisions flowing from them.

authority, and is geared towards maintaining the established social and economic order. As such, it reminds its users that the conception and production of space remains the prerogative of the powerful, and especially of the state.

For Hooper, (male) desire and fantasy are influences that planning simply cannot escape. She emphasizes the importance of addressing 'the presence of unannounced fantasies and desires that work themselves unconsciously and unexplicitly into the good, even the best, intentions of planning's knowledges, histories and plans' (Hooper 1998: 248). However enlightened it attempts to be, planning appears fated to produce environments which set out to discipline, and result in alienation and disenfranchisement. Its main outcome, intended or otherwise, would seem to be a diminishment of human life.

Feminist and Marxist critiques of spatial planning share common ground in adopting a hermeneutics of suspicion. As an interpretative mode attentive to assumptions, prejudices and ideological blind spots, a hermeneutics of suspicion is vital both analytically and politically for understanding the motivations, implications and consequences of an intervention like the *Schéma directeur*, which had a bearing on the lives of millions. At the same time, however, I would agree with Rita Felski that we need to remain attentive to what such a hermeneutics can itself elide or occlude.

Felski reminds us of Paul Ricœur's distinction between a hermeneutics of suspicion and a hermeneutics of trust, 'between a reading which tears off masks and one which seeks to restore and recollect meaning' (Felski 2011: 228). My aim in this chapter and the next, on the *Schéma directeur* and the new town of Cergy-Pontoise, is to mobilize and navigate between these two modes of interpretation. Doing so means unearthing the assumptions and prejudices in play in spatial planning, but it also involves investigating what Hooper acknowledges might be the planners' *well-intentioned* aims, and revisiting (or 'restoring', to use Felski's term) what it was they were setting out to achieve.

This in turn means bringing the human dimension of spatial planning back into play. In seeking to understand the transformations it wrought, as Kenny Cupers suggests, 'we need to favor situated agency over abstract forces and contingency over determinism' (2014: xv). On the more abstract level, spatial planning is undoubtedly about what Lefebvre calls 'la puissance de l'argent et celle de l'État politique' [the power of money and the political state] (1974: 65) and their shared imperatives, with the latter working to maintain a productive environment for the former. Yet on a more immediately human level, it is about Delouvrier touring the Paris region in a convertible car in order to get a better feel for the lie of the land (Murard & Fourquet 2004: 119), or the chief planner of Cergy-Pontoise gesturing to a scale model as he talks to an interviewer in a television news report (Fig. 2.2). In other words, mobilizing another of Felski's terms, we need to 'recollect' spatial planning as a profoundly human activity, guided by historically situated individuals filled with their own feelings, desires and beliefs, and involving a lived process of creation and negotiation between different actors on the ground.

Bridging these differing realities involves paying closer attention to planning as a realm of the imagination. It means exploring the ways in which the planners articulated their visions, ideas and activities, how different modes and techniques

FIG. 2.2. Situated agency: Bernard Hirsch (on the left) gestures towards a
scale model of Cergy-Pontoise during a television news interview in 1970.
ORTF, journal télévisé de 13 heures, 16 December 1970.

of representation are imbricated within their work, and how the activity of spatial
planning is portrayed. One of the most striking aspects of post-war *aménagement* was
the amount of representational material produced by the planners as they designed,
developed and mediated their visions for a modernized France. But also striking is
how little critical attention that material has received. Not that it has been invisible
in recent scholarship. On the contrary, its reproduction in books such as Busbea
2007, Cupers 2014, Wakeman 2016 and others has helped draw attention to its
range, variety and centrality in the process of spatial production.

What has been lacking to date, though, is sustained interpretative engagement
which investigates its semiotic, rhetorical and material qualities; that is to say, how
it works to give shape to the planners' imagined worlds and communicate the
planning vision, and how symbolic, discursive and iconographic forms become
active participants in the production of new spatial realities. Reflecting on spatial
planning's representational machinery is an important part of re-inscribing the
human into the enterprise. It reminds us of planning's curious position as an activity
unfolding in the symbolic as much as the empirical realm, mediating between
imagined and real space, and producing one from the other.

In thinking through what is at stake in *aménagement du territoire*, and how the
planners conceive of their intervention, an illuminating perspective comes from
a body of critical and theoretical work that was taking shape simultaneously in
France, and concerned precisely with how power and desire run through and shape
the social formation. What is more, that work frequently took as its starting point
the nature and consequences of spatial production, as well as the economic and
political forces which drove it. Indeed, it is easy to overlook the extent to which,
during the 1960s and 70s, the relationship between spatial planning, on the one

hand, and the emergence of radical critical, social and spatial theory on the other, is causal and not merely coincidental.

After all, Lefebvre for one was clear that his research on urbanism and the production of space developed in direct response to the work of the DATAR in the 1960s: 'la création de villes et le remaniement de villes existantes, étaient tout de même quelque chose de tout-à-fait nouveau par rapport aux descriptions classiques du phénomène urbain' [the creation of towns and the reshaping of existing towns was really something quite new in relation to classic accounts of the urban phenomenon) (Lefebvre & others 1983: 51). In *L'Invention du quotidien*, whose roots lay a government research contract awarded as part of the preparations for the seventh Plan in the mid-1970s, Michel de Certeau saw the shaping of daily life in terms of tactic, ruse, subversion and spatial incursion: necessary but nevertheless creative responses to the imposition of 'espace technocratiquement bâti, écrit et fonctionnalisé' [space built, articulated and functionalized by technocratic means] (1990: xlv).[2]

Similarly, it is arguably no coincidence that during the early 1970s, Michel Foucault's work was increasingly concerned with the nature of government as the management and regulation of populations within the framework of a national territory; or that around the same time, Foucault collaborated with Gilles Deleuze and Félix Guattari on the relationship between government, planning and infrastructure as part of the work of the Centre d'études, de recherches et de formation institutionnelles [Centre for institutional study, research and development] (CERFI), set up by Guattari in 1967, and financed by a series of government research contracts until the mid-1970s (Fourquet 1982: 10–12).[3]

Verena Andermatt Conley is right to underscore the increasing preoccupation with space in French theory from the late 1960s. There is plenty of evidence to suggest as well that it arose in direct response to the French state's spatial planning policies during the same period. Moreover, not only did *aménagement du territoire* galvanize critical theory as a response to the impact of new social and spatial formations, but critical theory also elucidates the assumptions behind planning action to a remarkable degree. One of the aims of this chapter is to consider how spatial planning was at once provoking and illuminated by the theoretical work of social and spatial critique taking place at the same time, thereby helping to fuel the emergence of 'space as a critical concept', to borrow Conley's phrase (2012: 1). The chapter focuses in particular on Delouvrier's *Schéma directeur* for the Paris region because it seemed to exemplify the problematic nature of power in Gaullist France, the unaccountable nature of technocratic government, and its manifestation in gendered terms as a largely male domain. Indeed, we shall see that Jean-Luc

---

2   Luce Giard writes about the origins of *L'Invention du quotidien* in her introduction to the Folio edition (Giard 1990: i–xxx). In the sort of neat irony produced by the recycling of high-ranking civil servants within French state administration, de Certeau's research contract was awarded by a committee chaired by Paul Delouvrier (Giard 1990: viii), who had moved on from his role as prefect of the Paris region in 1969 to be president of Électricité de France.

3   On Foucault's involvement with CERFI, see Mozère 2004 and Elden (2016: 83–85). On the history of CERFI more generally, see Fourquet 1982.

Godard, with typical alacrity, portrayed it precisely as such in his 1967 film, *2 ou 3 choses que je sais d'elle* [Two or Three Things I Know About Her].

On the one hand, the contemporary critical theory of Deleuze, Guattari, Foucault and others could offer analytical purchase on the *Schéma directeur*, the motivations of spatial planning, and the dynamics of power and desire which were latent within them. It opened up ways of thinking about planning as a human activity, bound up in and produced by a complex set of ideas, preconceptions, passions and emotions. On the other, there are points at which planning and theory converge quite strikingly, in terms of conceptualising how societies work, what governments do, and how spatial planning shapes both territory and population. If this is the case, it is because planning was itself a process attempting to work with the strange and unpredictable energy of human life, locating it in space and time, and recognizing it as matter in flow, circulation and flux. Put another way, French spatial planning could be seen as something approaching a live experiment or demonstration of the social, psychical and political processes preoccupying French critical thinking at the time, and how chief amongst them were the workings of power and desire.

Seeing like a State: Planning, Power and Vision

At first glance, spatial planning is most obviously about power. It is about the will, means and ability to make things happen on a large scale. In terms of its impact, it is also one of the most obvious expressions of state power and government in post-war France. To this day, the outcomes of the *Schéma directeur* structure lived experience in and around Paris. Its legacy is navigated by anyone who travels via Roissy-CDG airport, takes the RER to La Défense or Marne-la-Vallée, or changes trains at Châtelet-Les Halles underground station. Yet what has now become part of the fabric of everyday life once formed a horizon anticipated with varying degrees of enthusiasm.

In 1967, two contrasting perspectives appeared on what the future held for the Paris region and its inhabitants. First came Godard's *2 ou 3 choses que je sais d'elle*, released in March of that year. A few months later, at the start of July, the front cover of *Paris Match*, the popular weekly news magazine, carried the headline 'Paris in Twenty Years' Time', next to a dramatic artist's impression of the city skyline to come. Between them, they offered two portraits of Gaullist power, as well as diverging ways of understanding the stakes and consequences of French spatial planning.

Godard already had form in predicting urban futures, and warning of their dangers. In 1965, he released *Alphaville*, a science fiction movie set in a repressive city state run by a sophisticated mainframe computer (Alpha 60) and managed from control rooms by lab-coated technicians. The film offered a dystopian vision of an urban future where the rational planning and organization of society converge with authoritarian government; or more specifically, where the latter proved to be the logical conclusion and requirement of the former.

Appearing in the same year as *Le Plan, ou l'anti-hasard*, Pierre Massé's celebration of planning as enabler of civilizational advance, *Alphaville* offered a thinly-veiled

FIG. 2.3. Planning as command and control in Jean-Luc Godard's *Alphaville* (1965).

FIG. 2.4. Landscapes of the future in *Alphaville* (1965).

allegory and critique of the Gaullist, technocratic state (Fig. 2.3). In an encounter with central character Lemmy Caution (Eddie Constantine), the city's youthful and sinister chief engineer observes, using words that would resonate with Massé, that 'le principe d'Alphaville 60 est de calculer et de prévoir les conséquences auxquelles Alphaville obéira ensuite' [the principle of Alpha 60 is to calculate and predict the consequences which Alphaville will subsequently obey]. The parallels were reinforced by occasional glimpses of Alphaville, whose modernized landscapes of infrastructure (power lines, pylons, tower blocks) were those that Godard could film in and around contemporary Paris (Fig. 2.4).

To that extent, there seemed to be plenty of evidence to suggest that Godard's imagined future was already lurking in the present. *2 ou 3 choses que je sais d'elle* would confirm it to be the case, as Godard set out to document the development of the Paris region. In effect, the film was a report on how the science fiction of Alphaville was taking shape in (and shaping) the reality of 1960s Paris. Godard suggested with some mischief that, given how it sought to understand the implications of the *Schéma directeur*, Delouvrier himself should have commissioned the film (Godard 1971: 12). Its documentary intent comes through in its opening sequence, with sounds and images of construction work around Paris, and a title card stating (in the blue, white and red of the French tricolour) 'elle: la région parisienne'. More accurately, as Douglas Morrey notes (2005: 62), the viewer is presented initially with sounds *then* images of construction. Godard decouples the two, switching between sound and silence for the first minute of the film as he finds ways to disorient the viewer and raise the problems that the film will go on to investigate.

The opening twenty seconds or so show the film title (with '2 ou 3' also in the French national colours) against a black background, accompanied by the insistent and startling sound of a pneumatic jackhammer. Cutting to the first shot of the film reveals the elegant, geometric curve of a new slip road occupying much of the screen, with sunlight glinting on its freshly laid tarmac, and a construction site in its shadow beneath. The sound of construction stops abruptly with the cut, leaving us to contemplate the scene in silence for a few seconds. The next cut reunites sound and image, and startles us again by locating us near a motorway overpass which amplifies the noise of the traffic rushing beneath it. Silence returns for the start of the next shot, which shows an elevated expressway under construction, receding into the distance beneath an expanse of sky and a scattering of tall buildings.

We are clearly somewhere on the edge of Paris — in fact, as Jacob Paskins notes (2016: 58), the northern stretches of the Boulevard Périphérique being built around the Porte de la Chapelle — even if Godard gives no explicit clues as to the location. Rather, the opening sequence seems intent on foregrounding the difficulty in understanding what is going on. Indeed, it does not present difficulty as a problem, so much as subject its viewers to it. As Morrey suggests, by springing the sound of the jackhammer on the audience, the film's opening seconds 'associate knowledge (the *savoir* of the title) with *noise* and thereby with uncertainty' (2005: 62). The decoupling of sound and image, switches from sound to silence, shifts in sound level from one scene to another, jump cuts between locations and changes in perspective all combine to sow sensory and epistemological confusion, and disrupt our attempts to grasp how things (activities, spaces, locations) piece together. In any case, Godard had already promised only limited and partial knowledge (of two or three things) in the title of his film.

Morrey interprets Godard's preoccupation with knowledge in *2 ou 3 choses que je sais d'elle* primarily in philosophical terms, as an investigation into the provisionality of thought, the limits of cognition and the difficulty of making sense of the world. Yet the challenges to knowledge are as much spatial and political as they are philosophical. More precisely, the film roots phenomenological problems of understanding in the spatial and political transformations affecting Paris and

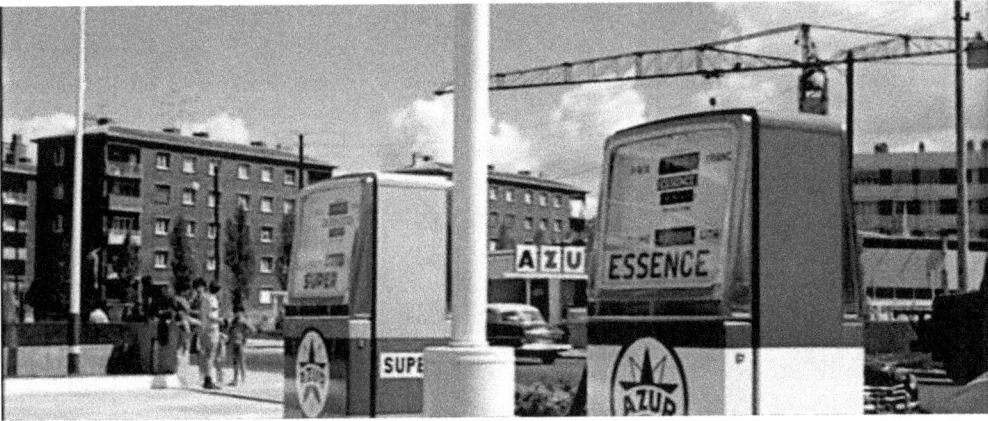

FIG. 2.5. The politics of building in Jean-Luc Godard's *2 ou 3 choses que je sais d'elle* (1967).

its inhabitants (Fig. 2.5). The relationship between the three emerges in another aspect of the film's sonic environment in the opening few minutes. The silence accompanying images of construction, traffic and new space is broken by Godard's whispered voiceover, which signals recent developments in the government of the Paris region. Noting the publication on 19 August 1966 of a decree on the administrative reorganization of the Paris region, Godard observes that 'deux jours après, le Conseil des ministres nomme Paul Delouvrier préfet de la Région parisienne qui, selon le communiqué du secrétariat à l'Information, se trouve ainsi dotée de structures précises et originales' [two days later, the Council of Ministers named Paul Delouvrier prefect of the Paris region which, according to the communiqué published by the government press service, acquired specific and distinctive structures as a result] (Godard 1971: 20).[4]

I have noted elsewhere (2018: 107) how Godard's theatrical whisper creates the impression of secrets being revealed and shared with the audience. While the film foregrounds the challenge of knowledge in philosophical terms, it nevertheless seems more confident in diagnosing what might be afoot politically in the noise and confusion of urban development. If the changes are difficult to fathom, it is because they are scattered discontinuously across the landscape, an effect staged in the opening sequence by jump cuts from one location to another. But woven through

4   The creation of a regional prefect completed the administrative reform of the Paris region initiated by prime minister Michel Debré in the early 1960s. While distinct from the development of the *Schéma directeur*, it expressed the same Gaullist desire to restore order to a region felt to have become, in Jean Millier's words, 'ungovernable' (Murard & Fourquet 2004: 155). In 1964, the existing *départements* of Seine and Seine-et-Oise were replaced by seven new ones: Paris, Hauts-de-Seine, Val-de-Marne, Seine-Saint-Denis, Yvelines, Essonne and Val-d'Oise. The latter two would have the new towns of Évry and Cergy-Pontoise as their prefectures. The 1966 decree created Godard's 'specific and distinctive structures' by introducing a new tier within the prefectural hierarchy, and enhancing Delouvrier's powers by placing the departmental prefects under his command. It also subsumed his existing functions as *délégué général* of the District, a role whose strengths (an agility derived from being outside the traditional power structures of state administration) simultaneously made it vulnerable to changes in the political weather.

the noise of construction and traffic, Godard's quiet articulation of administrative moves behind the scenes suggests a hidden agenda at work. It is as if the government creates then takes advantage of sensory and spatial confusion to do its work under cover (or rather, to hide it in plain sight).

Furthermore, that work seems invariably to be against the interests of the country's citizens. Godard's hermeneutics of suspicion frames the collusion between state and capital as fundamental to the aims and intentions of *aménagement*. Over shots of construction cranes, a petrol station and goods on display in a furniture store, his voiceover proposes that 'le pouvoir gaulliste prend le masque d'un réformateur et d'un modernisateur alors qu'il ne veut qu'enregistrer et régulariser les tendances naturelles du grand capitalisme' (1971: 21). Gaullist power might claim to be about reform and modernization, but in fact it is about securing and easing the path of capital.[5] Godard sets about mapping the consequences that derive, to recall Lefebvre's terms, from the accommodation between the twin powers of money and the state.

The first and most visible consequence is spatial. It is captured in the film's first image, that of the new slip road curving over the construction site beneath it (Fig. 2.6). A sense of beauty is to be found in the calculated precision of the bend and the freshness of its surfaces, one reinforced by the contrast between its smooth sheen and the jumble of moved earth above which it hovers. At the same time, there is something odd about the sharpness of that contrast. It has a two-dimensional, planar quality reinforced by the monochrome combination of black tarmac and light grey concrete border, its lack of depth, and the contours of the construction site below. It seems to have arrived from elsewhere, and bear no direct relation to its surroundings.

Indeed, the forms and locations filmed by Godard display all the qualities of the 'abstract space' that was characteristic of spatial production by the state for Lefebvre. He locates the effects of spatial abstraction in a combination of forms and materials: glass and stone, concrete and steel, angles and curves, solids and voids (Lefebvre 1974: 61). Not only is abstract space an imposition on its surroundings (something figured in Godard's shot of the slip road filling the screen and casting a shadow over the space below it), but its formal and material qualities diminish everyday life by evacuating the history, identity, difference and spontaneity that constitute it.

---

5   Godard's suspicions would surely have been confirmed when the film censor removed the previous sentence of the commentary, which claims that 'Paul Delouvrier, malgré son beau nom, a fait ses classes dans les groupes bancaires Lazard et Rothschild' [notwithstanding his name, Paul Delouvrier learned his trade working for the Lazard and Rothschild banking group] (Godard 1971: 21). In fairness to Delouvrier, the claim was inaccurate. While he had family connections with banking via his father (Chenu 1994: 18), Delouvrier spent all his career in the public sector. Nevertheless, his influential roles in the French Finance Ministry and the European Coal and Steel Authority meant he was part of the French banking and finance establishment. At the same time, he had a keen sense of the ethos of probity expected of a public servant, expressed in an anecdote about his embarrassment over a turkey received as a gift of thanks from (as it happens) the Rothschild family (Chenu 1994: 142). Delouvrier's liminal position between the public and private sectors is captured in Pierre Bourdieu and Monique de Saint Martin's analysis of French industrialists and the field of economic power in post-war France (Bourdieu & Saint Martin 1978).

FIG. 2.6. Abstract space in *2 ou 3 choses que je sais d'elle* (1967).

The second and more profound consequence is moral, which emerges as Godard explores the psychical and social consequences of modernization for the inhabitants of the Paris region, and in particular, for women. The film's opening sequence concludes its tour of the Parisian periphery by bringing us into a huge new housing development (*grand ensemble*) at La Courneuve to the north of Paris, known as 'Les 4,000' (a reference to the number of apartments it contained). There we meet the film's central character, Juliette Jeanson, played by Marina Vlady. Filmed on what we assume to be a balcony, she seems to hang in mid-air, an expansive view south to Paris behind her, but to her left the imposing wall of a tower block.

We encounter Juliette dwarfed, framed or enclosed by the monumental buildings of the housing estate at different points in the film, and it becomes clear that the alienating qualities and consequences of abstract space are manifested not just in infrastructure, but also, and more problematically, in the new dwelling places being built around Paris.[6] The film's starting-point was an investigation by the news weekly *Le Nouvel Observateur* into the phenomenon of female prostitution in the *grands ensembles* around Paris (Godard 1971: 17). Godard was struck by this, seeing in it a metaphor and symptom of a more generalized moral decline whose roots lay in Gaullist modernization and its stimulation of a consumer society. As he puts it in his commentary, 'en systémitisant le dirigisme et la centralisation, ce même pouvoir accentue les distorsions de l'économie nationale, et plus encore celle de la morale quotidienne qui la fonde' [in systematizing central control and organization, that same power further accentuates the distortions of the national economy, and even more so the moral foundations that underpin it] (1971: 21).

So much for the Gaullist desire to bring (moral) order to the 'bordel' of the Parisian suburbs through spatial reorganization. Instead, we follow Juliette through

---

6   Though the construction of Les 4,000 at La Courneuve predates the development of the *Schéma directeur*, having been built between 1957 and 1963 as part of the rush to resolve the capital's *crise du logement*. In Welch 2018, I discuss Godard's amalgamation of these two phases of urban development, what is at stake in the confusion, and how it resurfaces in later critiques of Parisian spatial planning such as Maspero 1990 and Ross 1995.

the film as she becomes caught up in the cycle of credit and debt fuelled by the demands, pressures and pleasures of consumption, and turns to prostitution in order to make ends meet. Godard thus begins to exploit the referential ambiguity of the pronoun *elle* as meaning both 'it' and 'her'. If the opening titles confirm that 'elle' refers to 'la région parisienne', it quickly also comes to mean Juliette, as well as prostitution, and a host of other themes identified in the film trailer ('the terrible law of the housing estates', 'life today'), all of which are constitutive of the Paris region as a whole. *2 ou 3 choses que je sais d'elle* is the story of each through and in relation to the others. It is an assemblage, a piecing-together of an ensemble which crystallizes around Juliette to afford a glimpse of the true picture. The story of Juliette is also the story of what the Paris region is 'about'; namely, the implications, complexities and risks of the policies being pursued by the Gaullist government that Godard wants to draw to the surface, even as their full effects remain just out of sight, obscured by the noise and confusion of construction.

Four months later, in July 1967, the omnipresent but elusive force at work in Godard's film materialized in the pages of *Paris Match* and gave account of itself (Fig. 2.7). The story about Delouvrier's plans for the Paris region offered a chance to see what planning power looked like, how it worked, how it viewed the world, and how it saw itself in action. Most importantly, perhaps, it showed what happens when a certain way of seeing the world is sustained and propelled by the resources of political and state power. Delouvrier was amongst friends at *Paris Match*. Not only was the magazine a firm supporter of the Gaullist regime and its vision of French greatness, but it could offer one of the country's most extensive readerships, at the time approaching ten million (or roughly twenty per cent of the population) on a print run of around two million (Hewitt 1991: 111).

The author of the piece, Marc Heimer, made no bones of the opportunity it could afford, observing to his readers that 'Paul Delouvrier comprit qu'il ne pouvait choisir meilleure tribune que "Match" pour s'adresser à tous les Français et leur dévoiler, d'un seul coup de baguette magique, ce que sera leur capitale aux confins du XXe et du XXIe siècle' [Paul Delouvrier understood that there was no better place than *Paris Match* for addressing all French people and revealing to them, with a wave of the wand, how their capital city will be at the dawn of the twenty-first century] (Heimer 1967: 43). While the *Schéma directeur* had been in the public domain since June 1965, and received extensive press coverage at the time of its launch, there had subsequently been little in the way of detail about what the plans might entail. Heimer joins with Godard in articulating the same sense of obscure activity and incomplete knowledge evoked in *2 ou 3 choses que je sais d'elle*:

> Les Parisiens ne percevaient que quelque chose se préparait que grâce aux chantiers qui compliquaient un peu plus leur circulation et aux quelques tours isolées qui, à la Défense et à Montparnasse, commencent à surgir au milieu des grues et des pelles mécaniques. (Heimer 1967: 42)

The only visible sign to Parisians that something was going on was building work, traffic disruption and a scattering of new buildings taking shape between cranes and diggers.

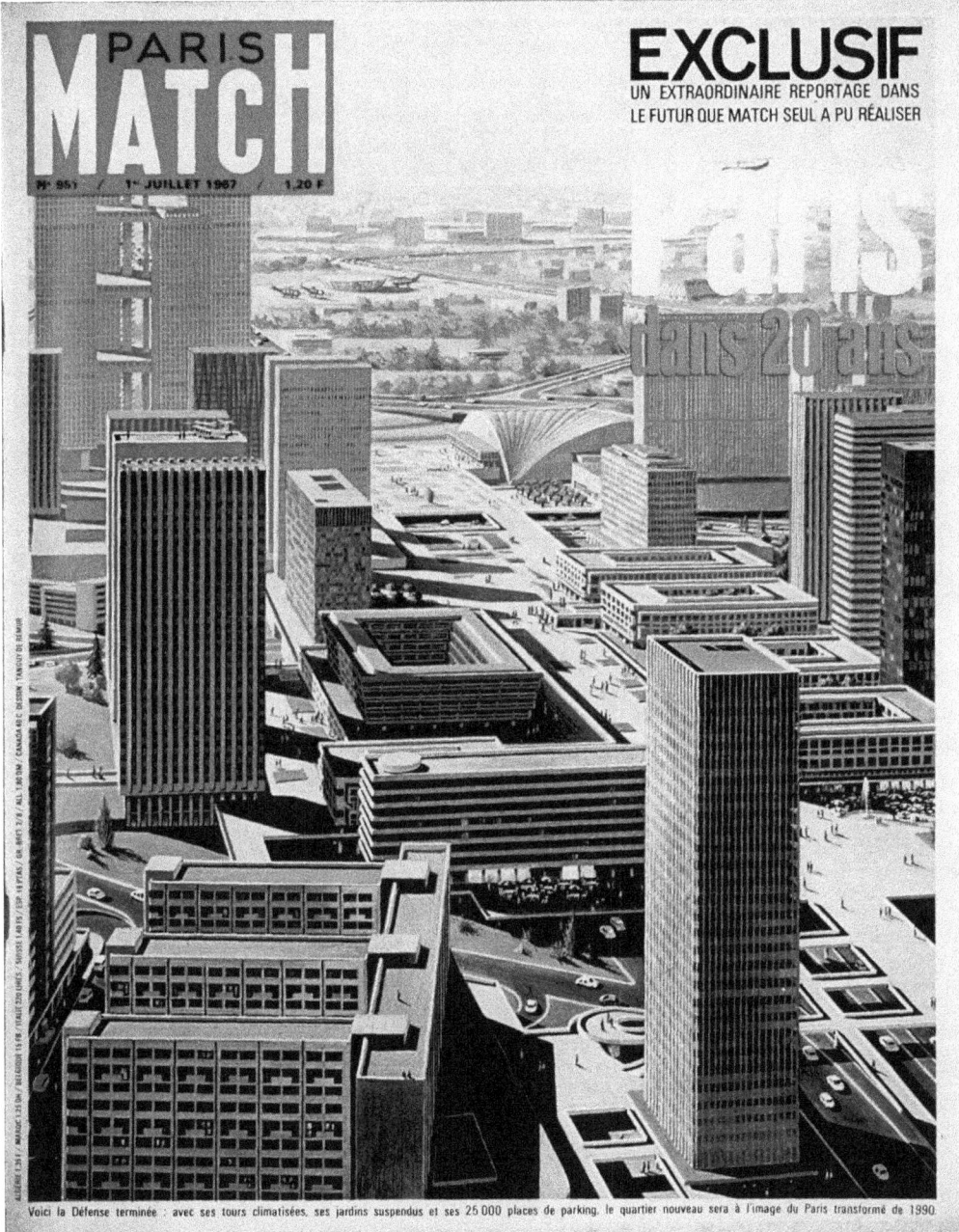

FIG. 2.7. 'Paris in Twenty Years' Time'. *Paris Match*, 1 July 1967.
© PARIS MATCH/SCOOP

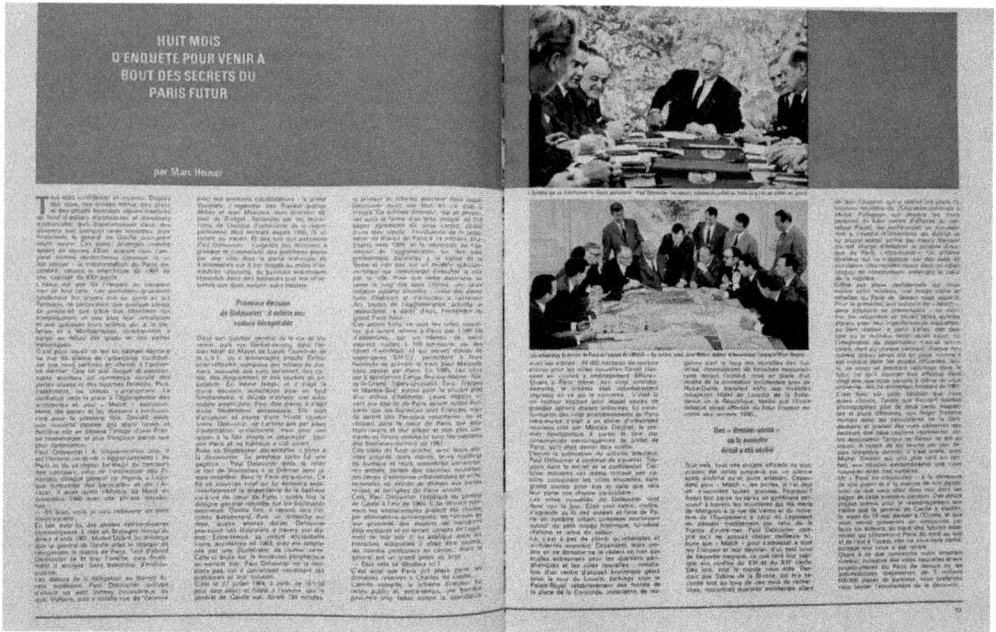

FIG. 2.8. Staging the planners at work. *Paris Match*, 1 July 1967. © PARIS MATCH/SCOOP

It was the happy role of *Paris Match* to bring enlightenment to the country in its 'exclusive' report, and reveal the vision guiding the movements of those cranes and diggers. It did so by helping its readers to a shift in perspective, from the partial view of the circulating citizen to the total view of the planner. Heimer's story offers an education in the planning perspective, as well as the centrality of vision and the visual in planning. If *Paris Match* was uniquely suited to the task, it was not only because of the privileged access to power afforded by the magazine's reach and political affinities, but also because of the privileged role it gave to images in its reporting of the world. It placed a premium on images for the communication of its stories, from full-page cover images to the extensive use of illustrations and the prominence of photographs on the page. In short, the fullest and best way to understand the world was visually.[7] The magazine's emphasis on the visual converges with planning as a mode of seeing, and as a practice which has vision and visual representation at its core.

Heimer's scene-setting story is accompanied by two revealing photographs of the planners at work (Fig. 2.8). Both images foreground the role played by visual modes of representation in the daily practice of spatial planning. They also make clear that we have entered a man's world. The upper image is familiar to us. Provided by the District's own planning arm, the Institut d'aménagement et d'urbanisme de la Région parisienne [Institute for spatial and urban planning of the Paris region] (IAURP), it shows Delouvrier in full flow against the backdrop of a huge aerial photograph offering a commanding view of the Paris region (Orly airport is visible

7   For a more extended discussion of the role of images in *Paris Match*, and the ways in which it mobilizes images to do political and ideological work, see Welch 2020.

La Seine : de Grenelle
à Bercy, elle coulera entre
tours et jardins

FIG. 2.9. Envisioning the sunlit future of planned Paris. *Paris Match*, 1 July 1967.
© PARIS MATCH/SCOOP

over his right shoulder). In the lower image, the planning team present the *Schéma directeur* to the magazine's reporters. On the wall behind them is a map showing the layout of the *Schéma directeur*, while they gather round a large table covered with maps and plans, as well as sundry items like marker pens and rulers.

It is instructive to see how transformations on an epic scale can be catalysed by small groups of people mobilizing a collection of drawings, plans and ordinary objects. If this is so, it is also because planning is a matter of confidence and agency, captured in the photographs through the bodily dispositions of those in the frame, and most obviously Delouvrier at the head of the committee table. In many respects, they offer an embodiment of the prospective attitude that, for Gaston Berger, was the defining quality of the age, geared towards the creation of the future in the present. The temporal and agential certainty of the prospective attitude is conveyed repeatedly in the story's images, which suggest the planners' seemingly seamless ability to produce space. It is captured especially in the image of the planners meeting in front of an aerial photograph of the Paris region. Not only does the size of the image convey the scale of their project, but it also serves to express their dominion over the territory it shows. The image gives them purchase on the Paris region by framing it, defining it, making it visible, and thereby opening it up to transformation.

Following the photographs of the planners at work are colourful double page spreads devoted to artist's impressions of what is to come (Fig. 2.9). They adopt the commanding perspective of the aerial view, including panoramas of the business district of La Défense and the redevelopment of the banks of the Seine in Paris. Tiny

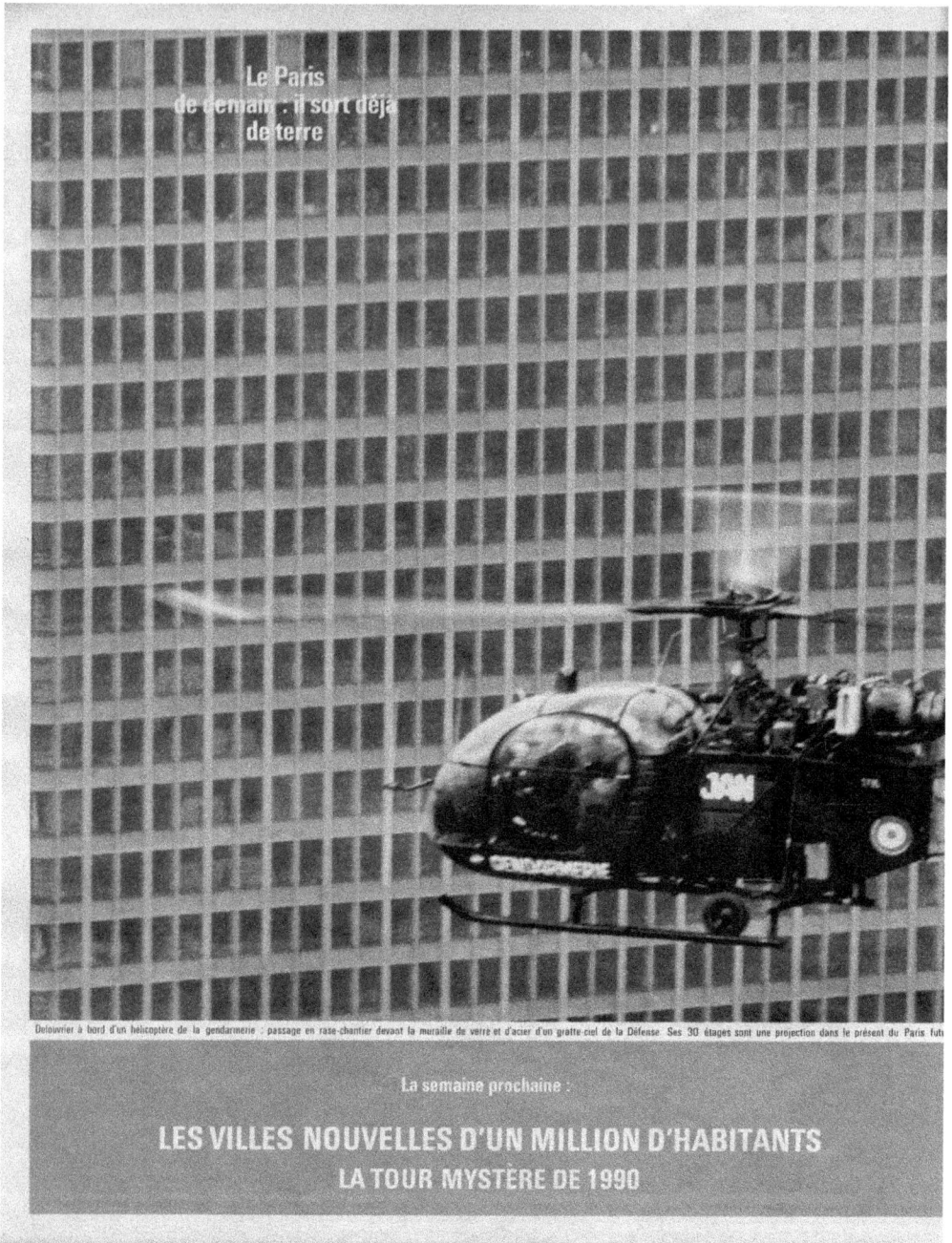

Le Paris
de demain : il sort déjà
de terre

Delouvrier à bord d'un hélicoptère de la gendarmerie : passage en rase-chantier devant la muraille de verre et d'acier d'un gratte-ciel de la Défense. Ses 30 étages sont une projection dans le présent du Paris fut...

La semaine prochaine :

LES VILLES NOUVELLES D'UN MILLION D'HABITANTS
LA TOUR MYSTÈRE DE 1990

Fig. 2.10. 'The Paris of tomorrow is already taking shape': Paul Delouvrier flies through La Défense. *Paris Match*, 1 July 1967. © PARIS MATCH/SCOOP figures stroll along expansive, sunlit boulevards as jetfoils and helicopters shuttle people around.

The biggest revelation is at the end of the story, which concludes with a full-page colour photograph of a police helicopter flying at speed past an office block in La Défense, with the imposing figure of Delouvrier visible in the passenger seat (Fig. 2.10). Already, notes the image caption, the Paris of tomorrow is taking shape on the ground (Heimer 1967: 56). The planners are confirmed in their role as the mediating agents between the present and the future, working with their maps, plans and models to translate their imagined worlds into built realities.

In its staging of the work and vision of the planners, the *Paris Match* exclusive can be seen to sum up the nature of the planning enterprise and the prospective attitude as the encounter of two things: on the one hand, what historian René Rémond calls the 'volonté d'agir' [will to action] that defined the *esprit de corps* of the French planners, and which Delouvrier himself was seen to exemplify (2005: 10; see also Welch 2018); on the other, what Michel Foucault calls the state's 'pouvoir sur la vie' [power over life] (1976: 182) as it regulates, manages and disciplines the population under its purview. The planners had both the will and the power to produce new worlds, and in so doing, shape the lives of millions of people. Godard could see the dangers posed by that will. *Paris Match* preferred to let its readers revel in the promise of 'un "Paris en majuscules" à la démesure de son avenir et à la mesure de son passé' [a 'Paris in capital letters' that promises a glorious future in keeping with its past] (Heimer 1967: 43).

There is perhaps no better expression of planning power than the shot of Delouvrier in a police helicopter flying over La Défense, not least because it serves to make explicit a militaristic quality to spatial planning that is latent in the other photos of the planners at work. Whether strapped into a helicopter or chairing discussions before an aerial photo, Delouvrier takes on the appearance of a general or colonial governor surveying the territory under his control. In fact, Guichard for one was explicit in highlighting the parallels between spatial planning and war, given that strategic intervention on the ground is central to both: 'l'art de la guerre étant pour une bonne part, un art du terrain, il y a entre l'état de militaire et les spécialistes de l'aménagement du territoire une sorte de langage commun qui leur a souvent permis de se comprendre' [given that the art of war is in large part an art of terrain, the military and the spatial planners share a sort of common language that allows them to understand each other] (Guichard 1965: 182).

If planners and the military had similar ways of seeing the world, then their lingua franca was the map. When the time came to present the *Schéma directeur* to de Gaulle in 1964, Delouvrier was convinced the president would best understand it through the medium of the map: 'j'ai averti Bonneval [de Gaulle's chief of staff] et je lui avais dit, "il faut qu'on arrive avec des cartes, il faut lui montrer des cartes". [...] C'était un militaire, il voulait voir les cartes, je les lui ai montrées' [I alerted Bonneval and said 'we need to take maps with us, we need to show him maps'. He was a military man who wanted to see maps, so that's what I showed him] (Murard & Fourquet 2004: 139). De Gaulle's training as a military man would give him the visual and cartographic fluency to interpret what the map was telling him. Delouvrier's instinctive turn to the map, on the other hand, responded to de Gaulle's perception of the Paris region as a theatre of operations in which the strategic objective was the restoration of 'order'.

Planning's military impulse also lurks in its preoccupation with speed and efficiency of circulation. It was not for nothing that the *Schéma directeur* was predicated on the development of a network of motorways and rapid transit rail systems. Nor that, when Godard set out to film evidence of Gaullist modernization, its most visible manifestation was the construction of an urban expressway, the Boulevard Périphérique around Paris. The defining role of infrastructure in the *Schéma directeur* supports Paul Virilio's argument that speed is of fundamental military, political and economic importance for the state (Virilio 1977).

Speed, movement and efficiency of circulation are amongst the state's central preoccupations because they are the key to military success and effective territorial control; but they are also essential for sustaining economic activity and the flows of people and goods that constitute it. The pursuit of speed and the creation of speed space (space designed to enable speed) drive the growth of state and capital, and are beneficial for both. At the same time, as *Paris Match* reveals in its closing photo, even the pursuit of speed for civilian ends cannot help but appear in militarized form from time to time, and remind us of its coercive and disciplinary origins.

De Gaulle's programmatic instruction to Delouvrier ('mettez-moi de l'ordre là-dedans') confirmed that spatial planning, from the state's point of view, was a matter of territorial control. It was an essential means through which the state could command, organize and govern its territory. As the repeated foregrounding of photographs, maps, plans and illustrations in accounts of spatial planning would suggest, doing so effectively also relied on a range of techniques, tools and methods to envision the territory under the state's purview. Guichard's book on *aménagement du territoire* establishes the metropolitan territory as his theatre of operations in large part through the repeated use of national maps for data visualization (Fig. 2.11).

The benefit of mapping, Guichard suggests, is that it 'permet de ramener l'échelle de vision du territoire à un document que l'on peut considérer facilement' [scales the territory down to a document that can be easily studied] (1965: 182). By scaling down the country, a map creates a totalizing perspective and makes visible ('fait apparaître', as Guichard has it) trends and patterns. Framed by the page, moreover, France's hexagonal outline lingers in the eye and reinforces an impression of a unified national space. Meanwhile, Delouvrier could deploy the resources at his disposal, including the IAURP, to translate the Paris region into various discursive, iconographic and symbolic forms. The maps, plans and models produced by his team could be put into circulation, placed before interested parties, inscribed, annotated, redrawn, enlarged and otherwise manipulated. All offered ways in which territory was made at once more legible and more malleable.

The mobilization of maps, aerial photos and other prosthetics of vision (including the helicopter that sweeps Delouvrier over his territory), as well as their centrality in the business of spatial planning, provide a paradigmatic illustration of what James C. Scott (1998) calls 'seeing like a state'. It was not the first time such a synoptic and panoptic view had been mobilized: the long history of aerial photography, mapping

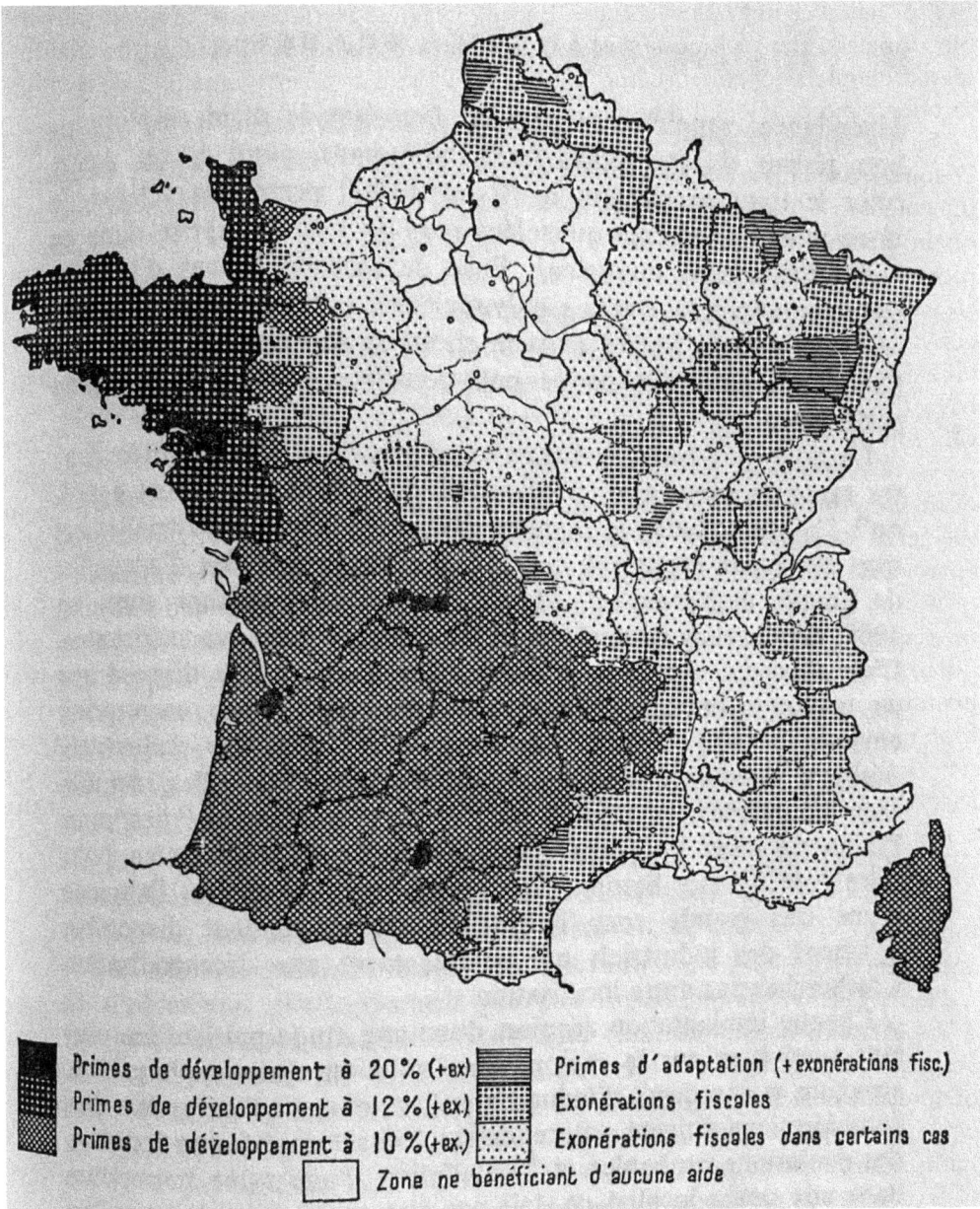

FIG. 2.11. Hexagonal France as a theatre of operations in Olivier Guichard's
Aménager la France (Paris: Laffont-Gonthier, 1965). Author's personal collection.

and surveillance in France has been traced by Jeanne Haffner (2013) amongst others. Nevertheless, the techniques of visuality and representation deployed by Gaullist spatial planners to enhance the legibility of French territory are one of its most sustained and developed manifestations.

At the same time, the investment in mapping made by both Guichard and Delouvrier would seem to confirm Scott's sense of 'legibility as a central problem in statecraft' (1998: 2). Through processes of codification, measurement and quantification, the translation of the world into symbolic forms not only makes it more legible, but paves the way for intervention within it. Guichard was strikingly clear about the importance of representation in practices of spatial planning: 'il convient d'attacher du prix à l'expression graphique elle-même' [it is important to take care with graphical expression] (1965: 183). Scott concurs, observing that maps have the ability to 'transform as well as merely summarize the facts' (1998: 87). Once in the right hands — essentially, the hands of the powerful — maps and other forms of representation can change the world. So statecraft's problem of visibility, of making things legible, is also one of power. The ability to see, particularly from the aerial view, becomes the prerogative of the powerful, and at once implies and enacts a fundamental imbalance of power between the state and its citizens.

While Scott's focus is on the consequences of state intervention in colonial or neo-colonial contexts, such as the management or sedentarization of mobile populations, the factors he identifies behind it are germane to thinking about spatial planning in Gaullist France: the administrative ordering of nature and society; a high modernist ideology driven by faith in science and technology; an authoritarian state willing and able to use its coercive power; and a prostrate civil society that lacks the capacity to resist its plans (Scott 1998: 4–5). If this is so, it is because of the fundamental continuities between the projects of colonization and modernization in the French context. After all, France had only recently drawn a formal line under its colonial activities. When Delouvrier published the *Schéma directeur* in 1965, independence had been granted to France's West African colonies five years before, and Algerian independence had been won only three years previously.

Henri Lefebvre points out that colonial practices of state intervention did not disappear with decolonization, but could simply be reimported into metropolitan France (1970: 11). In effect, the post-colonial French state was embarking on a form of internal colonization, modernizing its metropolitan territory in the hope of ensuring more evenly distributed economic development, and repositioning itself within the emergent project of European cooperation (France had signed the Treaty of Rome in 1957). Almost literally, in fact: one of the immediate consequences of decolonization was the return of a civilian colonial corps which had developed considerable expertise in urban planning, public works and civil engineering, and had been at the forefront of the colonial project as modernizing force.

Of course, it was not only specific technical knowledge that was coming home, but also an embodied set of beliefs, practices and ways of understanding the function of the state and the relationship between state and territory. Alongside Delouvrier himself, several of those returning from the colonies became leading figures in

French spatial planning, such as Jean Millier (director of the IAURP) and Bernard Hirsch (in charge of building Cergy-Pontoise) (Murard & Fourquet 2004: 66–68). Millier had spent considerable time overseeing the development of Abidjan in Côte d'Ivoire, while Hirsch had been a director of public works in Mali and Mauritania. Both were graduates of the ENPC, where they had trained as civil engineers.[8]

As *délégué général* in Algeria, one of Delouvrier's main responsibilities had been to implement the so-called Plan de Constantine announced by de Gaulle in October 1958. The plan's broad strategic aim was to neutralize Algerian demands for independence by showing, via a sustained burst of modernization and economic development, that in Muriam Haleh Davis's words, 'prosperity would be found under the umbrella of French Algeria rather than with the FLN' (Davis 2010: 177).[9] As such, it was the last iteration of civilizational advancement through territorial planning that had been integral to the French colonial project since the nineteenth century (Rabinow 1989).

Modernization as a mode of colonial occupation could be converted readily into a mode of national rebirth. In the slippage between the two, we can again see reasons for Olivier Guichard's alignment of spatial planning and war. As Paul Virilio observes, de Gaulle's landmark *ordonnance* on national defence, published in January 1959, was noteworthy for blurring the distinction between peace and war by defining defence in terms of the permanent protection of national security rather than singular instances of military conflict (1977: 139). In its words, 'la défense a pour objet d'assurer en tout temps, en toutes circonstances et contre toutes les formes d'agression, la sécurité et l'intégrité du territoire, ainsi que la vie de la population' [the aim of national defence is to ensure in perpetuity, in all circumstances, and against all forms of aggression, the security and integrity of the territory, as well as the lives of the population] (*Journal officiel*, 10 January 1959: 691). Moreover, the ordinance established defence as a matter for the government as a whole, with each minister responsible for the 'preparation and execution of defence measures' appropriate to their department (*Journal officiel*, 10 January 1959: 692).

Every area of government activity, in effect, became in some way a part of the national defence strategy, mitigating threats which might be internal as much as external. We saw in the previous chapter how Guichard made the case for *aménagement du territoire* along precisely those lines. If spatial planning had strategic significance, it was in helping to reinforce the security and integrity of the territory through economic prosperity, and in turn, through political stability and civil

8   On the continuities between French colonization and post-colonial spatial planning, see also Fredenucci 2003, examining the extensive role played by civil engineers from the ENPC. Fredenucci notes how those returning from the colonies, used to having a substantial degree of professional autonomy, saw in the opportunities created by new spatial planning initiatives a liberating alternative to what they perceived to be the conservatism and inflexibility dominating state administration in metropolitan France (2003: 82–83). We will see in the next chapter that Hirsch was not averse to drawing parallels between his time in the colonies and the development of Cergy-Pontoise by a small band of adventurous 'pioneers'.

9   It was perhaps appropriate that Delouvrier's roles in Algeria and Paris shared the title of *délégué général*. Both situations involved him being dispatched by central command to troubleshoot problems on the ground.

peace. Indeed, we can go further and say that *aménagement du territoire* had such a crucial role to play because it is productive of territory almost by definition. By enacting state authority over its jurisdiction through the production and shaping of space, it is one of the most obvious and powerful forms of territorialization.

What also becomes clear is the extent to which spatial planning, and through that, the production of space as territory, is predicated on processes of representation and mediation by an array of discursive and visual forms. Guichard finds a nice formulation when he describes *aménagement du territoire* as a matter of 'la mise en œuvre des textes' [putting texts to work] (1965: 219). He has in mind the application of the legislation enabling territorial development, from urban planning zones to environmental protection. Shifting the perspective slightly, we might say that it is a question of the transformations on the ground which are framed, sanctioned and initiated by legislative texts; in other words, about how the new empirical realities produced by spatial planning emerge from the workings of language, text and discourse.

If the shift is important, it is because it draws out how discursive and symbolic forms mediate and create transformations in the world. André Trintignac's account of *aménagement du territoire*, contemporary with Guichard's, is similarly instructive in its emphasis on the legal texts and related administrative reforms that serve as the 'instruments' of spatial planning (Trintignac 1964: 62). In foregrounding legal texts and legislation as the catalysts for *aménagement*, Trintignac draws to the surface how the political and administrative command over language can harness its performative force, and in doing so, produce the conditions for new material realities.

By encoding and naming space in specific ways (for example, by designating 'zones' for urgent or deferred development), legal texts enable the state and other actors, such as public and private land developers, to intervene in and transform it. Equally important in such processes are the other representational tools that the planners mobilize as they take stock and measure up the world, and that we see displayed in the *Paris Match* story. They are everywhere and central to the work that planners do. Photographs, maps and plans might have less apparent purchase on the world than government legislation. However, they are fundamental to processes of territorialization by enabling the state to see and get the measure of its territory, and in turn, encode it in legal and legislative ways.

Between them, Deleuze, Guattari and Foucault provide us with some useful terms for describing the array of administrative devices, discourses, legal instruments, texts, images and other representational forms that the planners deploy to mediate and produce space and territory. Foucault might see them as constituting a *dispositif*, Deleuze and Guattari a *machine*. Both terms crystallized during the 1970s as ways of characterizing an assemblage or ensemble of forms, processes, structures and codifications which converge to organize and give shape to the world.

For Foucault, the *dispositif* is a way of conceiving how power flows through and structures society. It also captures how the exercise of power takes place in more or less tangible ways and is distributed across a range of sites, from institutions with disciplinary or administrative authority to the dissemination of ideas around informal networks of influence. As he put it in an interview in 1977, glossing the term he had introduced a year earlier in *Histoire de la sexualité*, a *dispositif* is:

> Un ensemble résolument hétérogène, comportant des discours, des institutions, des aménagements architecturaux, des décisions réglementaires, des lois, des mesures administratives, des énoncés scientifiques, des propositions philosophiques, morales, philanthropiques, bref: du dit, aussi bien que du non-dit. (Foucault 1994: 299)

> [A heterogeneous assemblage of discourses, institutions, architectural forms, regulatory decisions, laws, administrative measures, scientific conclusions, philosophical, moral and philanthropic propositions. In short, things both said and unsaid.]

Grasping the workings of this assemblage means establishing the links between its heterogeneous and apparently disconnected elements, and understanding how they coalesce into a form of strategic, regulatory or governmental intent.

For Deleuze and Guattari, machines take shape in response to, and because of, the nature of life as an endless force of energy and form of productive becoming, a 'process of production' (Deleuze & Guattari 1972: 11). Like Foucault's *dispositif*, a machinic assemblage operates at a more or less observable level, but produces tangible realities and social formations. One of its most basic components, suggests Guattari, is language itself (Chatelet & others 1973: 28). Language, discourse and other symbolic forms are the fundamental instruments by which human beings gain purchase on and articulate the world, in the real and tangible sense of dividing, combining and recombining its undifferentiated flows. Moreover, the structures produced by the operations of discourse (which might be physical, but also institutional, administrative or social) themselves combine to form so many other types of machinic assemblage which express, channel, shape and fix the constant flux of life's energies. Chief amongst those energies, from a human perspective, is desire (Deleuze & Guattari 1972: 35–36).

Power on the one hand, desire on the other. It might be said that we find the machinic assemblage of spatial planning balanced between these two forces. In the first place, it codifies, defines, demarcates and otherwise makes space legible, visible and malleable. In doing so, as Guattari's team at the CERFI make clear, it prepares the ground (literally) for intervention: 'sol labouré par les routes, transpercé par de canalisations, modelé par le béton, mais aussi cartes, schémas, "POS", tous les plans des stratèges' [earth worked by roads, pierced by pipelines and shaped by concrete; but also maps, masterplans, land use plans, all forms of strategic plan] (Chatelet & others 1973: 190). Its discursive and administrative apparatus enables the physical transformation of space through which the state makes and shapes its territory.

Second, as *Paris Match* demonstrated with its renderings of an imagined Parisian skyline, the spatial planning machine works to express and enable dreams and visions of the future. On the one hand, it is an instrument of power, the means by which things can be made to happen and lives organized. On the other, it is a channel through which desires and imaginings find their first contours on the way to them taking shape in reality. What it also serves to do, therefore, is draw power and desire to the surface as a key tension at the heart of the planning enterprise.

Planning Between Power and Desire

We have seen plenty of evidence supporting the analysis of Gaullist spatial planning as an exercise in state violence, and the expression of disciplinary power through the organization of space. From this perspective, planning takes the form of what Sandercock calls 'an ordering tool, a kind of "spatial police"' (1998: 27). Hence, perhaps, the planners' preoccupation with making space visible and legible, if planning is also a form of territorial surveillance. Meanwhile, if desire is considered to play a part in planning, then, as we have seen Hooper argue, it is as a working-out of male fantasies of control, an attempt to impose rational order on the chaos of the city. In Hooper's words, 'planning is desire, imagined and worked out in a sociospatial context' (1992: 53). Through their structurally privileged positions, the planners can translate their *volonté d'agir* into *pouvoir sur la vie*.

The costs of doing so are high, as a series of critical voices make clear in no uncertain terms. Not only, to recall Lefebvre's analysis, is state power expressed through 'violence exercised on space' (1974: 323), but the sorts of spaces it produces provoke an inevitable diminishment of everyday life and lived experience. Michel de Certeau (1990) concurs. For him, those caught up in spatial planning face a double disenfranchisement. Not only must ordinary city dwellers contend with the alienating nature of technocratic space, but they must also resort to ruses and incursions in order to occupy space that is by rights theirs — an occupation that, as the very notion of incursion implies, can only ever be temporary and provisional. Put another way, neither power nor desire seem to produce good outcomes as far as spatial planning is concerned; and from Hooper's point of view, as we saw, even good hands seem condemned to produce bad outcomes.

Yet while the critique of Gaullist spatial planning as an expression of (masculine) power and repression is important, it is not the whole story. Nor are the energies and desires articulated by planning necessarily just a matter of fantasies of control. Indeed, Sandercock acknowledges the danger of making totalizing assumptions about planning as 'a disciplinary practice essential to the maintenance of the social order' (1998: 27), in particular because it risks losing sight of the practices of resistance that emerge in response. Still further, seeing spatial planning in terms of a dialectic of discipline and resistance itself risks oversimplifying its complexity as a field of human activity.

François Fourquet, one of the founding members of Guattari's CERFI research group, puts it well when he notes how, in their analysis of the French state, CERFI came to understand the state not as a monolithic and abstract force but as an incorporated entity, a set of institutions constituted by human beings, each with their own beliefs, assumptions, energies, desires and emotions: 'pendant des années, nous fréquentons les hommes de l'État; et peu à peu nous apercevons les pulsions qui les animent et comprenons les idéaux qui les motivent' [we spent many years in the company of state administrators; and bit by bit, we noticed the drives that animate them and understood the ideals that motivate them] (Fourquet 1982: 11). Fourquet may well have in mind here the interviews he and his CERFI colleague Lionel Murard had carried out in the mid-1970s with Delouvrier, Millier and other key figures behind the *Schéma directeur* and the Parisian new towns. The interviews were finally published some thirty years later (Murard & Fourquet 2004), offering a valuable articulation of the planners' visions and motivations, as we have seen at various points. Fuelled by the drives, desires and ideals of individuals who coalesce into the corporate bodies that structure and perform its activities, like the ENPC or the DATAR, the state in turn becomes a desiring being.

Much also depends, of course, on how power and desire are understood. Foucault's work throughout the 1970s argued that power is fundamentally a productive rather than a repressive force. From his perspective, the state can be understood as an evolving set of institutions, discourses and governmental practices whose emphasis lies on management, organization and regulation as much as discipline and punishment. Alongside its 'formidable power of death' is 'un pouvoir destiné à produire des forces, à les faire croître et à les ordonner plutôt que voué à les barrer, à les faire plier, ou à les détruire' [a power intended to produce forces, to grow and shape them rather than block, break or destroy them] (1976: 179). In any case, as Fourquet points out, discipline in Foucauldian terms is not simply a matter of prevention, repression and restriction, but about the channelling, direction and concentration of energy. A primary goal of the state, he suggests, 'est de capter, non de tarir; de canaliser, non de faire barrage; de concentrer, non de bloquer' [to harness, not to cut off; to channel, not to dam; to concentrate, not to block] (1982: 64).

Meanwhile, in *L'Anti-Œdipe*, Deleuze and Guattari identified the energies of desire as fundamentally creative, a motive force of life and society. Not simply located in the individual psyche, desire is constitutive of the social body as a whole: 'le désir est de l'ordre de la *production*, toute production est à la fois désirante et sociale' [desire is a matter of *production*, and all production is at once desiring and social] (1972: 356). If this is the case, it is because life itself, an unending process of production, is fundamentally an expression of the flux and flow of energy as *élan vital*, or vital force. Machines emerge as devices (which might be organic or psychical, mechanical or bureaucratic) whose function is to divide, distribute, organize, channel, transmit or in some way intervene in the flow of energy and becoming (1972: 43–44). In doing so, they give shape and form to reality. One of the most powerful is the unconscious as a 'desiring machine', while another is that of capitalist production.[10]

Deleuze and Guattari make no bones about it. In their programmatic formulation, '*il n'y a que du désir et du social, et rien d'autre*' [*there is only desire and society, nothing else*] (1972: 38). Social realities, expressed in modes of social organization, the distribution and organization of labour, or in physical infrastructure and collective facilities, need to be understood as manifestations and inscriptions of human desire. Or rather, they are expressions of specific forms of desire. For as Deleuze and Guattari go on to argue, the energies of desire gravitate around two poles: revolutionary and disruptive on the one hand ('schizoid', in their terminology);

---

10 Thornton 2017 offers an incisive account of the emerging conceptualization of the machine in the work of Deleuze and Guattari, and how Deleuze was influenced by Guattari's notion of the unconscious as a 'desiring machine'.

repressive and controlling on the other (what they would term 'paranoid') (1972: 333). The latter is where desire manifests itself most explicitly as a will to power, and where Foucault's analysis of power as a productive process converges with Deleuze and Guattari's theory of desire as social force. In the terms of Fourquet's neat synthesis, the state's fundamental desire can be understood as the accumulation of power (Fourquet 1982). If this is the case, it is because the state must contend with the energies of desire in its unruly, disruptive and revolutionary forms, and attempts to do so through the sort of organization and regulation of life described by Foucault.

As a machine for making space and territory, Gaullist spatial planning is at the nexus of the complex interplay of power and desire as dynamic and productive forces. It is certainly the case that spatial planning has disciplinary and masculinist dimensions, with significant implications in terms of how space is produced and what consequences it has. Yet it is also true that the *Schéma directeur* expresses and gives material shape to drives, ideals and visions of the world, whether conscious or not. It is an expression of what Fourquet playfully calls an 'eros of the state' (1982: 28). A critique of spatial planning as an exercise simply in disciplinary power risks eliding the fact that it also derives from desire, affect and creativity, which are in turn bound up in conceptions of governance, territorial organization and futurity.

Put another way, it is possible for the disciplinary to coexist with the creative, and for spatial planning to be a productive as much as a repressive force. Drawing on the theories of power, desire and government developed by Deleuze, Guattari and Foucault opens up a perspective which makes the activities and intentions of Gaullist spatial planning more legible, and allows us to grasp some of the ideas and assumptions which drive it. At the same time, and in some ways more interestingly, doing so also reveals common ground between the two fields in terms of how they conceptualize human life, the social world and the ways in which they might be shaped, managed and governed. One offers critical purchase on the other; but in many respects, they show similar thinking about how the world works.

To use Fourquet's terms, spatial planning is a negotiation between space as territory and space as flux (Fourquet 1993: 166). On the one hand, the *Schéma directeur* and the DATAR work towards organizing, distributing and spatially fixing populations and economic activity (for example, through the creation of new towns). At the same time, economic activity at once demands and is predicated on movement, flow and circulation. Spatial planning attempts to channel and regulate those flows and energies, which otherwise risk running out of control and thereby threatening the state's control over its territory (something intimated by de Gaulle in his instruction to Delouvrier). The state must navigate constantly between stasis and dynamism, discipline and regulation, repression and production. In particular, it must work to contend with the unruly energies of capitalist production, whose unique power lies in its disruption of attempts to contain and stabilize it within a social order. As Deleuze and Guattari make clear, capital is a force at once embedded within modern human societies, and an endless challenge to the structures and fabric of those societies, which must find ways to accommodate it as best they can (1972: 42–45).

Fundamental to doing so is the development of the infrastructure, communal facilities and other installations (what the French term *équipements collectifs*) that are typically the most tangible manifestations of *aménagement*. In 1973, CERFI published a special issue of its journal *Recherches* on *équipements collectifs* as an instrument of government and a means through which the state can exert authority over its territory. It included a discussion between Deleuze, Guattari and Foucault during which attention turned to the regulatory functions of infrastructure and *équipements*. Foucault proposes roads as an illuminating example of how infrastructure is deployed to control, manage and regulate circulation and flow. He identifies three functions: stimulating production (by enabling the circulation of raw materials, goods and labour); stimulating demand (by connecting producers and consumers to markets); and, through the work of civil engineers, forming a standardized system that reaches the whole population and catalyses activity across the territory (Chatelet & others 1973: 184–85).

Foucault's analysis is borne out by the centrality of infrastructures of mobility and speed (motorways, airports, rapid transit rail networks) in the thinking of the DATAR and the team behind the *Schéma directeur*. Moreover, the planners' preoccupation with the need to engineer speed is a reminder of its centrality to the prospective view, and the assumption that acceleration is the defining characteristic of human advance. Striking too is the degree of congruence between the analysis of planning and governmentality by Foucault and others, and the ways in which the planners conceptualize spatial development. It is not simply that the logic of what the planners do can be uncovered by critique from a Foucauldian, Deleuzian or Guattarian perspective. They themselves articulate a similar sense of life and human society as a dynamic flux and flow of energy to be channelled, managed and shaped. The principle is intrinsic to the philosophy of *la prospective*, and it weaves its way through the texts and documents that frame spatial development. The structures and places they create, imagine and articulate through so many maps, models, images and texts are an inscription on the ground of their desire to harness, modulate and redirect the energies of life.

The guiding principle of the *Schéma directeur*, for example, is that 'le dynamisme de l'agglomération parisienne ne peut être brisé: il doit seulement être canalisé' [the dynamism of the Paris region cannot be broken: it must solely be channelled] (DGRP 1965: 83). Likewise, Guichard devotes a chapter of his book to mobility, which he defines as 'un signe de santé et de vitalité d'une nation' [a sign of a nation's health and vitality] (1965: 48). In an echo of Foucault's analysis of the road system, Guichard argues that the state must engineer mobility in order to 'libérer l'homme de son milieu géographique' [free people from their environment] (1965: 45). Physical infrastructure simultaneously breaks down barriers to movement by facilitating circulation round the territory, and opens up all parts of the territory to the productive flow of labour. Yet if Guichard's text equates mobility with freedom, it reveals spatial planning's disciplinary tendencies in the same moment. For as Guichard notes, 'la civilization de 1985 sera marquée par la mobilité' [the civilization of 1985 will be defined by mobility] (1965: 35).[11] Creating opportunities for mobility is also about training the population for a future in which mobility (of the workforce especially) will be the norm.

The tension between stasis and dynamism, flux and fixed space, found its most significant theoretical and ideological expression in the battle between the *Schéma directeur* and the *Plan d'aménagement et d'orientation générale de la région parisienne* [Plan for the development and orientation of the Paris region] (PADOG) in the early 1960s, as opposing approaches to the spatial development of the Paris region. The PADOG had been approved by presidential decree in August 1960, twelve months prior to Delouvrier's nomination as *délégué général* of the District de Paris, and he had been tasked by prime minister Michel Debré to manage its implementation (Hirsch 2003: 36). The PADOG had been developed by Pierre Gibel, head of the Service d'aménagement de la région parisienne [Planning service for the Paris region] (SARP), and had its origins in the *Plan d'aménagement de la région parisienne* [Development plan for the Paris region] (PARP), otherwise known as the Plan Prost, which had been approved in 1939 but had stalled because of the war.

The PARP was overseen by Henri Prost as head of the Paris planning office. Winner of the prestigious Prix de Rome for architecture (in 1902), a member of the Académie des Beaux-Arts, and co-founder of the periodical *Urbanisme*, Prost was an eminent member of France's planning and architectural establishment. Gibel had completed a doctoral thesis on the Paris region under Prost's supervision in the 1930s (Murard & Fourquet 2004: 26). Like many *aménageurs* who came after him, Prost cut his planning teeth in the colonies, working for General Lyautey in Morocco on plans for Rabat, Casablanca and other Moroccan cities (Rabinow 1989: 296–315). Also like them, Prost was preoccupied with how to bring a 'rational ordering' to spatial development (Rabinow 1989: 238). The PARP was the first attempt to extend coordinated spatial planning beyond Paris in an effort to control haphazard urbanization in the *banlieue*. Industrial development had driven population growth through migration, which in turn fuelled the rapid expansion of poorly regulated private development on individual building plots (*lotissements*), often without the necessary infrastructure. Prost's solution was to establish a 'périmètre d'agglomération' [agglomeration boundary] beyond which further urban development would be prevented (Murard & Fourquet 2004: 38).[12]

Gibel maintained the 'périmètre d'agglomération' as the organizing principle of the PADOG, containing the development of the Paris region within an established boundary, and assuming that decentralization would result in a stable population. In many ways, the PADOG was a product of its time. The desire to restrict the region's expansion reflected the persistent influence of Jean-François Gravier's

---

11   1985 being the horizon adopted by prospective planning, as we saw in the previous chapter. I return to the planners' preoccupation with life in 1985 in Chapter 4, not least in order to consider what life was actually looking like by the time the year had come to pass.

12   On the development of the Plan Prost, see Olson (2018: 221–67). Rosemary Wakeman (2009: 289–312) discusses how the principals of the PARP were carried over by the SARP under Pierre Gibel's leadership after the war, as well as the continuing post-war influence of planning initiatives and administrative structures for Paris developed under the Vichy regime.

arguments about the distorting effects of the growth of Paris on the rest of the country. Jacques Michel, who was part of Gibel's team at the SARP and would subsequently work for Millier at the IAURP, notes that 'le principal problème, à l'époque, était que l'esprit général, au niveau politique ambiant, était dominé par Paris et le désert français: il fallait donc limiter la croissance de Paris de manière à ne pas nuire à l'aménagement du territoire' [the main problem at the time was the political consensus around the idea of Paris and the French desert, which meant that the growth of Paris had to be controlled in order not to constrain the development of the territory as a whole] (Hirsch 2003: 31). Gibel himself sums up the PADOG as 'une politique de non-accroissement' [a non-growth policy] (Murard & Fourquet 2004: 46). In effect, the physical extent of the Paris region would simply be frozen in time as that defined by the PADOG in 1960.

Restrictions on spatial and demographic expansion were precisely where Delouvrier and his team saw the problems with the PADOG. As Millier describes it, 'c'était plutôt un plan d'interdiction qu'un plan de permission' [it was a plan that was more about forbidding than permitting] (Murard & Fourquet 2004: 103). Their critique of the PADOG was grounded in oppositions between stasis and growth and between disciplinary versus regulatory mechanisms of spatial development. The political work of replacing the PADOG with the *Schéma directeur* was done by projecting anticipated population growth for the region over the following decades, to show that the limits imposed on the agglomeration meant there was insufficient land to build the housing required to absorb it; but also by arguing that the growth of the Paris region reflected the broader trend of urban development as a 'mutation profonde' affecting France as a whole (Hirsch 2003: 42).[13]

It was enabled too by the emerging consensus over the prospective view as the key to shaping the nation's future, and those were the terms in which the *Schéma directeur* was introduced when it was published in 1965:

> Tracer le schéma directeur du Paris de demain, ce n'est pas dessiner un Brasilia français sur un plateau désert; c'est prévoir à la fois l'adaptation aux besoins de demain de l'agglomération parisienne d'aujourd'hui et les extensions en surface de cette agglomération, que commandent les chiffres de l'avenir. (DGRP 1965: 35)

> [Tracing the master plan for the Paris of tomorrow is not about designing a French Brasilia on a deserted plateau. It is about planning the adaptation of today's region to the needs of tomorrow and the extent to which the agglomeration needs to grow, determined by data based on future projections.]

The *Schéma directeur* is striking in its emphasis on spatio-temporal flow and circulation, as if to build in the forward-flung dynamism inherent in the prospective view. Where the PADOG established an administrative frontier round the agglomeration, the *Schéma directeur* insisted on its continuity with the rest of the national territory. It channelled development through 'preferential axes' running along the line of

---

13   Interviews with Delouvrier, Gibel and others in Murard & Fourquet 2004 and Hirsch 2003 offer first-hand accounts of the debates around the PADOG, and the political manoeuvres required to supersede it with the *Schéma directeur*. A historian's perspective is provided by Vadelorge 2014.

FIG. 2.12. Plan d'aménagement et d'orientation générale de la région Parisienne (1960). Image courtesy of the Institut Paris Région.

the Seine river basin, connecting to the west with Rouen and the Channel port of Le Havre. Construction of motorways and rapid transit rail networks (the RER) would accelerate circulation and improve quality of life through time-space compression, 'raccourcissant les distances en réduisant les temps et les fatigues du parcours' [shortening distances while reducing travel time and fatigue] (DGRP 1965: 67). New towns had a crucial role to play in distributing development across the region, but they had to be situated in the right locations. Place them too far away from Paris, suggested the commentary to the *Schéma directeur*, and they 'n'inscriraient dans aucune ligne de force géographique ou économique à l'échelle du bassin parisien et, plus largement, du territoire national' [would not be integrated into geographic or economic lines of force, within either the Paris region or the national territory] (DGRP 1965: 82).

Indeed, the different philosophies of the PADOG and the *Schéma directeur* are expressed neatly in their respective cartographic forms. The map of the PADOG demarcates and encloses through a combination of colours and lines (Fig. 2.12). The dark grey of the *zone d'économie urbaine* [urban economic zone] is distinguished from the pale greens of the rural areas around it by a distinct black line, while the red line

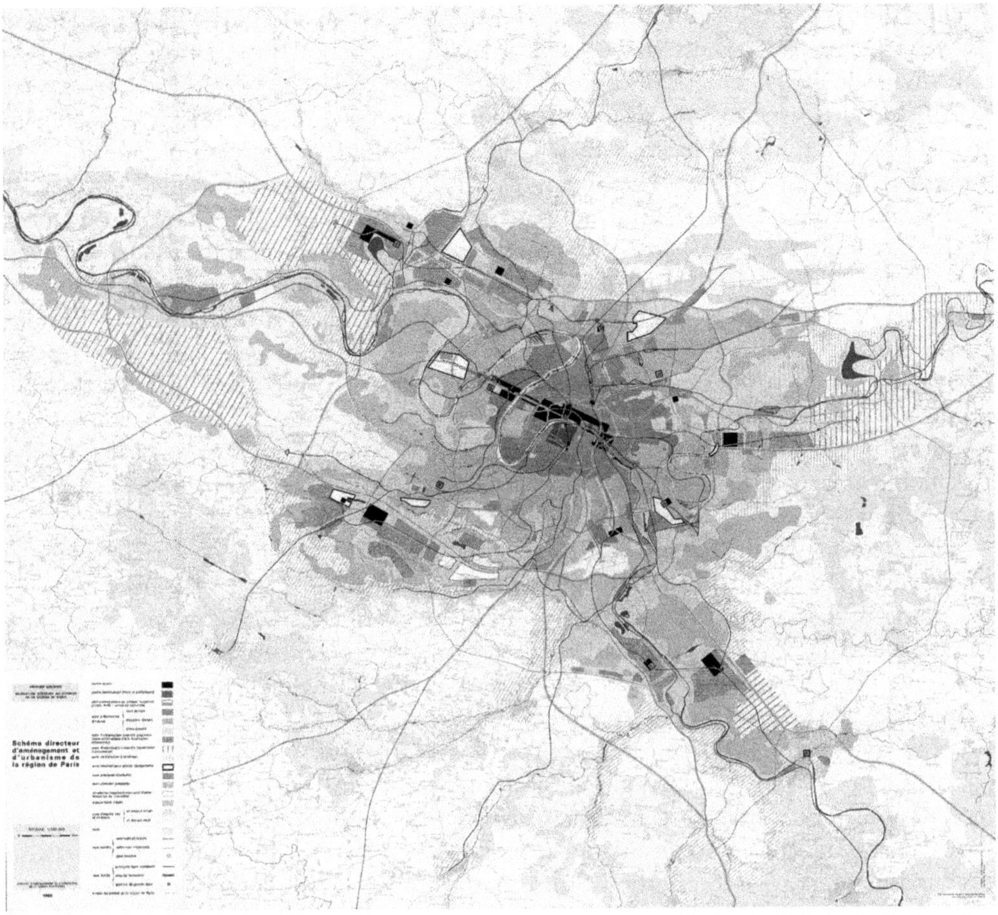

FIG. 2.13. Schéma directeur d'aménagement et d'urbanisme de la région de Paris (1965).
Image courtesy of the Institut Paris Région.

of a proposed orbital motorway encircles the agglomeration. In contrast, lines of communication lead off the edge of the map showing the *Schéma directeur* in a visible sign of connection to the world beyond, while shadings and hatchings convey the orientation of the development zone along the east-west axis, defined by the prominent blue lines showing the course of the Seine and its tributaries (Fig. 2.13).

There is something fitting about the fact that Delouvrier and his team were drawn to a river basin as the structuring principle for the *Schéma directeur*, and that they understood it as an economic *ligne de force*. In their discussion of infrastructure, the researchers at the CERFI note that river basins historically have played a determining role as catalysts for territorial development. Rivers are one of the purest natural manifestations of energy as flow. As such, they also provide a raw material which can be harnessed for economically productive forms of activity and thereby surplus value (Chatelet & others 1973: 71–72). More than just a metaphor for the dynamic energies of production and flow, as 'deuxième fleuve d'Europe et premier "canal" de France' [Europe's second river and France's main 'canal']

(DGRP 1965: 98), the Seine was a motive source of those energies which the *Schéma directeur* set out to harness through its machine of spatial production in order to galvanize the advancement of region and nation.

All this returns us to the relationship between state and capital as it plays out in spatial planning, and in particular to Godard's critique of the Gaullist regime in *2 ou 3 choses que je sais d'elle* ('le pouvoir gaulliste prend le masque d'un réformateur et d'un modernisateur alors qu'il ne veut qu'enregistrer et régulariser les tendances naturelles du grand capitalisme'). In many respects, Godard's insight is correct, even if the assumptions behind it might be less so. For what Godard reads as evidence of collusion could also be understood as the manifestation of a fundamental tension. If the aim of Gaullist power is in some sense to control or regulate capitalism, it is because its 'natural tendencies', as Deleuze and Guattari would subsequently argue, are precisely towards excess and disruption. The state's efforts to channel and regulate the flows of capital through spatial production and territorialization always risk being overwhelmed by the deterritorializing force of capitalist production as its inherent tendency.

The tension would be sustained through the 1970s and 80s, with the balance of power shifting steadily from state to capital. If the election of Valéry Giscard d'Estaing as French president in 1974 marked a political move away from state interventionism towards market-led liberalism, it also coincided with the end of the long period of growth that, at the end of the decade, Jean Fourastié (1979) would call 'les Trente glorieuses' [thirty glorious years], and that had done much to fuel the optimism embodied in the prospective attitude. By the early 1980s, large parts of France were enduring a period of post-industrial decline in the face of international competition, as multinational capital was increasingly able to assert its global reach, its ability to circulate across borders, and its rapid ebb and flow from one national territory to another. From that perspective, the directional arrows and lines of communication leading off the map of the *Schéma directeur* and away into the world appear eerily prescient of a future that the prospective view simply did not see.

Yet even as the political and economic context evolved from the one that enabled them in the first place, the modernized landscapes initiated by the spatial planners of the 1960s continued to take shape, give form to the territory and enact dreams of futurity and progress. In December 1977, a television news report on the inauguration of the RER line A between La Défense and Marne-la-Vallée would foreground its contribution to time-space compression by reducing the journey time across Paris from ninety to thirty minutes: 'such is the great miracle of the RER', the reporter tells the nation.[14] In 1975, however, *Enfance d'une ville* [Birth of a town], a documentary film by Éric Rohmer and Jean-Paul Pigeat about Cergy-Pontoise for French television, had offered a more nuanced account of the complexities of modernization, as the desires expressed in the vision of the new town were turned into the realities of built environments.

---

14   Michel Chevalet, 'La Traversée de Paris en RER', TF1 Actualités 20H, 7 December 1977.

Enfance d'une ville once more raises the question of who is making space, for whom and how. The film leaves us in no doubt that Cergy-Pontoise is a man's world, insofar as all those we see planning and building the new town are men. It also dwells on one of its most visible and striking buildings, the Tour Bleue des Cerclades, or 'Tour des jeunes mariés', given a prominent location at the heart of Cergy's main administrative and commercial centre and originally, as its nickname suggests, intended to house young married couples. In doing so, the film prompts us to ask the questions posed by Sandercock in terms of what effects planning had on the lives of women, and what assumptions were in play about their role (1998: 15). At the same time, it draws out how spatial planning is haunted by the ghost of colonial practices, not least in terms of how the site is 'settled' and land expropriated in order to do so.

The politics of expropriation would find fictional expression in *Trente hectares de bonne terre* [Thirty hectares of good land] (1981), a television film directed by Jean-Pierre Gallo about urban development and expropriation of land which unites a middle-aged white woman and a younger Berber man in a battle against the developers, inviting us to consider who is given space in a modernized France and who, in a literal sense, finds themselves displaced. Meanwhile, if Foucault's riff on roads in 1973 ends with a suggestion that the engineer and the vagabond symbolize the flipsides and consequences of modernization (one the embodiment of the norm in its social and regulatory senses, the other representative of the socially abnormal and unregulated), then it is intriguing to find the same pair given dramatic form a decade or so later in Varda's *Sans toit ni loi*. Released in 1985, prospective planning's talismanic year, the film tells the story of the life and death of a young female vagabond (also the film's title in English-speaking countries) whose aimlessness sparks unease as she wanders a south of France marked by the legacies and traces of *aménagement*.

So spatial planning is at once an expression of disciplinary power and a productive force, a machine fuelled by a collective imagination that can create realities from dreams. But if spatial planning has the power to turn imagined futures into present realities, it is also the case that those realities need then to be negotiated in different ways: as landscapes and environments, settings for everyday life, and objects of political dispute. The focus of the next two chapters is on what happens when dreams and visions take on material form, how they are perceived and portrayed, and how they influence lived experience. We turn first to the new town of Cergy-Pontoise as the manifestation of an imagined form of modernized life, and an example of how the temporal lag inherent in spatial planning creates a disorienting concatenation of past, present and future.

CHAPTER 3

❖

Cergy-Pontoise:
Building the Imaginary

The Strange Temporality of New Towns

It is worth recalling Olivier Guichard's observation, as head of the DATAR, that 'l'aménagement du territoire dialogue constamment avec le temps' (spatial planning is in constant dialogue with time) (1965: 26). Guichard's hunch in *Aménager la France* is correct, as we have already seen: spatial planning is as much about time as space. The need to work with time and to shape urban development over a long period of time was the key insight of Delouvrier's team at the District, reflected in the symbolic identification of the year 2000 as their planning horizon. In Kenny Cupers' terms, it articulated a conceptual shift on the part of the planners from *urbanisme* to *programmation* (2014: 199). Or, we might say, from the organization of space as the fixing of forms, to the organization of space-in-time as a more dynamic gearing of functions, management of activity and anticipation of future trends. In Chapter 1, I explored how the urge to do so was not just technical but philosophical, driven on by the prospective sense of progress as evolutionary advancement. Gaullist spatial planning was a project impatient with the present and intent on ushering in the future. While the production and organization of space were oriented towards the future, spatial forms and functions (architecture, urban design, transport infrastructure) could make manifest in the present what that future would look like.

Planning's drive for the future found its practical expression in a preoccupation with the passage of time, and the management of time spent. For the sociologist Sylvia Ostrowetsky, who worked at the IAURP in the 1960s, *aménagement* is about the state's attempts to 'gérer le temps productif, le temps du développement, la vie quotidienne tout comme l'espace social' [manage productive time, the time of development, daily life and social space] (Ostrowetsky 1983: 14). Spatial planning opened up the way to the future by making better use of time through improved efficiency of speed and movement. Hence the emphasis placed on transport infrastructure in Gaullist *aménagement*. Developing speed space to accelerate flows of traffic, people and goods was essential for increasing economic productivity and output. Simultaneously, making gains on time spent would also produce a surplus of time that could be used for leisure and other activities (based on the contemporary assumption that a leisure society, facilitated by technological advance, was the logical destination for mature liberal economies).[1]

Crucially, though, spatial planning cannot escape the fact that it is embedded in time and unfolds over a long duration. When Guichard commands spatial planning to outrun time and project itself into the future ('l'aménagement ne vit pas dans l'époque présente; il doit toujours la devancer, projeter sur l'avenir'), he captures the bold, forward-flung-ness of prospective thinking. Yet the urgency of his modal verb ('doit' meaning 'should' or 'must') intimates a nervousness that time could all too easily overwhelm it. In many respects, such an intuition would be right. The translation of imagined worlds into built realities cannot help but get caught up in the points of resistance, unforeseen obstacles, shifts in fortune and changes in political weather that constitute the fabric of life and society.

The complex temporalities of spatial planning surface most noticeably in the new towns initiated by Delouvrier's *Schéma directeur*, beginning with Cergy-Pontoise to the north west of Paris (in 1968) and Évry to the south east (in 1969). In the first place were the symbolic qualities with which they were invested. The new towns were intended and portrayed by the planners as emblems of a modernized France. Their architectural forms made them signifiers of modernity, while their blend of rural and urban living, beyond the built-up density of the existing agglomeration, at once proposed and created the conditions for the kind of post-industrial leisure society anticipated by prospective planning. As such, the new towns were realizations of urban futures as they were imagined at the time. Yet they also outlived their era, persisting in the landscape not simply as traces of the past, but as memories of how the past once conceived of the future. That is to say, the new towns simultaneously make manifest *and survive as a legacy of* the dreams and visions of Delouvrier's spatial planners. What is more, even as they persist as past visions of the future, they continue simultaneously to be the framework for life as it continues to be lived, and which works with and adapts to the environments bequeathed by the planners.

The move from concept to reality also meant the new towns began to exist in time, and encounter the inertia, resistance and unpredictability that the passage of time brings with it. An important factor here was the long duration of their development. The prefectures in Cergy and Évry were completed in a couple of

---

1   An enthusiastic theorist of the road to the leisure society was the economist and arch-moderniser Jean Fourastié, most notably in *Les 40,000 heures* (1965), published in the same series (Laffont-Gonthier's 'Inventaire de l'avenir') as Guichard's *Aménager la France*. Fourastié's premise was that technological advance, the expansion of the tertiary economy and an increasingly educated population would enable a substantial reduction of the working week from over forty to just thirty hours a week, and a working life of thirty-five years. Calculations using these two projections produced the 40,000 hours of the book's title. Assuming an average lifespan of eighty years, or 700,000 hours, only six per cent of life would be taken up with work, with the remainder devoted to leisure and other enriching activities. The prospect was an enticing one, not least in a context where the Western liberal democracies needed to find an alternative to the narratives of a worker's paradise being offered by the Soviet bloc. Nonetheless, it was tempered somewhat by Fourastié's prediction that France would realize the ambition somewhere between 2050 and 2100. The United States, meanwhile, ever the more advanced civilization, would achieve it a couple of decades or so earlier.

years, as if to assert the state's presence in, and claim to, the new urban territories it was creating (not least because they were the administrative centres for two of the region's new *départements*). But if the first residents moved into Cergy in 1973, the residential and commercial development of both sites as originally mapped out by the planning teams would not be complete for another two decades or so. For example, the construction of Cergy's final neighbourhood, St Christophe, on a plateau above the river Oise, began in 1979 and continued into the early 1990s (Saint-Pierre 2002: 62–68).

In particular, the long duration of the new towns' development meant they were exposed to the more rapid rhythms of political life, whose turbulence during the late 1960s and early 1970s had an important bearing on the political fortunes of state-led spatial planning. De Gaulle's authority had been eroded by the social unrest of May 1968 and he finally resigned in April 1969, to be replaced by Georges Pompidou. Given the momentum that had derived from de Gaulle's endorsement of the *Schéma directeur*, his departure inevitably left it vulnerable to its political opponents, who were becoming increasingly restive. The architect Guy Lagneau, who worked on the development of Évry, captures neatly the dynamic in play: 'le projet est passé de force, et après, la force de de Gaulle étant un peu moins présente, toutes les autres forces se sont conjugées contre' [the project was forced through, and afterwards, when de Gaulle's force was less evident, all the other forces began to marshal against it] (Murard & Fourquet 2004: 167).

Already in February 1969, Delouvrier had left his post as prefect of the Paris region, following increasingly difficult relationships first with Pompidou, and then with Albin Chalandon. The latter was a contemporary and acquaintance of Delouvrier. They had both been in the French Resistance and worked together as auditors at the Ministry of Finance. While Delouvrier had remained in public service, Chalandon had moved into the private sector, pursuing a career in banking and property development, before turning to politics (Hirsch 2003: 171–72). He was elected to the National Assembly as a member of the Gaullist UDR in 1967, and appointed Ministre de l'Équipement et du Logement in July 1968, in what would be de Gaulle's final government, keeping the portfolio until 1972.[2]

Chalandon's arrival at the ministry responsible for infrastructure and housing marked the growing influence of politicians more hostile both to the new town project and the broader philosophy of state intervention it represented. The change in mood was noted by Bernard Hirsch, in charge at the time of developing Cergy-Pontoise, and sensitive to the contrast in values, ethos and perspective that Chalandon embodied: 'cet ancien promoteur immobilier a conservé un réflexe de constructeur hostile à toute réglementation qui limite la libre entreprise, et en même temps à l'administration qui l'applique' [as a former property developer, he remained hostile to any regulations that limited free enterprise, and to the administration

2   Delouvrier's assessment of his colleague (and rival) is amusingly frank: 'c'était une intelligence et un tempérament... et l'habitude de brutaliser les choses. Je dirais: chacune de ses erreurs l'a grandi et lui a fait monter un étage. Il arrive, il est ministre. Il demande à voir ce que nous faisons' [he was intelligent and temperamental... and could also be brutal. Let's say that each of his mistakes elevated him. He comes to see us, he's a minister, and asks to see what we're up to] (Hirsch 2003: 171).

applying them] (Hirsch 2000: 179). The shift in political and economic orthodoxy signalled by Chalandon's appointment would be further confirmed in 1974. The death of Georges Pompidou and the subsequent election to the presidency of Valéry Giscard d'Estaing saw government policy move more clearly away from the state interventionism of Gaullism towards much greater embrace of market liberalism.[3]

The creation and development of the new towns also produced politics, of course, understood as a clash of interests, perceptions, beliefs and narratives. As Delouvrier remarks, 'même si nos relations individuelles étaient souvent excellentes, il est clair que j'avais indisposé les élus. Nous étions très directifs, c'est clair. Je crois que mon départ a soulagé les élus' [even if our individual relationships were often excellent, it's clear that I caused trouble for the elected representatives. We were very directive, for sure. I think they were relieved to see me go] (Hirsch 2003: 176). The new towns took on a steadily more political life as they were inscribed in reality and enmeshed in conflicting interpretations of their value, benefit and meaning. The construction of Cergy-Pontoise on a greenfield site in a largely agricultural area provoked disputes with the established community and its elected representatives, not least when its construction entailed the displacement of local farmers and the expropriation of their land. Meanwhile, the new inhabitants moving into Cergy's first neighbourhoods began to form groups and associations in order to give themselves a political voice as they navigated the realities and practicalities of life in an experimental urban development.

Put another way, we might say that Cergy-Pontoise and the other new towns became *things,* in the sense understood by Bruno Latour, whose notion of *Dingpolitik,* or a politics of things, mobilizes the etymological meaning of 'thing', or *ding,* as a place for assembly and debate (Latour 2005: 22–23). Things exist simultaneously in empirical and discursive form, at once talked about and constituted by talking. Their presence catalyses debate, and they become subject to contesting representations. They form an assemblage with the people who are drawn to them in their disagreement, and produce disagreement through their being-in-the-world. As the first of the five new towns initiated by the *Schéma directeur,* Cergy-Pontoise became the most visible, and soon acquired life as an object of dispute in the Latourian sense. While its development unfolded on the ground, it simultaneously gained discursive and visual form as it was filmed, reported on and written about. It was the focus of stories which relayed the translation of visions into realities. Then, as it gained substance as a place of life and work, attention turned to the political, social and psychical implications of the new town and the modernity it enacted.

In the early 1970s, television news reports captured Cergy's dramatic emergence out of the agricultural landscapes of the Val d'Oise. In 1975, the documentary film *Enfance d'une ville,* by Éric Rohmer and Jean-Paul Pigeat, portrayed the new town not just as a physical location, but as a process that (amongst other things) produced political disagreement and debate, and explored how one derived from the other (Welch 2018, 2021). Around the same time, a proliferation of research reports by

---

3   The involvement of the private sector in expanding and running France's motorway network, which Chalandon was instrumental in initiating, was an early example of this ideological inflection.

social psychologists and other experts examined the perceptions and affective impact of life in the new town on its first inhabitants. Cergy's currency as a landscape of modernity was sustained in the 1980s and 90s through the work of filmmaker Éric Rohmer, in *L'Ami de mon amie* [My girlfriend's boyfriend] (1987), and writer Annie Ernaux, who in *Journal du dehors* attempted to map the contours of what she calls 'cette modernité dont une ville nouvelle donne le sentiment aigu sans qu'on puisse la définir' [the acute sense of modernity that a new town gives you but which you can't define] (1996: 8).

Interviewed in 2002, Jean-Eudes Roullier, one of Delouvrier's key allies at the District, was asked whether there had been a utopian dimension to the new town project. He replied:

> Je ne sais pas si on peut parler d'utopie, puisque l'utopie est par définition quelque chose qui n'existe pas. *Il y avait une forme de rêve.* Il y a eu beaucoup d'investissement sur la conception des équipements, sur ce que pouvait être la vie sociale dans des ensembles nouveaux, sur l'éducation, sur les écoles, les premières bases de loisirs. (Effosse 2002: 31, my emphasis)

> [I don't know if we can talk in terms of utopia, since by definition, utopias don't exist. *There was a sort of dream.* A lot of energy was invested in developing facilities, in what social life might be like in the new towns, in education, schools, the first leisure parks.]

The aim of this chapter is to explore the shape of the planners' dream, and how their imagined worlds navigated their way from dream to reality. It homes in on Cergy-Pontoise as the first and most emblematic of the French new towns, setting out to grasp the drama and audacity of its creation, and the challenges which arose as it started to exist in time. The chapter considers how its realities are portrayed, how it forms the setting for peoples' lives, and how it exists as an object of dispute, sparking depictions and interrogations of modernized life. As the nature of women's lives in the new town became a focal point of discussion in the 1970s, the creation of Cergy returns us again to the question of the relationship between gender and space, the ways in which space is engendered and by whom, and the extent to which there is a gendered (and unequal) division of labour between men as producers of urban space and women as its practitioners. The chapter concludes by tracking Cergy's portrayal as a locus of modernity by Annie Ernaux and Éric Rohmer in the 1980s and 90s, and the sense they give of the adaptations it demands.

Dreams and Hauntings

The new towns were materializations of dreams of the future, but their creation was haunted by ghosts and legacies of the past. The most recent were the *grands ensembles* like those at Sarcelles, where the loneliness, isolation and sense of alienation felt by their residents earned the nickname *la sarcellite*, or the even more imposing development of Les 4,000 at La Courneuve that Godard had used in *2 ou 3 choses que je sais d'elle* as the setting for his exploration of the psychical implications of modernization. Yet the *grands ensembles*, built in haste as a response to the housing crisis of the post-war period, were simply the latest manifestation of the uncoordinated, unplanned and piecemeal development around Paris since the nineteenth century, which left housing dislocated from facilities, amenities, transport and employment. The problem was formulated in the text accompanying the *Schéma directeur*, as much planning manifesto as interpretative commentary:

> Quitter un taudis dans un quartier animé et varié avec de nombreux commerces et des emplois, pour le logement clair, bien équipé et plus vaste d'un grand ensemble uniquement résidentiel et mal desservi, fait toucher du doigt que la vie dans une agglomération ne dépend pas seulement de la qualité du logement, mais de son environnement et de ses 'liaisons'. (DGRP 1965: 62)

> [Leaving a slum in a varied and lively district with numerous shops and job opportunities for the bright, well equipped and larger accommodation of a housing estate which is nevertheless purely residential and poorly connected highlights the fact that urban life does not just depend on the quality of housing, but on its surroundings and its 'links'.]

Delouvrier put it more strikingly the following year in a programmatic speech, the 'Discours des ambassadeurs', when he argued that such deficiency 'fait des banlieusards des citoyens mutilés' [turns suburban dwellers into mutilated citizens] (Delouvrier 1989: 42). How to solve the problem, he went on to ask, of the boredom and frustration fuelled by long journeys on public transport from isolated housing estates?

The question was a rhetorical one, insofar as Delouvrier's team at the District had decided that the answer lay in the creation of 'centres urbains nouveaux' (Delouvrier 1989: 43), soon known more catchily as 'villes nouvelles'.[4] The new towns would be designed to accommodate substantial populations (Cergy's was projected to grow to around 400,000) and provide a range of employment opportunities, facilities and leisure amenities.[5] In some sense, it seemed, new towns would have a reparative and even redemptive function. They attended to the damage done to urban lives and the urban landscape in the preceding years. By offering jobs in situ for their inhabitants, as well as amenities for leisure and consumption, they would avoid the need for lengthy and tiring journeys across the region, saving time and energy and allowing it to be spent in other ways. In doing so, they would restore 'mutilated' suburban dwellers to a state of wholeness at once physical, psychological, affective and civic, and enable them to participate fully as citizens of the nation.

Yet if Cergy-Pontoise was going to be a 'proper' town, it would simultaneously be a reinvention of urban living. Such was the promise made in the first promotional brochure for the new town in 1968: 'offrir aux 400 000 habitants qu'elle accueillera peu à peu un cadre et un mode de vie nouveaux, adaptés à la civilization

4   Delouvrier: 'le mot [*sic*] "centre urbain nouveau" ne dirait rien à personne, tandis que le terme "ville nouvelle" était parlant' [the word 'new urban centre' wouldn't mean anything to anyone, whereas the term 'new town' was more evocative] (Murard & Fourquet 2004: 127).

5   In 2019, at the time of writing the most recent data available from the French government's statistics agency, the population of the Cergy-Pontoise urban area was just over 212,000 with a very gently rising trend <https://www.insee.fr/fr/statistiques/1405599?geo=EPCI-249500109> [accessed 22 August 2022].

contemporaine et actuellement inconnu dans la région parisienne' [offer its 400,000 inhabitants little by little a new way of life adapted to contemporary civilization and so far unknown in the Paris region] (IAURP 1968: 2). Moreover, its novelty seemed to lay precisely in disguising its urban character as far as possible. Cergy's distinctive and distinguishing feature was that, as Bernard Hirsch put it when describing the new town to Pigeat and Rohmer in *Enfance d'une ville*, 'c'est une ville dont le centre est un lac' [it is a town whose centre is a lake]. The site was positioned on an undulating plateau overlooking the Boucle de Neuville, a large meander of the river Oise, a tributary of the Seine. In the apex of the meander were flooded gravel pits which the planners had earmarked for transformation into a public park and centre for aquatic sports.

The new town would be developed over time in a horseshoe around the meander, placing the residential neighbourhoods within easy reach of the lake, and offering panoramic views towards Paris on the horizon. While the administrative centre, commercial and residential areas were built on agricultural land, Cergy-Pontoise (in common with the other new towns) was not an entirely greenfield site. Rather, it was co-located with two existing settlements that gave the new town its name: the medieval village of Cergy, by the river, and the market town of Pontoise, slightly inland. Grafting the new town on to long-established places was another way in which the planners set out to dodge the failures of the *grands ensembles*, and the lack of connection, locatedness and sense of identity that had plagued them.

From that point of view, the presence on the horizon of the Paris skyline was also important. It reflected the planners' sensitivity to the symbolic opportunities afforded by topography, and the ways in which topography can be turned into spectacle. Hirsch captures the idea when he observes, 'combien de fois sommes-nous montés au belvédère de Gency pour essayer de faire vivre dans l'imagination de nos visiteurs cette ville qui pour nous était devenue une réalité' [how frequently we went up to the belvedere at Gency in order to help our visitors picture in their imaginations what for us had become a reality] (2000: 75). Selecting a spectacular location for Cergy-Pontoise enacted the promise that it would afford a 'new way of life' by providing its inhabitants with the opportunity to derive aesthetic pleasure and satisfaction from their surroundings.

At the same time, Cergy's location endowed the new town with meaning and identity by positioning it within the symbolic and historical topography of the Paris region. The site was more or less directly in line with the so-called *axe historique* running from the Louvre to La Défense via the Champs-Élysées and the Arc de Triomphe, a structuring alignment of landmarks rich in symbolism and history that stood metonymically both for Paris and for the nation as a whole. That Cergy was aligned with the *axe historique* seemed to confirm its historical significance as an important moment of national renewal and progress.

Indeed, Cergy's function as a coda to the *axe historique* was given material form in the 1980s with the development of the Axe majeur, a park by Israeli sculptor Dani Karavan covering more than three square kilometres on the plateau at Puiseux, not far from where Hirsch had taken his visitors to admire the view (Fig. 3.1). The

FIG. 3.1. The Axe majeur in 2022, looking out over the Boucle de Neuville with the hazy profile of La Défense on the horizon. Photograph by the author.

site's symbolic connections with the *axe historique* were asserted by using paving taken from the Cour Napoléon at the Louvre, and basing measurements for twelve columns on the Arc du Carrousel in the Tuileries gardens (Saint-Pierre 2002: 67). Its paths led the walker from an equally monumental, semi-circular block of apartments by Catalan architect Ricardo Bofill (home to one of the characters in Rohmer's *L'Ami de mon amie*) to an esplanade with views over the Oise towards La Défense and Paris, whose expansiveness offered metaphorical resonances exploited by filmmaker Céline Sciamma in *Naissance des pieuvres* [Waterlillies] (2007), as if to confirm the planners' intuitions about the aesthetic potential of the location.

In a way, the planners' sensitivity to viewpoints and perspectives summed up their broader relationship to the landscape, which was derived in turn from their fundamental preoccupation with the readability and visibility of the Parisian suburbs. The problem of legibility emerges early on in the commentary to the *Schéma directeur*:

> En vérité, on se perd dans ce magma urbain. On s'y perd physiquement, dès que l'on quitte les nationales ou son quartier de banlieue; y retrouver quelqu'un devient une expédition. On s'y perd intellectuellement: l'agglomération n'est devenue une réalité statistique depuis très peu d'années, et depuis moins longtemps une réalité d'urbanisme. (DGRP 1965: 37)

[In truth, one gets lost in this urban magma. One gets lost physically, as soon as one leaves the main road or one's neighbourhood. Trying to meet someone becomes an expedition. One gets lost mentally: the region became a statistical reality only a few years ago, and only more recently still a reality of urban planning.]

If sorting out the 'mess' of the *banlieue*, as de Gaulle had instructed, meant bringing order and clarity, then being able to situate oneself within it was an essential part of that process. In the stories they tell, the planners return insistently to their embodied engagement with the region, which they investigate on foot or by car, and the extent to which the decisions they take are rooted in perception and lived experience. As Guy Lagneau puts it,

> On a vraiment vécu la région pendant deux ans. Et puis après, on a décidé le dispositif général, je ne dirais pas par intuition mais presque, par une espèce de volonté d'aménagement, une volonté physique, qui résultait de ce qu'on avait senti dans la région. (Murard & Fourquet 2004: 97)

> [We really lived the region for two years. Then we established the general framework, not quite through intuition though almost, by a sort of will to plan, a physical will that stemmed from what we had felt in the region.]

Delouvrier led the way. Swapping the panoptic view of the helicopter for the individuated perspective of the car driver, he bought a convertible Studebaker with which he spent his Saturdays exploring the region. For the car to be convertible was important: 'avec cet engin, on peut regarder, observer, s'intégrer au paysage urbain et rural' [with this thing, you can look, observe and integrate yourself into the landscape] (Chenu 1994: 255). As if to illustrate how planning decisions were shaped by sensorial immersion in the landscape, Delouvrier concludes his anecdote by recounting the day he came across the location where Cergy-Pontoise would be built:

> Un jour, ayant quitté Pontoise pour gagner le plateau là où il commence à descendre vers l'Oise et la Seine, je découvris l'endroit d'où, par temps clair, on apercevait Notre-Dame, distante de trente kilomètres. Il faisait un temps exquis et, comme souvent en Ile-de-France quand brille le soleil après la pluie, la vue était à la fois nette et lointaine: on devinait les tours de Notre-Dame. [...] Rentré rue Barbet-de-Jouy [where Delouvrier's team had its offices], je téléphonai à Jacques Michel: 'est-ce que près de Pontoise...?' Il y avait pensé mais ignorait si des terres étaient aisément disponibles. (Chenu 1994: 255)

> [One day, having left Pontoise to head up to the plateau where it begins to descend towards the Oise and Seine rivers, I found the place where, on a clear day, you could see Notre-Dame thirty kilometres away. The weather was perfect, and as is often the case in the Ile-de-France when the sun is shining after the rain, the air was clear and you could see a long way: the towers of Notre-Dame were visible in the distance. [...] When I got back to the office, I telephoned Jacques Michel: 'what about near Pontoise...?' He'd thought about it, but didn't know if the land was easily available.]

Hirsch would in turn describe the view from the plateau above the Boucle de Neuville in similarly picturesque terms, which foreground the perspective of the viewing subject:

> Des hauteurs de Gency, la vue est très belle. Elle change avec les saisons, avec le ciel, avec le soleil. Au printemps, les cerisiers et les pruniers sauvages sont en fleur. L'Oise coule au pied, quatre-vingts mètres plus bas, à peine perceptible au milieu des arbres. (Hirsch 2000: 42)

> [The view is beautiful from the heights of Gency. It changes with the seasons, the sky and the sun. In the spring, the wild cherry and plum trees are in blossom. The river Oise flows by, eighty metres below, barely visible through the trees.]

Delouvrier and Hirsch see the view in strikingly similar ways. At once attuned to the aesthetic potential of the landscape, they are able to express their perceptions in aesthetic terms. What they say also carries an assumption that the view would be universally recognized as having picturesque qualities and aesthetic value. That they have shared tastes in landscape is maybe not a surprise, reflecting sensibilities shaped in similar ways by education and class, with eyes trained to interpret a landscape in aesthetic terms, and extract aesthetic value from it. Nonetheless, the startling fact remains that those shared tastes and sensibilities, stimulated perhaps by a serendipitous turn down a country road, could be the basis for decisions about where the new town would be built.

Emerging from these stories is a sense of the complex phenomenology of planning action. On the one hand is the planners' embodied engagement with the region, which emphasizes their situated position in the landscape. On the other is their mediated relationship to space, articulated in the photos we see of them gathered round plans and scale models, or the brochures which imagine, promise and promote the urban futures arriving with the new towns. Connecting the two is the desire to establish vantage points, perspectives and locations as a means of bringing clarity and order to bear on the *banlieue*.

The need to navigate between the two positions is captured neatly in the way Delouvrier deploys both a helicopter and a car, takes to the air and circulates on the ground, in his efforts to get to grips with his domain. Here too is another reason why the *Schéma directeur*'s principal form is cartographic, a 1:100,000-scale map of the Paris region. A map is not just the most efficient way to communicate the objectives of the plan, nor the expression of a panoptic desire for control of the territory. It is also a metaphor for, and manifestation of, the planners' need to orient themselves within the *banlieue*, the essential gesture of representation on which the restoration of order and clarity can be predicated.

The planners' preoccupation with territorial legibility, and their desire to organize Cergy around perspectives and views, make manifest how the new town forms part of an imagined construct, and exists as a place whose imagined forms in the minds of the planners precede its reality on the ground. Those forms were mediated through plans and scale models, but also took shape around locations such as viewpoints and perspectives, which are less tangible, insofar as they are enacted by a viewing subject, but in many respects no less mediated. That is to say, they are recognized as viewpoints because they correspond to culturally-constructed conventions of the aesthetic and the picturesque. Hence Hirsch's insistence on taking his visitors to admire the view from the heights of Gency, in the hope that they too could conjure up the vision of 'cette ville qui pour nous était devenue une réalité'.

Doing so also reflected another important impetus in play, which explains why Cergy's contours took shape not only in plans and models, but also in promotional brochures which underscored the uniqueness of the site and the opportunities it would afford. 'Par son site, par sa forme,' argued the first of these in 1968, 'cette ville dont le centre est un plan d'eau ne sera semblable à nulle autre' [thanks to its location and its form, this town whose centre is a lake will look like no other] (IAURP 1968: 5). Cergy needed not simply to be an expression of urban modernity but an object of desire, one capable of appealing to several different audiences: property developers and housing contractors, commercial and industrial businesses which could bring employment to the new town, individuals and families who could be lured by the promise of a new *mode de vie*.

As I noted above, and as Cupers also underlines (2014: 189–93), the new town programme found itself between the twin poles of state intervention and market liberalism that structured France's political economy in the post-war period. Moreover, the new towns began construction precisely as political momentum was swinging away from the former towards the latter. Cergy-Pontoise needed to chart a path through what Cupers terms 'the volatility of a flourishing consumer society' (2014: 197). It could not develop without securing investment and harnessing the power of private capital through the relocation of commerce and industry and the construction of its residential neighbourhoods. Exposed to the unpredictability of the market, it had to find ways to give itself a competitive edge. The prospect on offer from the heights of Gency was one such selling-point.[6]

At the same time, and notwithstanding the evolving political and economic orthodoxies of 1970s France, it is important not to overemphasize the retail, market-driven dimensions of Cergy's development. Its creation remained rooted in the prospective vision of spatial planning as a motor of social progress, understood as the social mixing of its inhabitants, an expansion of the middle classes through rising incomes and prosperity, and increased space and time for leisure.

The sense of ethical commitment with which the planners undertook their work is expressed by Hirsch in his memoirs: 'nous avons conscience d'accomplir une mission grave qui va engager pour toujours l'avenir de ces gens qui nous entourent' [we were conscious of carrying out a serious mission with important consequences

---

6   In his memoirs, Bernard Hirsch recounts his efforts to attract corporate investment in Cergy. Johnson & Johnson set up a factory there, and industrial conglomerate 3M moved its French headquarters to the new town (Hirsch 2000). For 3M, architect Paul Depondt built a modernist, cruciform tower of eleven storeys with a dark steel frame and mirrored windows (Ruidiaz 2003). Annie Ernaux notes in *Journal du dehors* how seeing the 3M building lit up at night brings back memories of getting lost driving round Cergy when she first arrived, 'trop affolée pour m'arrêter' [too flustered to stop] (1996: 29). Designed to give a sense of occasion and identity to the new town's urban environment, its modernist architecture seemed instead to accentuate its strangeness. The 3M building was demolished in 2018 and the company's headquarters relocated elsewhere in Cergy to less eye-catching premises.

for the future of the people around us] (2000: 87). In effect, Cergy was the product of all these forces and motivations simultaneously. It was a social experiment and statement of national intent that was also a retail proposal in a market offering a range of lifestyle opportunities for an expanding middle class. It was a magical place, promising a bright future in a hybrid landscape of modern urbanity, proximity to nature and sweeping, open prospects.

As such, it was perhaps appropriate that Cergy's promise found one of its most vibrant expressions in a glossy, full-colour promotional brochure that *Paris Match* produced for the new town in 1971. Not only had *Paris Match* already proved its use as an ally in helping the government to communicate its spatial planning agenda, as we saw in Chapter 2; but as France's most successful illustrated magazine, it also knew how to tell and sell a story, and how to exploit textual and visual forms in doing so. Here, the two converged in an object designed explicitly to sell the government's wares. 'Les villes nouvelles sont avant tout une nécessité' [first and foremost, the new towns are essential], ran the copy, recycling the central argument of the *Schéma directeur*. 'Dans une région parisienne qui atteindra 14 millions d'habitants en 1995, leur rôle est d'être un contrepoids à l'emprise de la capitale' [in a region where the population is expected to reach 14 million by 1995, their role is to serve as a counterweight to the capital] (*Paris Match* 1971: 7). *Paris Match* also offered the advantage of significant reach and resources. It included the brochure as an insert to the Paris edition of issue 1179 (11 December 1971). A report on the publicity campaign filed in the archives of the Cergy development corporation (*établissement public d'aménagement*, EPA) noted that the Paris edition of the magazine had a print run of 300,000, while an additional 400,000 copies of the brochure were printed for distribution to households and companies across the *département* of the Val d'Oise.[7]

The front cover, carrying the title *Cergy-Pontoise: naissance d'une ville* [Cergy-Pontoise: birth of a town] alongside the *Paris Match* logo, is given over to an aerial view of architect Henri Bernard's imposing new prefecture, completed the previous year. An inverted pyramid of steel, concrete and glass, it serves as a metonymical expression both of the new town's modernity and the state's guiding presence in its development. Photographed on a sunny day, the prefecture is surrounded by quiet roads and open space, against a backdrop of fields and wooded hillsides in the distance. Sitting discreetly in foreground are the planning offices of Hirsch's team. Light, space and greenery dominate the image, and the prefecture seems to add to the luminosity of the scene through the way its materials reflect the sunlight.

Over the page, next to an excitable headline in red ('The new town is here already!'), is the sort of image at which *Paris Match* excels, drawing together a series of signifying threads into a dense weave of connoted meanings (Fig. 3.2). Bernard's prefecture fills the upper third of the image, in the background but nevertheless an unmistakable presence, as if presiding over the scene before us. We are in a park planted with young cherry trees, through which two groups of people stroll. In

---

7   Fonds de l'Établissement public d'aménagement de Cergy-Pontoise, Archives départementales du Val d'Oise, 1087 W 41.

Cergy-Pontoise

LA VILLE NOUVELLE EXISTE DÉJÀ!

A 30 km du centre historique de Paris, autour des plans d'eau de la boucle de l'Oise, une étonnante aventure a commencé : Cergy-Pontoise, une ville nouvelle qui se veut différente des grands ensembles. Il y a cinq ans, une poignée d'urbanistes se sont installés sur place, dans une baraque au milieu des champs avec, comme seul viatique, une lettre de mission de Georges Pompidou leur donnant carte blanche pour construire et faire vivre une ville nouvelle de 300 000 habitants. Cinq années difficiles où il a fallu convaincre les sceptiques, rassembler les terrains, percer les canalisations, électrifier le chemin de fer, installer le téléphone. Les bulldozers ont déterré des haches et des pierres taillées : étonnante convergence de l'histoire, la ville de demain se construit là précisément où nos plus lointains ancêtres avaient installé une de leurs premières communautés. Aujourd'hui, la ville commence à vivre et les premiers habitants se promènent loin des voitures, parmi les cerisiers qui entourent la préfecture ouverte sur la vie. Savent-ils qu'ils deviennent les pionniers d'un monde nouveau ?

FIG. 3.2. Nurturing the future in Cergy-Pontoise. © PARIS MATCH/SCOOP

the central foreground is a toddler, running in front of his parents up an incline in the direction of the camera. The father carries a second baby, while his wife (an assumption, but a relatively safe one) has her arm through his.

From the parents' attire and appearance, not least that of the father (blazer, slacks, tie, short hair, horn-rimmed glasses), we can tell that they represent the sort of energetic middle-class arrivals Cergy was designed to attract. Here, perhaps, we have *un cadre* (a middle manager) enjoying a lunchtime walk with his young family, benefitting from the fact that he can both live and work in the new town. Shadowing the nuclear family at a distance is a second, younger couple (also heterosexual). Though not yet, it seems, with children of their own, they nonetheless reinforce the image of Cergy as a place where France's future is being nurtured, thanks not least to the state's foresight in creating the social and economic conditions in the present that will enable that future to take shape. (Notable too is that everyone in the photo is white, a telling but not unexpected detail to whose implications I return later.)

Cergy's modernity, a blend of efficiency, space and leisure, is variously staged through the remainder of the brochure. Young children are at work in a bright and airy classroom, pedestrian walkways pass over roads placed in cuttings, horse riders pause by one of the lakes in the Boucle de Neuville. The last page takes us elsewhere, quite strikingly, to a motorway junction at night (Fig. 3.3). Alongside the heading, 'l'acte de naissance de Cergy-Pontoise: son nom sur les panneaux de l'autoroute A15' [Cergy's birth certificate: its name on the signs of the A15 motorway] (1971: 12), we see a large black arrow on a white background pointing down towards the exit slip road for Cergy-Pontoise, and into the world we, as readers of the brochure, have just been visiting. In one sense, an image of a motorway exit sign at night could seem an odd way for the brochure to conclude. Yet like Bernard's prefecture, the sign functions metonymically, standing not just for the new town, but for the larger system of which it is part.

Indeed, the exit sign for Cergy might be one of the purest expressions of post-war France's modernity-in-progress, which is at once symbolized and advanced by the infrastructure on display.[8] The calm and effortless lifestyle we have just witnessed

8   Bernard Hirsch understood the symbolic importance of the road sign in lending the new town material and conceptual reality. Writing in December 1967 to M. Forgerit, in charge of designing the signage for the A15 motorway between Paris and Pontoise, Hirsch requests that 'les caractères de "Ville Nouvelle" soient aussi grands que possible'. The photograph taken a few years later for the *Paris Match* supplement suggests that his wish was fulfilled (letter to M. Forgerit, 19 December 1967, Archives départementales du Val-d'Oise, fonds Bernard Hirsch, 1287 W 28). Meanwhile, at the bottom of the page is the promise of a more futuristic form of transport, Jean Bertin's turbine-powered hovertrain (*aérotrain*), whose development had received government backing, and whose inaugural line would have connected Cergy to La Défense. There was prescience in the relative space afforded to slip road and *aérotrain*. Bertin's project was beset by technical, financial and political difficulties and was abandoned by the government in 1974, though not after it had funded a prototype line across open country near Orléans, where sections remain to this day. On the *aérotrain* and its fate see Hirsch (2000: 266–74) and Guigueno 2008, who notes the suspicion with which Bertin's project was viewed by the SNCF, busy undertaking research into high-speed rail technology that would produce the TGV (*train à grande vitesse*), inaugurated in 1981.

L'acte de naissance de Cergy-Pontoise : son nom sur les panneaux de l'autoroute A 15

Aujourd'hui les liaisons entre Paris et Cergy-Pontoise n'échappent pas aux difficultés rencontrées dans toute la région parisienne. Mais des efforts gigantesques sont entrepris partout. Sept ponts nouveaux vont être jetés sur l'Oise. L'autoroute A 15 est en construction et à son achèvement, Cergy-Pontoise ne sera qu'à 20 mn du boulevard périphérique. Dans quatre ans, une liaison autoroutière sera assurée avec la Défense. Avec l'aérotrain, glissant silencieusement à 180 km/h, aller à Paris deviendra un plaisir, plaisir que partageront les Parisiens qui voudront découvrir les théâtres, les musées et les centres de loisirs de Cergy-Pontoise, tout autant que les « Cergypontins » partiront explorer Paris. De plus, l'aérodrome très proche de Cormeilles s'équipe pour l'aviation de tourisme et d'affaires, ce qui permettra à la Ville Nouvelle d'être desservie, dès 1975, par les courriers des lignes intérieures qui la mettront à moins d'une heure de Marseille et de Nice. Cherchant à penser la ville de demain, « les hommes du rêve sont passés à l'action », mais ils n'oublient pas pour autant les réalités quotidiennes des premiers habitants d'aujourd'hui.

L'aérotrain :
la Défense à 12 mn des bords de l'Oise
En 1976, il faudra 12 minutes pour passer des tours de la Défense aux bureaux de Cergy-Pontoise : grâce à l'aérotrain dont la station d'arrivée sera située à proximité de la préfecture de la Ville Nouvelle (sur notre photo, à g., l'ingénieur Bertin devant la maquette de son aérotrain). Mais déjà, sur l'autoroute A 15 dont quelques kilomètres sont achevés et dont les travaux se poursuivent en direction de Paris, les panneaux lumineux (ci-dessus) indiquent la direction de la Ville Nouvelle. Là où se prépare la ville de demain sans méconnaître les réalités d'aujourd'hui.

Publi-reportage PARIS-MATCH

PHOTOS ANDRÉ LEFEBVRE

FIG. 3.3. The slip road to modernity. © PARIS MATCH/SCOOP

is enabled by an expanding and highly engineered transport system, whose fluidity and speed are signalled by the red and white streaks of car lights caught in the long exposure. As such, the image works to convey the planners' dream as an emerging realization. The closing sentence of the text concurs in its assessment of the planners' work, even as it reassures us that their success has not divorced them from awareness of the everyday realities of life: 'cherchant à penser la ville de demain, "les hommes de rêve sont passés à l'action", mais ils n'oublient pas pour autant les réalités quotidiennes des premiers habitants d'aujourd'hui' [setting out to conceive the town of tomorrow, 'the men of dreams have swung into action', but they haven't forgotten about the everyday realities of today's inhabitants] (1971: 12).

However, the drama of Cergy's creation as it unfolds during the 1970s stems precisely from an evolving tension between vision and reality inherent in the project. Cergy persists simultaneously in the empirical and symbolic realms, at once a real place on the ground emerging from muddy building sites, and a vision and promise of the future where things are shiny and new. Hirsch articulates the planners' liminal and instrumental position between these two states in describing his insistence that they move into offices on the site of the new town as soon as possible:

> Nous voulions être les premiers sur le terrain, voir de nos fenêtres les chantiers s'ouvrir et la ville grandir, souffrir de la boue et de l'isolement, constater au jour le jour les défauts et les corriger sans retard. Nous voulions que chaque urbaniste n'hésite pas à aller vérifier sur place un détail, si minime soit-il, avant d'arrêter définitivement le projet. (Hirsch 2000: 69)

> [We wanted to be the first on the ground, to see from our windows the building sites begin and the town grow, to suffer the mud and the isolation, to identify the faults and correct them quickly. We wanted the planners to go on site without hesitation to check even the smallest detail before signing off on the project.]

Here lies another reason for Cergy's existence in mediated form, and why it starts to circulate as brochure, pamphlet or television news item.[9] The new town becomes a matter of commercial, retail and political persuasion, particularly once the building work starts and planning visions run into the realities and perspectives of those already in situ. Different constituencies needed to be persuaded of the reality and viability of the vision, but also of the benefits the new town would bring when it seemed above all to bring problems. While Cergy started to exist in built form in the landscape, it also took shape discursively through, with and for those involved in its creation. This meant the planners first and foremost, but also those caught up in its development, including those who resisted or opposed it. In effect, Cergy begins to oscillate between being an object of desire and an object of dispute, and it does not take long for the friction of political contestation to emerge.

Cergy's double life between the empirical and discursive realms, its existence as both place and thing (in the Latourian sense), is a key theme of *Enfance d'une ville*,

---

9   I explore some of the ways in which French television news portrays the construction of Cergy in Welch 2021.

the television documentary by Pigeat and Rohmer. Broadcast in August 1975, it was the first in a four-part series on urban planning for French television, and marked the start of Rohmer's persistent interest in Cergy and the new town experiment. He would return to Cergy as a more finished product in the mid-1980s for the setting of *L'Ami de mon amie* (1987), and shot a preceding film, *Les Nuits de la pleine lune* [Full moon in Paris] (1984), on location in Marne-la-Vallée. But the *Ville nouvelle* series itself reflected a long-standing concern with space, architecture and urban planning, and the relationship between space and its inhabitants (as well as how the moving image can portray those things).

In 1969, Rohmer directed *Entretien sur le béton*, which explores the qualities of reinforced concrete as a building material through interviews with architects Claude Parent and Paul Virilio. Parent and Virilio argue that concrete's plasticity is ideally suited to an urban environment geared towards flow and circulation (a point *Paris Match* would go on to prove in its evocative photograph of the exit slip road for Cergy, the sort of speed space they perhaps had in mind). In 1964, Rohmer made *Métamorphoses du paysage*, a documentary for schools on industrialization, modernization and urban development. The film is concerned at once with the nature of space and landscape, and with how space changes through time; but it also dwells on how film captures that change, revealing his preoccupation with what Ivone Margulies calls 'cinema's special affinity for transience' (Margulies 2014: 173).

Métamorphoses du paysage draws out how the landscape is not fixed and immutable but constantly evolving, a trend magnified by the turnover of urban and industrial forms. Even the most imposing of industrial buildings have surprisingly rapid half-lives as they are overtaken by advancing technology:

> Dans le monde de la technique, tout vieillit avant l'âge, et ces usines à peine quinquagénaires nous semblent être les aînés des immeubles centenaires de Haussmann. Elles ont cette mélancolie de choses destinées à disparaître à plus ou moins brève échéance.

> [In the technical world, everything gets old before its time, and factories that barely date back fifty years appear older than Haussmann's buildings from last century. They have that melancholic air of things destined to disappear sooner or later.]

As it depicts environments at first glance disfigured by the uncompromising forms of modern industry and infrastructure, the film suggests that while they might appear rebarbative, we can learn to recognize the beauty latent within them.

As Marion Schmid puts it, 'seen with the fresh eye of a camera sensitive to the lines, textures and rhythms of industrial modernity, the shafts of cranes and telegraph poles take on a weightless elegance' (Schmid 2015: 350). The film's closing words converge with the Surrealist belief that enchantment can be found in things and places that seem otherwise to bring about the disenchantment of the world: 'nous osons garder l'espoir que le cadre futur de notre existence laissera dans sa rigueur une porte ouverte à la rêverie' [we dare to hope that our future surroundings, in all their rigour, will leave open a doorway to dreams]. Schmid notes that the words are spoken over shots of looming new tower blocks, whose functional rigour seems to contradict the voiceover's 'guarded optimism' and imply instead that the latest urban forms are 'little conducive to reverie' (2015: 353). Nevertheless, Rohmer's subsequent work on Cergy would suggest that, in the new towns at least, the door to dreams and enchantment remained open.

Like Godard in *2 ou 3 choses que je sais d'elle*, Rohmer in *Métamorphoses du paysage* films the construction of the Boulevard Périphérique around Paris as an instance of urban transformation. What differs is how they interpret what they see. In Rohmer's film, its construction is part of a natural phenomenon of change as space moves through time and society advances, rather than evidence of a politically motivated intervention in the landscape in order to reinforce the existing socio-economic order. *Enfance d'une ville*, on the other hand, brings politics back into the frame by making more visible the human agency behind spatial change, investigating the tensions which arise as change is brought to bear on the landscape, and encountering the people involved in it. It captures Cergy in its transition from planners' vision to lived reality, and what that transition implies in human terms. In many respects, there was perhaps no clearer demonstration of the transience of space in human hands than the installation of bold new urban landscapes in a rural setting.

By the time Pigeat and Rohmer came to make their film in 1975, some seven years after construction had begun, they appeared to take as a given that the new town had emerged in the landscape as an object of dispute, whose presence catalysed clashing perceptions, representations and narratives. The tensions around Cergy's development were heightened in particular by the fact that it required land to be expropriated from local farmers and landowners, which was the most obvious expression of the asymmetries of power inherent in state-led planning.

In contrast to Godard in *2 ou 3 choses que je sais d'elle*, who locates state agency in the determining absent presence of remote administrative structures and shadowy figures, Pigeat and Rohmer embody it in specific individuals, most notably Hirsch as director of Cergy's *établissement public d'aménagement* [state development agency] (EPA), an interview with whom is woven through the film. Doing so underscores how the creation of Cergy is bound up in the energy and personal investment of the planners who are tasked by the state with envisioning the new town and giving it material form. It returns us to the fact that spatial planning and the birth of the new towns are first and foremost human adventures, produced through the dynamic which takes shape when humans encounter each other and form social, political and affective relationships.

Loïc Vadelorge is wary of what he terms the 'biographical illusion' colouring historical accounts of spatial planning and the new towns (2014: 37). It is easy to get caught up in the myth-making of those involved, he argues, and the stories of planning as the resolute actions of a small and charismatic band of pioneers. Yet at the same time, those stories are important in terms of illuminating their perceptions and understanding of planning, agency and decision making. They also reflect a reality of spatial planning as an activity contingent on human relationships embedded within a specific administrative culture and political context. Hirsch articulates the value placed on fostering and reproducing a corporate ethos, an *esprit de corps*, as he describes putting together his planning team at Cergy:

> J'attachais une très grande importance au choix de mes collaborateurs et aucun n'a été recruté sans un entretien très approfondi qui portait moins sur ses références personnelles — c'était pour la plupart des débutants — que sur ses goûts, ses motivations, ses activités extra-professionnelles. (Hirsch 2000: 71)

> [I put a great deal of effort into choosing my collaborators, and none was recruited without an extensive interview which focused less on personal references — they were nearly all at an early stage in their careers — than on tastes, motivations and activities outside of work.]

Hirsch's interest in personality more than experience signalled that he was looking for the kind of free-thinking potential his generation had recognized in themselves, not least thanks to their time in the colonies. Indeed, he is open about his preference for 'ceux qui avaient fait un séjour outre-mer' [those who had spent time overseas] because it was indicative of the initiative and entrepreneurial spirit (the attitude, Gaston Berger might have said) that building a new town would need: 'cela traduit un esprit d'aventure et une aptitude à se débrouiller sans aide extérieure, tout à fait dans la ligne de la construction d'une ville nouvelle' [it signalled a spirit of adventure and an ability to sort things out independently, both of which were in line with building a new town] (Hirsch 2000: 71).

Notwithstanding Vadelorge's caution over reducing the history of Gaullist planning to the life stories and charismatic force of a few men of action, in play once more is an understanding of planning that favours, to recall Cupers's words, 'situated agency over abstract forces' (Cupers 2014: xv). From that point of view, the planners' memoirs, interviews and anecdotes can be read as delineations of their agency, and the points of resistance it encounters. Moreover, the distinctive character of Gaullist planning lies precisely in the fact that the planners' situated agency might express itself in the authoritarian impulse present within French political and administrative culture, be reflected in their pharaonic ability to select locations for new cities, or take on the appearance (particularly for those affected or concerned by its outcomes) of determinism and abstract force.

Through interviews with Hirsch and his team at the EPA, *Enfance d'une ville* maps the contours of the planners' situated agency and the extent of its power. As the film moves back and forth between interior and exterior locations, from planners at their drawing boards in offices overlooking construction sites to completed residential and commercial districts, it stages Cergy's process of becoming, and the translation of the planning imaginary into material reality. The headiness of bringing a new world into being is summed up by Hirsch towards the end of his interview: 'c'est quand même assez vertigineux de voir que ce qui a été d'abord étudié sur des maquettes se réalise grandeur nature comme cela a été prévu' [it's really quite something to see what started as a scale model take shape in real life in the way it had been conceived].

Hirsch is the first person we meet after Pigeat and Rohmer have introduced the film, and throughout he remains in the same interior location. Concomitantly, our

FIG. 3.4. Bernard Hirsch introduces Cergy-Pontoise in Jean-Paul Pigeat and Éric Rohmer's *Enfance d'une ville*. ORTF, série 'Ville nouvelle', 10 August 1975.

first encounter is with representations of Cergy, rather than the place itself. While Hirsch talks about the project, a vast map on the wall behind him shows the new town development area, with the Oise and the Boucle de Neuville clearly visible as a thick dark line running in from the top right-hand corner. From the start of the film, we are made aware of Cergy's existence primarily as an imaginary construct, as something taking shape in the imaginary realm through maps, drawings and models, before it finds its way out into the world. When Hirsch moves to the map in order to describe the development plan and its key principles ('c'est une ville dont le centre est un lac'), he illustrates once again how the planners' engagement and interaction with discursive and iconographic forms are fundamental to the creation of the new town, and how it gains conceptual and material substance through being mediated by them (Fig. 3.4).

Hirsch's opening exchanges with the filmmakers are also where a second ghost makes an unsettling appearance as part of the planning imaginary. In accounting for the specificity of Cergy, Hirsch volunteers immediately that many of the residents share a common background:

> Vous avez peut-être remarqué que dans la ville nouvelle il y a beaucoup d'anciens coloniaux, des Africains. Et… je crois que ceci s'explique parce que, d'abord, ce sont des pionniers, et qu'une ville nouvelle c'est un peu analogue au défrichage des territoires d'Afrique.

> [You've perhaps noticed that many people in the new town spent time in the colonies, came from Africa. And… I think the reason is that, above all, they are pioneers, and that a building a new town is a bit like clearing land in Africa.]

We saw in the last chapter how Gaullist *aménagement* was driven by a large cadre of planners and engineers returning from France's former colonies in North and

West Africa. Amongst them was Hirsch himself, who had been director of public works in Mali and Mauritania during the 1950s (2000: 9). As Hirsch suggests in his memoirs, they came back not just with the technical expertise they had acquired, but also with the sort of attitude he was looking for as he recruited his colleagues. If the new towns were haunted by the ghost of colonialism, then in the first instance, it was as a habit of thought and action, a certain way of seeing the world and acting upon it.

Henri Lefebvre had been quick to recognize the implications for metropolitan France of a returning cadre of colonial administrators. Their redeployment would initiate 'une espèce de transfert du colonialisme dans la métropole, un semi-colonialisme des régions et des zones mal développées par rapport aux centres de décision, et notamment au centre parisien' [a sort of transfer of colonialism to the mainland, a semi-colonialism of regions and zones poorly developed in relation to the decision-making centres, and the capital city in particular] (1970: 11). As a form of internal colonization, spatial planning's view of the metropolitan territory was shaped by the same ideas of underdevelopment, and concomitantly, of civilizational improvement through construction and infrastructural modernization.

Moreover, like the colonial projects that preceded it, while the conceptual work of development might be the domain of a bold and adventurous group of pioneering individuals, large amounts of the physical labour of metropolitan modernization, as I noted in the Introduction, were done by workforces drawn from France's former colonies in North and West Africa. Here was the second colonial ghost haunting Gaullist modernization, one glimpsed occasionally in news reports as North African workers on construction sites pass through the shot in the background, but occluded discursively from narratives of civilizational advance.

There is no more revealing illustration of Lefebvre's analysis than Hirsch's mobilization of the trope of the pioneer, nor its figuration in the noticeable whiteness of the couples in *Paris Match*'s brochure. The life of the colonial administrator provides the template for life in Cergy, which could become its continuation, fulfilment and uncanny echo: 'on sortait du bureau, trois minutes après on était chez soi, et cinq minutes après au tennis. Est-ce qu'on peut refaire ça à Paris?' [three minutes after leaving the office we were back home, and five minutes later we were on the tennis court. Can we do something similar in Paris?]. Meanwhile, the idea of *défrichage*, of clearing the ground and starting afresh, is the central promise of Cergy's marketing: as a new town, it was also 'une ville pilote et un lieu d'accueil pour toutes les expériences' [a pilot town and a place of welcome for those with experience of all kinds] (IAURP 1968: 8). That Hirsch could frame the new town project in such unselfconsciously neo-colonial terms is at once striking and disconcerting for a contemporary viewer (Schmid describes the analogy as 'unfortunate'). Yet the fact that he does so quite openly at once reveals the persistent currency of those terms among the planners as a way of conceiving territorial development, and indicates that the ideological assumptions behind them had yet to accumulate the negative political charge they would acquire in subsequent decades.

FIG. 3.5. The view of the expropriated in *Enfance d'une ville*.
ORTF, série 'Ville nouvelle', 10 August 1975.

Hirsch's colonial reflexes break the surface again when Pigeat pursues the analogy in their conversation. Colonization requires expropriation, suggests Pigeat. Hirsch concurs, albeit with a telling qualification: if there was a problem of expropriation in Cergy it was because, unlike in Africa, 'the land was already occupied'. Trained not to see existing claims to land in the colonized territories, the colonial administrator in Hirsch had to negotiate the troublesome thickets of land ownership back home (Chapter 5 explores some of the legal and administrative devices developed by the French state to enable the work of metropolitan *défrichage*).

After Hirsch explains in neutral terms that the farmers and market gardeners were relocated to a 'zone horticole' and now 'sell their carrots at the Cergy market', the film cuts to a local farmer in a field, M. L'Echaudé, expressing his disgruntlement as he gestures towards the new town in the distance (Fig. 3.5):

> Ces cultivateurs qui étaient sur le plateau où maintenant la ville nouvelle commence à s'élargir se sont trouvés à cultiver dans cette zone agricole qui nous a été laissée, mais qui se prête beaucoup moins à la culture maraîchère que la partie du plateau de la préfecture.

> [The market gardeners who were on the plateau where the new town is being built are now farming in the agricultural zone that has been allotted to us; but it is much less suited to market gardening than the part of the plateau where the prefecture has been built.]

The expropriation of land became the first political conflict of the project on the ground, and a recurrent theme in the memoirs of Hirsch, who was embroiled in disputes with the existing farmers and landowners, including an occupation of the site designated for the prefecture in July 1967 (2000: 111–14).[10] For this

10   On the politics of expropriation in relation to Cergy's development, see also Engrand & Millot (2015: 40–43).

to be the case was at once inevitable and appropriate, given that land was the commodity essential for the imagined worlds of the planners to take shape as built forms and landscapes. In many respects, it represented the point of contact between imagination and reality, a flashpoint enacted by cutting from Hirsch to the expropriated farmer. Doing so captures the human nature of the dispute as an encounter between embodied points of view; but as the farmer gestures towards the completed prefecture visible in the distance, it also makes plain the unequal balance of power between the two sides.

The farmer's gesture is important too for making us aware of the new town as a physical presence, an object in the landscape that demands our attention. Over the course of *Enfance d'une ville*, we gain a sense of Cergy as a place, made up of different neighbourhoods and locations (the prefecture, the Trois Fontaines shopping centre, schools, public squares, pedestrian areas). As a physical presence in the landscape, though, it is also a thing in the Latourian sense, gathering people around it and catalysing reactions and responses. Alongside the planners and the expropriated farmer, we meet a range of different constituents: the first of Cergy's residents, who must navigate the administrative complications arising from a new town that straddles the boundaries of fifteen different *communes*, the priests reflecting on what sort of building best represents the church in a new town, or the mayors of the local *communes* who need to find an accommodation with the EPA and the physical change to their world that the arrival of the new town represents.

Through these encounters, we see Cergy taking shape as an assemblage of structures and people, in which structures (physical and administrative) frame the lives of people, and people respond and adapt to structures. As deputy mayor of Éragny, one of the *communes* affected, Jacques Fournier's starting-point is to acknowledge the reality of the new town as a physical, political and administrative fact with which he must negotiate: 'elle est là, la ville, vous comprenez?' [the town is there, if you see what I'm saying]. If the making of Cergy was a human adventure, then it was so not just for the planners setting out to create a city of the future, but also for those whose lives became entangled with the new town, and for whom the new town became a setting for, or obstacle in, their lives. Its different constituencies negotiate with the new town, and negotiate with each other because of the new town. From that point of view, *Enfance d'une ville* is a film about how politics takes shape, and about how the new town takes shape with and through politics. Indeed, the film manifests politics in its most fundamental or etymological sense as about the life and running of the *polis*. At once a physical space and a location for political encounter, the new town itself becomes the subject of often intense political debate.[11]

At the heart of the new town's politics lay its residents. They were both actors themselves (in 1973, a local residents' association launched *À propos*, a mimeographed

---

11   In Welch 2018, I draw on Bourdieu and Foucault to explore the relationship between state power and civil society in Cergy, and how *Enfance d'une ville* depicts the emergence of local action groups as a response to the problems of governance and political representation posed by the new town cutting across the established electoral boundaries of the *communes* on whose territories it was built.

newsletter in which they aired their political and practical concerns about life in Cergy), and a group whose experience was debated and allegiance sought by other actors. As Cergy's translation from vision to reality progressed during the mid-1970s, the nature of the life it produced, and its emotional and affective impact on the residents, became the subject of close scrutiny. *Enfance d'une ville* was only one such example.

Around the same time appeared a flurry of research reports on life in the new town, with titles like 'Habiter une ville nouvelle' [Living in a new town] (1974), 'Cergy-Pontoise ville nouvelle vue par ses habitants' [The new town of Cergy-Pontoise seen by its residents] (1975) and 'Vivre à Cergy-Pontoise, ville nouvelle' [Living in Cergy-Pontoise new town] (1978). Commissioned from sociologists, social psychologists and market researchers by the state (EPA and CGP) and by private organizations such as the Jeune Chambre économique de Cergy-Pontoise, their dominant theme was the challenge of living in the new town, one which derived from the gap between the promise it made and its lived reality. According to the authors of 'Habiter une ville nouvelle', a study carried out for the CGP by the Compagnie française d'économistes et de psychosociologues [French company of economists and social psychologists], at stake in particular was 'cette inadéquation que l'on ressent sans cesse entre l'"offre" et la "demande", entre l'espoir ou les prétentions des concepteurs et l'indifférence ou les désillusions des habitants, entre la ville rêvée et la ville nouvelle' [the constant misalignment people feel between the 'offer' and the 'demand', between the hopes or the pretensions of the planners and the indifference or disillusionment of the inhabitants, between the dreamed town and the new town] (Grière & others 1974: 167).

Contracting research into life in Cergy as it began to unfold reflected the integration of the social sciences into spatial planning, part of a pluri-disciplinary approach that was itself a conscious gesture of innovation (Cupers 2014: 200–01). Doing so also illuminated how a modernizing France had set out to equip itself with the means to diagnose and analyse modernization's social and psychological effects.[12] The turn to a hybrid discipline like social psychology was an instance of how theories of motivation, business and organizational management had been imported from the United States during the post-war period by a modernizing avant-garde which, as Luc Boltanski (1982) notes, positioned itself at the intersection of academia, government and business.

---

12   I noted in the Introduction that Guattari's CERFI research group was sustained over a number of years by government research contracts. Hirsch's memoirs offer a somewhat sceptical perspective on his encounters with the sociologist Alain Touraine, who visited Cergy to research the planners' decision-making processes. 'J'analysai les structures de décision et l'appui que nous recevions de Paul Delouvrier qui nous avait dit, en nous lançant dans la nature: "Débrouillez-vous au mieux, je suis là pour vous aider et non pour vous contrôler". Alain Touraine m'interrompit et me déclara d'un ton solonnel: "Il faut maintenant que vous tuiez votre père, que vous vous affranchissiez de l'influence de Delouvrier". J'en restai coi' [I analysed the decision-making structures and the support we received from Paul Delouvrier, who had sent us on our way with the words, 'sort yourselves out as best you can, I'm there to help and not to monitor you'. Alain Touraine interrupted me and declared solemnly, 'Now you must kill your father, and break free of Delouvrier's influence'. I didn't say anything] (2000: 148).

Social psychology had established itself during the 1960s as both a field of academic enquiry (its proponents, like Max Pagès and Guy Palmade, often held posts in universities or the CNRS) and in commercial form as part of a burgeoning industry of consultancy and market research (Boltanski 1982: 210–12).[13] The latter was driven by the acceleration of consumer capitalism and an urgent need to understand the consumer's mind, wants and desires. At the same time, social psychologists themselves, often working for independent consultancy firms like the Compagnie française d'économistes et de psychosociologues, exemplified the expansion of France's service economy and the *cadres* of the aspiring middle classes to whom Cergy was designed to appeal.[14]

On the one hand, then, were the promises laid out in the new town's brochures and publicity material of a fresh start and a new way of life unlike any seen previously. On the other was the daily reality of life as it came to be lived in the neighbourhoods, streets and shopping centres. In the first instance, the surge of investigations and reports in the mid-1970s was responding to the perhaps inevitable gap that began to appear between those two things. At the same time, both their proliferation and their preoccupation with the nature of lived experience in the new town suggested a sense of uncertainty about what Cergy represented and what was happening there. In effect, the reports were so many attempts to fathom the affective and psychical implications of the new town, implications which emerged as it developed, and would play themselves out over time.

'D'abord vous serez désorienté'

In 1979, Hachette published a travel guide to the Parisian new towns in its venerable *Guides bleus* series. The lead author was Denise Basdevant, one of the series's seasoned writers, with books on the Nile Valley, the Emirates and the Indonesian islands of Java and Bali to her name. In many ways, the bracing modernity of the new towns was an unexpected subject for a *Guide bleu*. As Roland Barthes put it in a typically acerbic article in *Mythologies*, 'le *Guide bleu* ne connaît guère de paysage que sous la forme du pittoresque' [the only form of landscape the *Guide bleu* really knows is the picturesque] (Barthes 1972: 113). The fact that the guide was co-published with the Groupe central des villes nouvelles (GCVN), the government's co-ordinating agency for the new towns, was a clue that, like *Paris Match* a decade or so earlier, the series might have been persuaded to lend the new towns some of its symbolic capital by endorsing them as places worth seeing.[15]

13   For accounts of the development of social psychology from within the field, see (for example) Martin & Vannier 2002, Meynaud 2008 and Pagès 2008.
14   Social psychology's novelty, and its ambiguous position between science and commerce, also opened it up to satire. Georges Perec spotted its significance in *Les Choses* (1965), his exploration of the psychology of desire in a consumer economy. The novel's central characters are at once prone to the lure of consumerism and in part responsible for enabling its effects. They find (precarious) work as social psychologists carrying out opinion polls and market research, before becoming established partners in a marketing firm by the end of the novel, all the while dogged by an unshakeable feeling of dissatisfaction. William Klein's film *Le Couple témoin* (1977) satirized both the futuristic lifestyle promised by prospective planning and attempts to observe it in the name of science (Schilling 2018).
15   And financial capital, come to that. France's national archives hold the papers relating to the

An arbiter of conservative taste and interest for the bourgeois tourist since 1916, the *Guide bleu*'s dominant mode was imperative, structuring the tourist visit around what Jules Gritti calls 'injonctions du devoir-regarder' [instructions about what to look at] (Gritti 1967: 51). What also mattered, alongside seeing the right thing — the 'chose-à-voir', to use Gritti's term (1967: 52) — was attending to the aesthetic or affective response it provoked. Thus, just as Delouvrier and Hirsch shared the same sentiment of beauty before the view from the heights of Gency, and imagined Cergy's residents doing the same, so in their turn the authors of the *Guide bleu* felt that the visitor's first response to the spectacle of the new towns should be uncertainty and disorientation:

> D'abord vous serez désorienté, car il est toujours difficile de saisir l'avenir à travers un commencement. Les grandes voies routières qui mènent aux villes nouvelles, avec leurs courbes à travers des chantiers et leurs parkings immenses, vous paraîtront peut-être énigmatiques, voire absurdes. (Basdevant, Chatin & Milleron 1979: 10)

> [At first you will be disorientated, because it is always difficult to grasp the future from a beginning. The large main roads taking you to the new towns, curving through building sites to massive car parks, will perhaps seem mysterious or even absurd.]

The book's implied readers were those who might venture nervously to the new towns to see what the future had in store: 'c'est une ville pour demain qui va vous être proposée' [what is being proposed is a town for tomorrow] (1979: 10). Its front cover prepared the ground with a photograph showing architectural details of a contemporary building (the Cité artisanale des Champs-Élysées at Évry) whose modernity is connoted through a combination of building materials and design (Fig. 3.6). A dark brown brick wall in the foreground is set against the eye-catching primary colours that dominate the upper half of the image. A metal spiral staircase painted in yellow runs diagonally down against the backdrop of a blue-painted wall. The combination of lines, shapes and curves gives the image an abstract feel. It serves almost to anticipate and stage disorientation by the way it immerses its viewers in the scene, leaving them unable to grasp a full sense either of the building itself or its location. The view beyond is blocked by the blue wall, with only a small rectangle of blue sky visible above it.

While they might be put off by what they found, visitors could take comfort from the fact that the new towns were performing a function vital for Paris and the nation: 'elles restent, en le préservant de l'anarchie, les seules garants de l'avenir de Paris' [by protecting Paris from anarchy, only they can guarantee its future] (1979: 65). Their visible modernity, implied the *Guide bleu*, belied their role in preserving

---

publication of the *Guide bleu* on the new towns, which reveal that its projected budget was in the region of half a million francs, with the GCVN and new town EPAs contributing a total of 120,000 francs. In December 1977, writing to Jean-Eudes Roullier, head of the GCVN, his colleague Jean-Marie Duthilleul reported on a positive meeting with Gérald Gassiot-Talabot, the *Guide bleu* series editor at Hachette and an architectural historian. Gassiot-Talabot, felt Duthilleul, was 'personnellement assez motivé pour promouvoir les villes nouvelles' [personally quite keen to help promote the new towns] (Archives nationales 19840342/400).

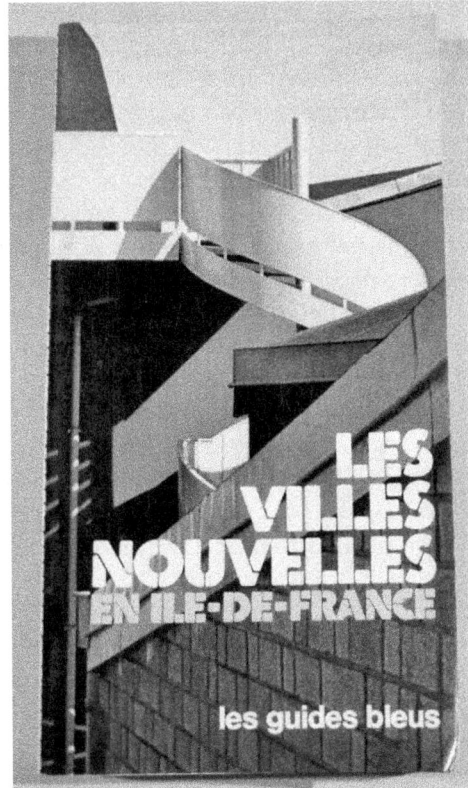

FIG. 3.6. The cover of Hachette's *Guide bleu* to the Parisian new towns (1979). Archives départementales du Val-d'Oise (BIB 8/4568).

stability and order. Or rather, it was through a modernity of forms that a politics of stability and order was best practised. From that point of view, the *Guide bleu* succeeded in aligning the new towns with the Giscardian style of technocratic conservatism. In fact, as a mediator of conservative values whose view was also pragmatically adapted to the realities of the time (not the least of which were 'current economic difficulties'), it could suggest that having been conceived during a time of 'plans, dreams and grandiose projects', the new towns had now to make their own way in the world: 'elles existent humainement, avec leurs difficultés financières et leurs exigences quotidiennes' [they exist on a human scale, with their financial difficulties and their daily demands] (1979: 65). In coming of age, like responsible adults, they would learn to live life with all its trials and tribulations.

Yet disorientation was not simply reserved for the readership of the *Guide bleu*. It was a recurrent theme of reflections on what it meant to 'exister humainement' in Cergy during the 1970s. At stake was how, to borrow Kenny Cupers's phrase, 'subjectivity is produced' in the new towns (Rice & Cupers 2017: 121), and what forces had a bearing on that process. We have seen already that prospective planning was concerned as much with producing modern subjectivities as it was with creating new built environments. More specifically, it grasped how one would flow from the other. The new towns represented its most concerted attempt to anticipate the lifestyles of the future by creating the conditions necessary for them in the present.

But we have seen as well how Delouvrier recognized that modernization required adaptation, and that it would fail as a project if the population did not learn to 'play the game' of new urban living as mobility and relocation (1967: 30).

The string of reports in the mid-1970s into life in Cergy signalled that Delouvrier's intuition was correct. As they investigated the psychical and affective impact of life in Cergy on its first inhabitants, those reports not only articulated the gap between anticipated future and experienced reality, but also made clear the difficult labour of adjustment and adaptation it required. Chief amongst the new town's effects were indeed confusion and disorientation, according to 'Vivre à Cergy-Pontoise, ville nouvelle', produced by the Société d'Étude et de Coopération (SEC) for the EPA and the Ministère de l'Équipement et de l'Aménagement du Territoire. The disorientation was partly spatial, the report suggested. It was produced by a layout perceived on the ground to be 'mal structuré topographiquement' [poorly structured from a topographic point of view] (SEC 1978: 6) and thereby creating 'difficultés de repérage' [problems of orientation] (1978: 3). Moreover, spatial disorientation was compounded by a perhaps greater sense of temporal dislocation, and here we return to the peculiarities of Cergy's relationship to time.

Modernity was central to Cergy's pitch as a new town. The authors of an earlier report, 'Habiter une ville nouvelle', had already observed that the promise to be of or ahead of its time functioned as a 'principe de garantie qu'on en a fini avec les cités dortoirs, l'anarchie urbaine, et que la scientificité qui préside à la création de Cergy évitera de recommencer les erreurs passées' [a guarantee that there were to be no more dormitory towns and anarchic urban development, and that the scientific approach behind the creation of Cergy would avoid the repetition of past errors] (Grière & others 1974: 145). As the authors of 'Vivre à Cergy-Pontoise' discovered, however, the new town's performance of modernity in turn became a source of unease for the inhabitants it interviewed. The new town's look, feel and organization — its sheer material newness — inescapably made manifest 'l'absence d'histoire vers le passé, l'incertitude d'une histoire future' [the absence of history and uncertainty over the future] (SEC 1978: 2). Cergy's very embodiment of a vision of urban modernity seemed to cut it adrift from time, with no clear links to the past and an uncertain future ahead.

The peculiar sense of a-temporality infusing Cergy was reinforced by the emphasis placed on *cadre de vie* [quality of life] as the new town's defining feature, an idea whose foregrounding of setting over time was captured in the bright light of the *Paris Match* brochure, with its eternal now of sun and open prospects. For the authors of 'Habiter une ville nouvelle', 'c'est au fond ce concept de cadre de vie que l'on essaie de vendre, peut-être plus encore que le concept d'urbanisation volontaire' [fundamentally, quality of life is the concept they are trying to sell, perhaps more than that of concerted development] (Grière & others 1974: 156). The temporal or existential anxiety provoked by Cergy's newness could be mitigated by promoting its *cadre de vie* as a calming antidote to the problems posed by contemporary urban life. The snag, they go on to point out, was that 'de l'aveu même d'un responsable interviewé, le concept de cadre de vie reste indéfinissable' [as one of those in charge admitted, the notion of quality of life is impossible to define] (1974: 157). In order to be effective, the notion needed to be translated into terms that were less abstract, more recognizable and more meaningful, not least in a situation where Cergy's *cadre de vie* and its uncertainties seemed precisely to be the problem.

One response to the challenge emerged in the autumn of 1976, when the EPA published the first issue of *Cergy magazine*, its new municipal publication (Fig. 3.7). From its second appearance in November 1978, the glossy and colourful A4-size magazine would appear twice a year until publication ceased in September 1983 after seventeen issues. Its launch coincided with the end of *À propos*, the residents' own newsletter created in 1973 that had aired the challenges of life in Cergy as it took shape, and had frequently been critical of the EPA (Saint-Pierre 2002: 24–27). *Cergy magazine*, far better resourced and with a much greater reach (by 1979, it claimed an estimated readership of 700,000 on a print run of 250,000 free copies), represented a significant shift in voice and perspective, from the contestatory grassroots of the Touleuses neighbourhood to an office in the EPA building and the orbit of the new town's decision-makers.

Nevertheless, the magazine's first editorial made a notable rhetorical move. For the thousands of people who had made Cergy their home, 'la ville nouvelle n'est pas un point sur une carte, ni une querelle de sociologues, ni une conjugaison au futur. Elle est leur vie quotidienne' (Mirimanoff 1976: 7). The new town was not an abstract concept, nor material for sterile academic debate, but a matter of real and daily life. Here was the EPA positioning itself on the side of its residents, mobilizing print media to fashion an 'imagined community' (Anderson 1984) of residents with a shared identity ('les Cergy-Pontins') and common ground. But in underscoring the theme of everyday life ('thousands of people work, study, marry, have children'), the editorial also signalled that the magazine would play a role in translating Cergy's *cadre de vie* into more tangible and recognizable possibilities. Put another way, its function could be understood to be helping to organize the confusion and disorientation uncovered by researchers on the ground (and expressed by the residents themselves in *À propos*) into something more familiar, reassuring and workable.

The rest of the first issue suggested how it would do so, focusing notably (as the cover image had adumbrated) on women and children as the main vectors of social life and the community. A long essay by Marie Cardinal, whose novel *Les Mots pour le dire* (1975) had established her as a leading exponent of women's writing in France, positioned Cergy as a progressive solution to everyday life for women, arguing that it offered them the opportunity to flourish and grow through self-realization and self-knowledge: 'je l'écoute, elle est en train de se façonner elle-même comme elle façonne un vase ou un cendrier sur le tour du potier, mais elle ne s'en rend pas compte tout à fait' [As I listen to her, she is making herself in the same way that she makes a vase or an ashtray on the potter's wheel, even if she doesn't realize it] (Cardinal 1976: 36). Cardinal had moved to Cergy and was on the magazine's editorial board.

Meanwhile, paediatrician Annie Gozlan gave scientific endorsement to the new town with her assessment that its *cadre de vie* provided a conducive setting for young children and early years education: 'je crois pouvoir dire qu'à Cergy,

FIG. 3.7. The first issue of *Cergy magazine*, published by the EPA in autumn 1976.
Archives départementales du Val-d'Oise (PER 24/187).

FIG. 3.8. The cylindrical shape and bright blue colours of the Tour Bleue des Cerclades at Cergy-Pontoise, photographed in the 1980s. Image courtesy of the Archives départementales du Val-d'Oise (1694 W 1).

l'environnement, le mode d'habitat, les structures qui existent, sont faits pour qu'un petit enfant soit heureux et trouve les conditions nécessaires à son développement tant physique que psychologique' [I can say that in Cergy, the environment, the housing and the structures that exist are designed to ensure a child's happiness and all it needs for its physical and psychological development] (Gozlan 1976: 21). Subsequent issues investigated teenage life ('Ville nouvelle, nouvelle jeunesse?' [New town, new youth?], a question rhetorically posed, issue 2), happiness ('Le bonheur est-il à Cergy?' [Is there happiness in Cergy?], likewise, issue 11), or education ('À l'école de l'imagination' [A visit to the school of the imagination], issue 13). All these topics reflected a demographic fact about Cergy's population, while at the same time mining the symbolic implications of that fact: Cergy was a place of the future and, as it welcomed and fostered new generations, where the future was taking shape.

The *Guide bleu* had nevertheless put its finger on something in its characterization of the new towns and their role. At Cergy's heart lay a fundamental tension between the visible modernity of its built environment and more conservative assumptions about its population. The tension found material expression in one of its iconic buildings, the Tour Bleue des Cerclades, a blue-painted, cylindrical apartment block near the prefecture designed by architects Martine and Philippe Deslandes (Fig. 3.8). Completed in 1974, with a crèche on the ground floor, it was intended to provide starter accommodation for young couples, and soon became known as the 'Tour des jeunes mariés'.

Its hetero-normative orientation was accompanied by architectural experimentation. Reflecting the block's cylindrical construction, the apartments featured curved walls, while plastic partitioning dividers offered flexible living spaces. Taking up the whole of the bedroom was a large circular bed, a feature that gained some notoriety, as if to make clear the building's role in sustaining the growth and reproduction of Cergy's population. Its presence at the centre of the new town was also striking confirmation of CERFI's analysis that a principal function of housing and related *équipements collectifs* was to sustain the nuclear (or 'conjugal') family as the fundamental socio-economic unit in a capitalist society (Chatelet & others 1973: 122, 127–28).

Consciously or not, moreover, the pages of *Cergy magazine* brought out how the social, familial and psychical labour of adaptation to life in the new town divided along gender lines, and fell to women in particular. More precisely, its articles on childcare and self-fashioning invited women to recognize that labour as part of their role in the new town, a manoeuvre articulated in the conclusion to the first issue's editorial:

> Dans le fond, tout le monde sait bien que Cergy c'est quelque chose de différent. Qu'il s'y passe on-ne-sait-quoi qui rend les femmes plus responsables, les enfants plus vifs, les hommes plus dynamiques, les personnes âgées moins nostalgiques et les adolescents moins pessimistes. (Mirimanoff 1976: 7)

> [Deep down, everyone knows that Cergy is something different. A certain something is happening there that makes women more responsible, children more lively, men more dynamic, older people less nostalgic and teenagers less pessimistic.]

While the new town made men more dynamic, it made women more responsible. Meanwhile, everyone was better adapted to (and better disposed towards) the future. While men had created the environment, it was for women to work out how to live there. In its distribution of gender roles and expectations, through its modernity of forms, and as per the *Guide bleu*'s reading, the new town promised more of the same, socio-culturally, but — from the perspective of the status quo at any rate — newer, better and more efficient.

Alienation and Adaptation

Annie Ernaux was another writer who, like Marie Cardinal, had made her home in Cergy-Pontoise. In 1993, she published *Journal du dehors*, a diary of her life over seven years as an inhabitant of the new town and the Paris region. As she observed her fellow passengers on the RER, shopped in Cergy's Trois Fontaines shopping centre, or described the expansive prospects opening up along the A15 motorway, she created a portrait of life modernized by the *Schéma directeur*.

At various points, Ernaux notes scenes and impressions which echo the concerns uncovered by the social psychologists investigating life amongst Cergy's pioneers. There is spatial and sensorial disorientation: 'quand j'ai commencé de vivre dans la Ville Nouvelle, je me perdais toujours et je continuais de rouler, trop affolé pour m'arrêter' [when I began living in the New Town, I was always getting lost and would keep driving, too flustered to stop] (1996: 29); or a sense of unease and anxiety generated by the built environment: 'en sortant dans l'ascenseur, dans le parking souterrain, troisième sous-sol, le vrombissement des extracteurs d'air. On n'entendrait pas les cris en cas de viol' [leaving the lift on the third floor down of the underground car park, the noise of the air extractors. No-one would hear the cries of someone being raped] (1996: 29). Ernaux's persistent reference to Cergy as the 'Ville Nouvelle', each time capitalized like a proper name, lends it a daunting grandeur and agency, while at the same time reinforcing its remote and indefinable quality: 'je vis dans la Ville Nouvelle depuis douze ans et je ne sais pas à quoi elle ressemble. Je ne peux pas non plus la décrire, ne sachant pas où elle commence, finit, la parcourant toujours en voiture' [I've lived in the New Town for twelve years and I don't know what it resembles, or how to describe it. I don't know where it begins or ends, because I always drive round it in the car] (1996: 64). Cergy seems to slip beyond words, defying her attempts to describe it even as she tries to do so.

Then, in the preface to a second edition of the text published in 1996, came a notable declaration: 'j'ai aimé vivre là, dans un endroit cosmopolite, au milieu d'existences commencées ailleurs' [I've liked living there, in a cosmopolitan place, in the midst of lives begun elsewhere] (1996: 7–8). On closer inspection, *Journal du dehors* emerges as a story of adaptation, a working-through of alienation to produce a subjectivity fit for life in the new town. The preface from 1996 helps us piece together the text's prehistory, and read it as evidence of Ernaux's adjustment to modernized life. She has lived for twenty years in Cergy-Pontoise, Ernaux tells us in the preface. If she began her journal in 1985, then nine years had to pass before she could begin to describe the experience of living there. Those nine years were defined by confusion and uncertainty, a psychological disturbance brought about by the strangeness of planned space: 'j'étais submergée par un sentiment d'étrangeté, incapable de voir autre chose que les esplanades ventées, les façades de béton rose ou bleu, le désert des rues pavillonnaires' [I was submerged by a feeling of strangeness, unable to see anything other than windy esplanades, pink concrete façades, empty residential streets] (1996: 7).

Emerging from what she terms 'this schizophrenia' meant readjusting her vision and taking notice of what was happening around her, 'tout ce qui, d'une manière ou d'une autre, provoquaient en moi une émotion, un trouble ou de la révolte' [everything that in some way triggered emotion, unease or revolt] (1996: 8). Her diary entries are not just observations, but traces and signs of her affective engagement with her new world. One of its attractions seems to be that it is a place without history, one full of people with a multiplicity of backgrounds; or that, as Bernard Hirsch had pointed out in *Enfance d'une ville* a year before Ernaux arrived in Cergy, 'tous les habitants de cette ville, quoiqu'on y fasse, sont des déracinés' [whatever we do, all the inhabitants of this town are rootless]. The 'intense satisfaction' (1996: 105) felt by Ernaux at the view from the motorway makes clear that the eyes which have adjusted to the world around them now see the new town as home.

The year 1985 was when Ernaux felt able to begin writing about life in the new town. It was also when Rohmer began preparing for his feature film *L'Ami de mon amie* by visiting locations in and around Cergy-Pontoise. A few years earlier, Cergy had been the setting for a contemporary thriller set in an unnamed country, involving a presidential assassination and political conspiracy. If the director, Henri Verneuil, had chosen Cergy as the main location for *I... comme Icare* (1979), *Cergy magazine* reported, 'c'est parce qu'elle symbolise, à ses yeux, la cité moderne par excellence' [it is because for him, it is the ideal symbol of the modern city] (Bugat 1979: 32). Left unsaid was the fact that, in staging the drama in Cergy, and in an echo of Godard's *Alphaville*, the film appeared to reassert a link between the modernist landscapes of planning, the impulse of authoritarian government and intimations of secrecy at work behind the scenes (the film ends with the prosecutor investigating the assassination himself being assassinated).

L'Ami de mon amie, released in 1987, depicted the romantic intrigues of a pair of white, middle-class, heterosexual couples, and presented a more ordinary picture of life in Cergy; or rather, presented the new town as a more ordinary place to live. Where Ernaux gave a starker sense of the alienating qualities of Cergy's built environment, Rohmer's characters spend time by the Oise and windsurfing at the aquatic sports centre developed out of the old gravel pits. Blanche, one of its central characters, lives in Ricardo Bofill's semi-circular apartment block up on the heights at Gency and enjoys the vast, open prospect towards Paris, as Delouvrier and Hirsch imagined might one day be the case.

On the one hand, it might be tempting to see the film as an optimistic portrait of modernized middle-class life, confirming the promises made by the planners. On the other, it creates the uneasy impression that Cergy maintains its inhabitants in a bubble of the imaginary, safely disconnected from the developing realities of the rest of the country and what, by the mid-1980s, were becoming the increasingly unsettled suburbs beyond the precincts of Cergy. Marion Schmid (2015: 359) notes how the whiteness of Rohmer's Cergy caused controversy when the film was released, not least in a context of growing race-based tension elsewhere in the *banlieue*. Yet in many respects, it was entirely consistent with the imaginary construct of the new town that had been forged since its inception. Rather than representing a political blind spot on Rohmer's part, it was perhaps more a demonstration that the new town project had in fact fulfilled its socio-economic objectives, notwithstanding the actual socio-economic divisions within the country (themselves spatially distributed, as we shall discuss in Chapter 5) that it helped at once to feed and lay bare.

The year 1985 was significant as well for being the symbolic horizon established by Massé and the prospective planners of the 1960s. From that point of view, Rohmer and Ernaux converge in offering portraits of life in the future anticipated by the planners, and doing so in one of the totemic locations of the prospective enterprise. Their work raises the question of how the environments of the *Schéma directeur* produce the everyday realities of life, how those realities are lived and perceived, and the extent to which they align with the visions and dreams of the

1960s. At stake above all is how the futures imagined in the 1960s, having gained material form, had a sustained and lasting influence on forms of life, and how they did so even as they existed as relics of the past, as memories of the time of 'plans, dreams and grandiose projects', to recall the elegant words of the *Guide bleu*'s Denise Basdevant. While it can be easy for us to overlook the signs and traces of modernized landscapes, or for their presence to grow familiar, they nevertheless persist in giving shape to life in significant ways.

The next chapter continues to explore how modernized landscapes are present and portrayed in French culture, how they can be seen to frame and inflect life in modern France, and the extent to which the future anticipated by the prospective view has become the reality of the present. It begins by going back to the future, and considering how the planners imagined the France of 1985. It then returns to the 1980s and 90s to explore further how Ernaux, Rohmer and others portray life in France's manufactured landscapes.

CHAPTER 4

❖

Manufactured Landscapes:
Scenes from a Modernized France

Back to the Future: *Réflexions pour 1985*

In 1964, after a year of work and twenty meetings, a crack committee of experts published its report on life in France two decades hence. *Réflexions pour 1985* was the fruit of investigations by the Groupe 1985, established by Pierre Massé in 1962 as part of his preparations for the fifth Plan (1966–70). It was chaired by Gaullist politician and administrator Pierre Guillaumat, who was Armed Forces Minister between 1958 and 1962 before taking charge of the French oil and gas industry.[1] The group's membership, presented at the start of its final report, was a constellation of French modernizers and prospective thinkers (Groupe 1985 1964: 7). It included Claude Gruson, head of the Institut national de la statistique et des études économiques (INSEE), the national statistics agency; Eugène Claudius-Petit, France's pioneer of *aménagement*; Bertrand de Jouvenel, who had become the leading advocate of prospective thinking after Gaston Berger's untimely death on the motorway in 1960; and the unavoidable Jean Fourastié, economist and theorist of modernization.[2] The committee took evidence on the economy from liberal philosopher Raymond Aron, on the development of the Paris region from Paul Delouvrier and on ethnology's contribution to *la prospective* from Claude Lévi-Strauss. Among the secretariat that drafted the report were Jérôme Monod, who was at the DATAR with Olivier Guichard, and Michel Piquard, part of Delouvrier's team at the Paris District.

Réflexions pour 1985 had chapters on all aspects of life, from education, training and scientific development to leisure, consumption and aesthetics, or 'le droit de chacun à vivre dans le beau' [everyone's right to live in beauty] (Groupe 1985 1964: 83).

---

1   On Guillaumat, see Soutou & Beltran 1995.
2   On Bertrand de Jouvenel, his notion of *futuribles* ('futurs possibles'), and its relationship to *la prospective*, see Andersson (2018: 58–66). As Andersson notes (2018: 60), while his work had caught the attention of the Ford Foundation in the United States, Jouvenel remained a marginal figure in the French intellectual field after the war, in large part due to his involvement with Drieu La Rochelle, Jacques Doriot and other figures of French fascism in the pre-war period (see also Winock 1999: 284–97). Jouvenel's membership of the Groupe 1985 was indicative of an intellectual and political rehabilitation, no doubt helped by the political capital accrued by prospective thinking at that point, as I discussed in Chapter 1.

Its wide-ranging scope exemplified the inherent confidence of the prospective method — a confidence both that the future could be scouted out, and that a future defined by progress and development was axiomatic. It was safe to assume, for example, that factory output would have doubled given that, by 1985, the number of factories in the country would also have doubled (1964: 11). Since decisions taken now could have significant long-term consequences, it surely made sense to identify, as Massé put it in his preface to the report, 'les propriétés du futur utiles pour les décisions à prendre dans le présent' [the features of the future useful for decisions being made in the present] (1964: 6). Reaching for a far temporal horizon was the key to freer thinking, by enabling the planners to look beyond *prévision* as mere budgetary projection over the shorter term. Informed predictions derived from the future could better orient the present towards it.

If the group took 1985 as their horizon, it was also because the year had significance as a generational milestone. It represented the moment when the cumulative effects of modernization on French civilization would really begin to make their presence felt. Not only would those born in the present of 1964 have reached adult life as defined by the age of legal majority, but the generation currently entering productive life would (as the writers unabashedly put it) be at the height of their powers.[3] As the first generation to grow up in an era shaped by prospective planning and modernization, the youth of 1985 would embody new ways of seeing the world: 'ainsi pourront avoir changé profondément les manières d'appréhender et de traiter les problèmes' [as a result, ways of understanding and solving problems will have changed fundamentally] (1964: 10). By joining forces with their elders, they would be able to propel the country even further into the future.

The group's report tempered such visionary moments with a rhetorical emphasis on the practical applicability of prospective research. Massé set the tone in his preface, adopting the technocratic pragmatism that characterized his other writing on planning. Far from being a speculative flight of fancy, 'l'étude prospective demandée au Groupe de Travail lui a permis d'extraire du champ des possibles quelques figures de l'avenir intelligibles pour l'esprit et utiles pour l'action' [the prospective study asked of the Working Group enabled it to identify from a range of possibilities some clues to the future understandable by the mind and useful for action] (1964: 5). Prospective planning's navigation between the philosophical and the techno-pragmatic materialized in the report's treatment of liberty, one if its oft-recurring themes. While it took as a given that ensuring and promoting the conditions for freedom were fundamental to (liberal democratic, as opposed to communist) society, it moved quickly to translate the grand principle into the more concrete and tangible question of mobility: 'parmi les manifestations les plus importantes de la liberté, le pouvoir de mobilité est apparu comme ayant une particulière importance' [amongst the most important forms of freedom, the power of mobility emerged as being of particular importance] (1964: 15). Looking at the country from the vantage point of 1985 would help shape territorial development

---

3   Twenty-one was the age of legal majority in France until 1974, when Valéry Giscard d'Éstaing lowered it to eighteen as one of the first modernizing measures of his presidency.

in a way which anticipated the material and practical forms that French freedom would take.

The group's concern for freedom was one it shared with Delouvrier's *Schéma directeur*, as we saw in Chapter 2. Indeed, the relationship between liberty and planning emerges in a revealing exchange during Delouvrier's retrospective interview with Bernard Hirsch, Jean Millier, Michel Piquard and others in 1984. Prompted by Millier, their discussion turns to liberty as a guiding principle of the *Schéma directeur*. How, wonders Hirsch, does a planning framework enable freedom? 'Comment se traduit la liberté dans un schéma directeur?' Millier's response is unequivocal: 'par une organisation sur des axes de transports, qui ont été tout de même une organisation de transports en commun et une organisation d'autoroutes assez extraordinaires' [by using transport axes as an organizing principle, which meant using public transport and motorways in a way that was really quite extraordinary] (Hirsch 2003: 71).

Engineering the conditions for liberty was literally a question of engineering. If infrastructure was the guarantor of freedom, it was because it was the key to mobility. With mobility came the ability to pursue opportunity and to live more comfortably. Millier's emphasis on infrastructure signals the extent to which the planners interpreted the notion of *cadre de vie* in material and physical as much as conceptual terms. At stake above all was the physical infrastructure framing the country's citizens, what *Réflexions pour 1985* calls 'le cadre matériel de leur existence' [the material framework of their lives] (1964: 17), and which catalysed liberty as mobility by setting them in motion.

At stake as well was the proleptic nature of spatial planning, and the implications that derived from it. Predicating spatial development on predictions about the future meant introducing future modes of life into the lived reality of the present. Bridging the gap between the two would be the work required of those caught up in the changes being engineered. Brian Sudlow highlights the relationship between the 'probable' and the 'desirable' (*le souhaitable*) in *Réflexions pour 1985*, and its coercive tendency to prefer the latter over the former (Sudlow 2017: 694). What concerned the Groupe 1985, in other words, was how lives were to be managed in directions appropriate for France's successful modernization.

The tension between the *probable* and the *souhaitable* has lexical manifestations in their report. If it foregrounds liberty and mobility as defining features of life in 1985 (thirty-one occurrences of *liberté*, sixty-four of *mobilité*), one of its key themes is also adaptation (twenty-seven occurrences of its verbal and nominal forms). The numbers are telling: in the first place, liberty is understood primarily in socio-economic terms as the ability to circulate and relocate in order to follow and create opportunity; but second, mobility was a lesson the French needed to learn. For France to progress, its citizens had to overcome their reluctance to move and, as Delouvrier would subsequently put it, 'prendre l'habitude d'intégrer la mobilité à leur vie' [get used to integrating mobility into their lives] (1967: 30). The offer of liberty thus came with a price, one expressed in the development of transport infrastructure and speed space. In fairness, the report makes no bones about it: 'l'homme n'a pas le choix. Il devra trouver son bonheur, son équilibre, son salut dans ces structures nouvelles' [mankind has no choice but to find happiness, stability and salvation in these new structures] (Groupe 1985 1964: 95). Freedom and happiness lay not just in mobility but in adaptation. France's evolving (infra) structures — its 'armature', to recall André Trintignac's term — would be both mechanism and setting for that change.

At the same time, *Réflexions pour 1985* was alive to the risks posed by a failure to adapt, not least at the level of the individual psyche. Indeed, its attentiveness to the psychological implications of modernization illuminates an inherent contradiction within its position, as it oscillated between care and control of the nation's citizens. On the one hand, planning's role was to create the environment required for France to flourish into the future. Doing so carried the weight of a moral imperative. On the other, the creation of a new *cadre de vie* placed demands on its citizens that required adaptation for the good of the nation and themselves (adaptation being the key to mobility and therefore to freedom). At the same time, it exposed them to the risk of psychical harm precisely because of that requirement. One of the potential outcomes of modernization, suggested the report, was an increase in cases of depression:

> Sur le plan de son comportement psychologique et social, l'homme de 1985 sera menacé d'une moindre adaptation qu'aujourd'hui à son milieu: angoisse de l'individu devant le monde extérieur, sentiment de la perte de l'autonomie individuelle, réaction à l'agressivité de l'environnement. L'une des manifestations sur le plan du psychisme en sera le développement des phénomènes de dépression. (Groupe 1985 1964: 34)

> [In terms of psychological and social behaviour, the man of 1985 will be threatened by being less well adapted to his environment than today: anxiety when faced with the outside world, a feeling of loss of individual autonomy, reactions to a threatening environment. One of the consequences of this on a psychical level will be the experience of depression.]

A central aim of prospective planning would thus be to mitigate the unchecked consequences of technological advancement and modernization through careful management. Recognizing the changes ahead enabled government and society to take action (1964: 103). Change required adaptation. But adaptation could be smoothed by training and education, by 'la formation des hommes' (1964: 38) (the French retains better than the English the sense of education as a shaping that is at once mental, corporeal and social). Through training and education, people could learn to be 'sains, équilibrés et heureux' [healthy, balanced and happy] (1964: 39).

On the one hand, the people of 1985 should be leaner, fitter, happier and more productive.[4] On the other, the risk of depression and other forms of psychical harm would be greater, not least because of the proliferating number of artificial environments in which life was lived, and the affective impact they might have. In raising the danger of alienation from modernization, the report was attempting to fend it off with a promise of enlightened action via the prospective method.

---

4   As Radiohead might say (*Fitter Happier*, Parlophone, 1997).

But in doing so, it nevertheless begged the question of the extent to which its prediction about the psychical effects of modernization would prove accurate, and to what extent responsibility for those effects lay (or were perceived to lie) with the outcomes of spatial planning. After all, by its nature, *Réflexions pour 1985* presented a hostage to fortune as a set of predictions that could be measured against reality when the time came.[5]

The economist Philippe Dubois of INSEE did just that in 1985. From a macroeconomic point of view, he found the group's predictions to have been quite accurate. The projections for population growth, economic expansion, the relative growth of different economic sectors and household consumption stood up well against the development that had been achieved. While as anticipated, the rate of growth in agriculture was low, industry and the tertiary sector grew more robustly (Dubois 1985: 6). However, if its predictions for levels of employment in different sectors of the economy were broadly in line with trends (a steady decline in agriculture, gentle increase in industry and strong expansion in the tertiary sector), it had overestimated the amount by which overall levels of employment would grow, in part because the decline in the agricultural sector was greater than anticipated as productivity increased (1985: 5–6).

As is often the case, the macroeconomic data failed to capture the full (human) drama of what had happened over the two decades since *Réflexions pour 1985* had been published, and how the skies had darkened on the project of modernization. Looking into the future as it was during a Gaullist time of certainty, *la prospective* appeared to have something of a blind spot in relation to the often significant effects of political turbulence. Already, the end of Gaullism had created headwinds for state-led planning, as we saw in Chapter 3. Then geopolitics, in the form of the oil crises of the 1970s and the recessions that followed, triggered an economic downturn that drew a line under the prolonged period of growth that France had enjoyed since the war.

By 1985, that period had acquired a name, which served to confirm it as a historical fact rather than a present reality. Appropriately, the name was coined by France's arch modernizer, as ready to call the end as he was to map out the future. In 1979, Jean Fourastié published *Les Trente glorieuses*. The book was at once a celebration of three transformative decades, a recognition — and mourning — of its passing and an account of what came next. What struck Fourastié in particular was that, beyond the hard facts of the macroeconomic data, the 'thirty glorious years' did not seem to have been *lived* as glorious. If anything, they were lived as a period of growing rancour and uncertainty:

> Les historiens qui, tôt ou tard, dépouilleront les journaux de la période 1946–1975 y trouveront peu de témoignages de l'ardeur de vie et de la joie du peuple français. Les grandes mutations du niveau de vie n'y apparaissent pas (on n'en parle guère qu'*a contrario* pour se plaindre de leur inexistence ou de leur lenteur); la morosité, l'inquiétude, l'annonce et le récit de catastrophes,

---

5   The report's authors acknowledged as much in a nice touch of humility (Groupe 1985 1964: 107).

accidents et troubles dominent beaucoup (allant des grèves, conflits sociaux et luttes politiques intérieures, aux crises et guerres internationales...). (Fourastié 1979: 233)

[Historians who, sooner or later, go through the newspapers between 1946 and 1975 will find little evidence of the French populace's joy and enthusiasm for life. The dramatic changes in living standards aren't visible (or at least only in negative terms, when people complain about how they don't exist, or how long they are taking to appear); talk is dominated by gloominess, worry and tales of catastrophe, accidents and disturbances (from strikes, social conflict and domestic political battles to wars and international crisis...).]

Certainly, the hangover they left behind was a pervasive sense of *morosité*. France had entered the time of crisis (*la crise*) that would linger into the 1980s, marked by economic stagnation, deindustrialization and unemployment.

One of Fourastié's most intriguing observations was that the end of the period coincided with (and in part derived from) a crisis of reason. The limits of reason and rational activity on the world had been reached, and faith in reason's ability to transform the world had started to wane: 'si l'homme a effectivement une raison, il ne lui est pas facile de *conduire* cette raison' [if mankind certainly has rational faculties, it is not easy for him to *guide* those faculties] (1979: 269). The work of reason had a struggle to contend with all the other factors in play in human behaviour, and the hormonal, neurological, biological and psychical forces that constitute the human animal (1979: 269).

More startling was Fourastié's contention at the start of his final chapter. The glory of the past three decades lay in France's completion of its Enlightenment project. It had made great strides in ensuring the health, prosperity and comfort of its people; but (and the qualification was significant) 'elle a tenté en outre — elle a cru le pouvoir — réaliser par ce progrès physique même, l'harmonie sociale et le bonheur personnel: c'est un échec' [it has also tried — and thought it possible — to bring about through this physical process both social harmony and individual happiness: it has not succeeded] (1979: 261). It was now clear that happiness, freedom and wellbeing could not be engineered into existence by the material improvement and development of living conditions. That France's most confident voice of modernization was casting doubt on the success of planned and rational action on the world — assumptions about which had underpinned the work of Fourastié and his colleagues in the Groupe 1985 — was a measure of how the mood had changed.

Nor was Fourastié alone in having such doubts at the end of the 1970s. In fact, 1979 was busy with reflexions on French modernity. Alongside the *Guide bleu* to the Parisian new towns, and its claim that their apparent modernity was in fact a guarantee of order and stability, the year saw the publication of François Lyotard's study *La Condition postmoderne*. Lyotard converged with Fourastié in identifying a crisis of epistemological confidence. Where Fourastié located it in the disruption of reason by the neuro-chemical complexities of the individual, Lyotard found it in growing 'incredulity' (Lyotard 1979: 7) over the 'grand narratives' which framed and legitimized scientific knowledge, and the social compact more generally. Broadly speaking, they were the narratives of truth, progress and justice by which the project of modernity had defined itself since the Enlightenment (1979: 7–8). There had arguably been no grander narrative in post-war France than the idea of accelerating human progress through the ever more sophisticated application of reason.

Also that year, two films were released that seemed to capture the mood of the times, and the sense that a crisis of reason had taken hold: Bertrand Blier's *Buffet froid* and Alain Corneau's *Série noire*. We can track the shift in the French mood over the course of the 1970s when we compare them with another cinematic moment from the start of the decade, Jean-Pierre Melville's *Le Cercle rouge*, one of the highest grossing films of 1970. Melville's thriller about a daring jewellery heist is also a reflection on the nature of Gaullist France as a managed space. As the film begins, a prisoner is being escorted on the night train from Marseille to Paris by a police inspector, Commissaire Mattei (André Bourvil). The prisoner makes a daring bid for freedom, jumping from the moving train as it journeys through the French countryside. Despite having lost his man, Mattei appears surprisingly unfazed. The reason becomes clear shortly afterwards, when he mobilizes an extensive apparatus of surveillance and pursuit with a phone call from a country hotel. Having gathered helicopters, cars and men, he commands them to begin the chase. Slowly but surely over the course of the film, the escapee is hunted down, as the periodic appearance of maps of the French territory, particularly in the police headquarters in Paris, reminds us of the visual reach and power of the French state.

The action of Blier's *Buffet froid*, released nine years later, was circumscribed by and played out in the planned spaces of contemporary France. It opens in the gleaming, spectacular, empty and disconcerting setting of the new RER station at La Défense, where on the platform late one evening the unemployed Alphonse (Gérard Depardieu) encounters an accountant (Michel Serrault) for whose subsequent death by stabbing he may or may not be responsible. It ends in a rowing boat on a man-made lake dammed as part of a hydroelectric project, which gathers together Alphonse, the police inspector who had been pursuing him (Bernard Blier), and the daughter of the stabbed accountant (Carole Bouquet) looking to avenge her father. The police inspector had retreated to the mountains after he became the laughing-stock of the men under his command and had a nervous breakdown. Following a tussle on the boat, he drowns having been shot by Alphonse, who meets a similar end at the hands of the accountant's daughter.

In *Série noire*, the psychologically troubled travelling salesman Franck (Patrick Dawaere) returns repeatedly to the same patch of *terrain vague* on the outskirts of Paris in the middle of winter, with the vast building sites of Créteil in the distance.[6] For Susan Hayward, Franck's psychical crisis is emblematic of a general national crisis fuelled by the economic downturn, where 'everything is in freefall' (Hayward 2014: 58). As such, the film can be seen as a portrait of an arrested modernity. Yet this would be to overlook the fact that the cranes are still present in Créteil and

6   While not one of the *villes nouvelles* of the *Schéma directeur*, Créteil was designated the prefecture of the new *département* of Val-de-Marne and underwent substantial development during the 1960s and 70s as a result.

that the building work is in progress. Modernization is present as a process as yet incomplete, but not necessarily stalled. The appearance in the landscape of a sign promising the coming of spring (albeit in the form of a new branch of the Printemps department store) can certainly be read as an ironic commentary on Franck's situation, and beyond him, that of the country as a whole. But it is also an unironic statement of fact. Spring is on its way and the world continues its trajectory. The question is perhaps more whether or not there is a place for Franck within it, or indeed for the likes of Alphonse. Their problem may simply be that they have been unable to adapt as modernity requires.

By placing their characters so clearly in dialogue with planned and managed space, the two films illustrate how cultural production starts to explore the nature of life in modernized France, and how the manufactured landscapes of modernization become protagonists in its depiction. I borrow the notion of 'manufactured landscapes' from the 2006 film by Jennifer Baichwal about the work of landscape photographer Edward Burtynsky, which depicts the human transformation of the environment as manifested in industrial plants, transport hubs, mines and dams. The term is also well suited to describing the production, look and feel of the outcomes of post-war French spatial planning. Where the landscapes of Burtynsky's work are often spectacular, or interpreted as examples of the industrial — or more strikingly, the toxic — sublime (Peeples 2011), it is also the case that many modernized landscapes appear obliquely or subtly, as traces, creases, lines or folds.

Sometimes the modernity of France's landscapes is obvious or foregrounded. *Buffet froid* would be one such example, in terms of how it frames and contains its action within man-made landscapes. Often, though, modernized space is just there in the background, unobtrusively present as a marker or fact in the writing, filming or photographing of post-war France. In the closing moments of Varda's *Sans toit ni loi*, for instance, traffic moves swiftly and soundlessly along a motorway in the depth of field, while the central character stumbles towards her death. Yet even in their unobtrusiveness, signs of modernization are showing and telling us something, and open up dialogues between characters, their settings, environments and habitats. The rest of the chapter sets out to investigate how France's managed and modernized spaces appear in French culture; how those spaces are lived, perceived and negotiated; the extent to which they can be disrupted, disturbed, evaded or escaped; and what they tell us about the state of post-war France's modernizing dream.

The Aesthetics and Epistemics of Infrastructure Space

Réflexions pour 1985 had optimistic things to say about the future in its chapter on aesthetics. Mass consumption would see the proliferation of beautiful things in the world and enhance the public's appreciation of aesthetic value (Groupe 1985 1964: 83). Meanwhile, 'la technique moderne engendre de surcroît une beauté propre'. Modern engineering was engendering its own forms of beauty, a sort of infrastructural sublime manifested in feats of construction from artificial lakes and hydroelectric dams to bridges and electricity pylons (1964: 85).

A sense of that infrastructural sublime is drawn out in *Métamorphoses du paysage* (1964), Éric Rohmer's contemporary film on the changing landscape, not least through images of pylons striding across country. It is also present in Godard's contemplative shot of the elevated access road at the start of *2 ou 3 choses que je sais d'elle* (1967). Even as we hear Godard's unfolding critique of Gaullist power, it is hard not to appreciate the curve's purity of form. Abstracted from the rubble below, its geometric qualities are enhanced by the play of light and surfaces between the matte of the concrete and the satin sheen of the tarmac. As a lowly form of construction technology, the wheelbarrow sitting on the road is at once a remnant of the old world beneath and a testament to how the old world has transcended itself.

The image recalls Le Corbusier's admiration (alighted on by Walter Benjamin in the *Arcades Project*) for the astonishing way in which the splendours of Haussmann's Paris were produced by rudimentary tools (Benjamin 1999: 133). Just as Benjamin tracks the phenomenology of modernity through its materialization in the Parisian arcades, so too Godard's camera, by dwelling on the spatial forms of Gaullist modernization, draws out their epistemic implications alongside their aesthetic qualities. That is to say, it points to the ways in which the material transformation of the landscape through spatial production and modernization shapes knowledge, perception and lived experience of the world.

The relationship between modernized space and human being emerges as a persistent concern of French culture throughout the subsequent decades. One of its most memorable instances is *Buffet froid*'s opening scene on the platform of the RER station at La Défense. It is important to remember the newness of the RER as an environment at the time the film was made. The *Réseau express régional* was a network of high-speed mass transit rail lines envisioned by the *Schéma directeur* to improve the mobility, flow and circulation of the regional population. While a section of the east–west route (RER A) between La Défense and the Place de l'Étoile had been running since 1970, it was not until 1977 that the whole of the route across central Paris was completed, connecting with the equally new north–south line (RER B) (the one explored by Maspero and Frantz a decade later) at the vast underground complex of Châtelet-Les Halles, nodal point of the system. We saw in Chapter 2 how the television news reporter on the RER A's first day of operation spoke in excited terms about the time–space compression engineered by the line, as he journeyed from La Défense in the west to Noisy-le-Grand in the east in a matter of thirty minutes.

The opening eight minutes of *Buffet froid*, released two years after that inaugural journey, offered its audience one of the first sustained looks at the RER's radically new spaces. Given that the encounter between Alphonse and the accountant begins a film about murder, revenge, corruption, anxiety and alienation (King 1993), it is no surprise that the setting becomes freighted with a sense of menace, nor perhaps that Blier saw in the station's disconcerting scale and newness an effective way of establishing the mood of the film. He does so by paying it noticeably careful attention over the long opening sequence. It is as if he is intent on capturing the particular qualities of this bold new development of the urban environment as he

FIG. 4.1. Welcome to the future: the RER in Bertrand Blier's *Buffet froid* (1979).

explores the look, feel and sound of its spatial configurations, and the effects it produces on the people who navigate it. In a way, the RER station becomes as much of a protagonist of the film's first minutes as the two characters who meet on the stage it provides.

The title sequence maps out the station in a series of still images which show it stretching down to a distant tunnel entrance, its roof supported by huge concrete pillars in parallel rows. All the while, the insistent, metronomic rhythm of the escalators running in the background echoes across the cavernous platform area. The station is deserted (we are seemingly late at night) but dazzlingly illuminated by white neon strip lights which reflect off metal surfaces and enhance the bold, bright colours of the station signage and furniture. The noticeable presence of French republican colours (blue and white for the signage, red for the seating) reminds us of the symbolic importance of the RER as an expression of French modernity and civilizational advancement.

The station's monumental quality is heightened by its emptiness, and the way in which emptiness amplifies sound. When Alphonse comes down the escalator and walks along the platform (passing in front of a billboard advert for the new Forum des Halles shopping centre down the line), his unhurried footsteps ring out and form an offbeat counterpoint to the escalator's mechanical clank (Fig. 4.1). The insistent presence of usually unobtrusive sounds sharpens our sense of the scale and function of a space engineered to manage the flow of large crowds: the open expanse of platform, the central position of the escalators, the arrow-like arrangement of the seating located midway between each direction of travel, the illuminated plans of the transport network showing the traveller's location in the system and an array of potential destinations.

FIG. 4.2. A decidedly modern encounter: Alphonse (Gérard Depardieu) and the accountant (Michel Serrault) in *Buffet froid* (1979).

When just two people occupy the space, monumentality quickly takes on the feel of hubris or civilizational over-reach, as its assertively mineral architectonics dwarf their presence and movements. Moreover, the setting in turn magnifies the tension and unease of the decidedly modern encounter between the unemployed Alphonse and the disillusioned and exhausted accountant locked into the temporal rhythms and rigidity of capitalist life ('Vous croyez que le travail repose? Le mien, il m'emmerde, il m'abrutit' [So you think work is restful? Mine winds me up and knocks me senseless]). If the oversized space of the station has its own oppressive or menacing quality, it also enables menace, generating the potential for violence and insecurity as a system that draws strangers together (Fig. 4.2).

When Alphonse tries to strike up conversation with the accountant, their exchange articulates the experience of modernity as at once an erosion of human relations, and a concomitant feeling of co-presence as threat rather than source of companionship ('Vous me suivez?' 'Oui.' 'Mais pourquoi?' 'Pour se parler. Les gens ne se parlent plus' ['Are you following me?' 'Yes.' 'But why?' 'So we can talk. No-one talks to each other anymore']). On Blier's reading at least, it was the fears more than the hopes of *Réflexions pour 1985* that were being borne out. Rather than making the population healthy, happy and balanced, the 'cadre matériel de leur existence' seemed instead to be creating the conditions for tension, anxiety, disillusionment and despair.

Blier's filmic investigation of the RER station anticipates two other extended treatments of mass transport environments, albeit in different styles and media: Luc Besson's *Subway* (1985) and Annie Ernaux's *Journal du dehors* (1993). Several scenes of Besson's film about a countercultural community living in the guts of the Paris underground system were shot in and around Châtelet-Les Halles. The huge new station, several storeys deep, had opened in 1977 on the site of the old wholesale food markets of Les Halles (Zola's 'ventre de Paris'). It was topped off by the Forum des Halles shopping centre, whose mirrored glass and steel construction, as Greg Hainge notes, was a (clumsy) reference to the profoundly more attractive iron and glass pavilions by Victor Baltard that had been demolished in 1971 to make way for the RER station (Hainge 2008: 203–04).

The convergence on Châtelet-Les Halles of both the RER lines and numerous Métro lines made it the nexus of the Paris region. It was the point through which millions of people flowed as they navigated the transport system, a fact expressed in the scale of its shopping arcade.[7] As such, the station represented one of the most significant pieces of infrastructure in post-war Paris, not least in terms of being integral to the engineering of mobility envisioned by the *Schéma directeur*. It was part of the radical transformation of the area around St Eustache and Beaubourg (Marchand 1993: 296–301), with the relocation of the food market to Rungis south of Paris (more 'efficiently' situated next to a network of motorways), the demolition of decaying housing stock and the construction of the Centre Pompidou, whose appearance as a major tourist landmark marked the area's abrupt shift from local to global networks of flow and circulation (Welch 2005).

Like *Buffet froid*, *Subway* is a film whose action is contained within, and determined by, infrastructures of modernization. It opens with a high-speed car chase which begins on the motorway heading into Paris, passes through the service roads under the Forum des Halles and ends when the central character, Fred (Christophe Lambert), pursued by gangsters because he has broken into the safe of a shady businessman, crashes through the doors of a Métro station. Abandoning the car, he escapes into the Métro system and loses his pursuers by dodging through a service door and into an obscure network of passages. There, he encounters a band of dropouts, misfits and thieves living a secret existence and forming a sort of radical alternative community in opposition to the routine world of the commuters on the other side of the corridor walls.

On one reading, as Hainge suggests (2008: 204), the film's revelation and celebration of a parallel community making disruptively playful use of the Métro invites us to reimagine it as a space where alternative modes of life can thrive in its niches, and challenge the hegemonic authority it represents. It is not for nothing, after all, that the local transport police have an important role to play in the narrative, as they attempt to keep the band under control and stop it from interfering with the smooth running of the system. As such, the film's suggestion that the energy of alterity and difference is there to be found represents an advance on the mood of crisis and alienation permeating the modernized worlds of *Buffet froid* and *Série noire* a few years earlier. Yet it remains the case that difference is pushed to the margins, even as the margins are celebrated as a place of liberation.

7   By 2019, according to RATP data, nearly 60 million people a year were starting their journey at the Châtelet-Les Halles complex. The RATP's data does not capture changes between lines, which account for a hugely substantial amount of additional traffic at Châtelet-Les Halles <https://data.ratp.fr/explore/dataset/trafic-annuel-entrant-par-station-du-reseau-ferre-2019/> [accessed 15 January 2021].

FIG. 4.3. A machine of transport and movement: the Métro in Luc Besson's *Subway* (1985).

Moreover, while it makes its presence felt at various points in the film (acts of petty theft, commandeering a bar after hours, the closing concert organized by the musicians in the band), difference has to make its home for the most part as the underside or other of 'normal' existence, producing what Mark Orme (2006) characterizes as the 'imprisoned freedom' that becomes the fate of a number of characters in Besson's films.

Revealing from that point of view, if initially less eye-catching, are what we might term the film's more documentary moments, when Besson captures the everyday business of the Métro system: point-of-view shots from the driver's cabin as a train enters the station, scenes of people waiting on platforms, flowing along corridors and riding escalators, or (even if it more obviously part of the filmic narrative) the portrayal of police activity (Fig. 4.3). The police occupy a pod-like command post with darkened windows, a strategic vantage-point over a main thoroughfare, and a bank of surveillance monitors. As they try with more or less success to keep the band in check, their presence makes manifest the nature of the Métro as a regulated system. Indeed, the Métro's very systematicity, its ability to function smoothly as a transport network, is shown at once to rely on policing and regulation, and to be constantly at risk of disruption, a machine on the verge of going awry.

In part, Besson's moments of ethnographic attention to the Métro as a space of regulation and discipline, where people have a function they must fulfil and where transgression risks punishment, serve to stage the contrast between two radically different worlds coexisting metres apart, into one of which the other makes rapid and disruptive incursions. They are also moments where, like Blier in *Buffet froid*, it seems Besson simply wants us to notice and absorb the sophistication of the Métro system as a giant machine of transport and movement. At one level, Besson's quite careful observation of the intricacy and functional beauty of the mass transport system might well have appealed to the planners as an appreciation of their endeavours. It offers a sense of the infrastructural sublime that has no real need of embellishment by his steam punk vision of the hidden structures — tunnels, pipes, gangways, cables and drains — making it all work behind the service doors.

The film's movement back and forth between the two parallel worlds, and its containment within the Métro system, make it an effective portrait of life in modernized space. The adventures of Fred and the underground band provide the means to explore the room for manoeuvre within a planned world. In many ways, *Subway* is an illustration of, or testing ground for, the kind of resistance that Michel de Certeau had recently been theorizing in his work on everyday life as a practice. In *L'Invention du quotidien*, first published in 1980, Certeau had modelled daily life as a series of tactical moves, ruses and tricks to create space and opportunity by exploiting the cracks in an apparently homogeneous system. Yet even as it celebrates the possibility of tactical incursion as a means of gaining purchase and advantage, *Subway* also illuminates the conundrum snagging Certeau's theory of spatial praxis: the populace's need for tricks, however inventive, is predicated precisely on the fact that the city is no longer really home. Having been displaced by a system geared towards liberty as economic mobility, those who will not or cannot adapt to it must resort to ruses in order to make use of a space that by rights is also theirs.

The perspective in Ernaux's *Journal du dehors* is that of the people Besson films going about their business in the Métro, those for whom it is a structuring component of their daily life. They may occasionally notice those who go against the flow of the tide, or disrupt it as they beg in the corridors, presenting themselves within the system as evidence of the discards it produces. Ernaux's text depicts her life as a resident of the Paris region, living in the new town of Cergy-Pontoise, circulating round the region by train or car, shopping and commuting. In doing so, it exemplifies the sort of mobility (and adaptation to mobility) the planners had set out to produce, and as such, represents a view from within the system, a sort of user account of life in the environments of the *Schéma directeur*.

Like all of Ernaux's writing, the text is also characterized by its reflexive self-awareness. Not simply a diary of things observed, it is a depiction of a particular state of being and knowledge, one made manifest by those observations and deriving from her existence in the planned spaces of modernization. What is more, as I noted in Chapter 3, it has its own pre-history of psychical adaptation to life in the new town and its attendant apparatus. When Ernaux observes her discomfort on encountering homeless people in the Métro and RER, the way she gives them a wide berth, the guilt she feels in doing so, and the fact that she does so nonetheless, she is acknowledging her compromise with the established socio-economic order. Her physical gesture of distance-keeping ('je suis passée très au large de lui, comme ceux qui ne lui donnent rien' [I skirted round him, like everyone else who doesn't give anything], 1996: 21) is a simultaneous expression of shame and complicity with the inequalities of the order she inhabits and sustains through her activities.

Through what she sees, hears and feels while circulating in the capital's infrastructures of mobility, Ernaux grasps the peculiar epistemological and ontological consequences of life in planned environments: what it means to play one's role as a component in systems of movement and transportation, what it feels like to do so, and what impact it has on our relationship with those around us. She realizes the extent to which her memories (and therefore identity) are triggered by chance encounters with fellow RER passengers or passers-by. She teases out how, in effect, our past is distributed amongst those around us, and can be brought unexpectedly to the surface depending on who happens to be in the queue at the supermarket or gets on the RER (1996: 106–07). The effect is a sort of infinite multiplication of the Proustian madeleine, but all the more powerful for being predicated on the specific lived experience of a commuting urban dweller, exposed every day to countless chance encounters and memory triggers through co-presence in the contained spaces of public transport and consumption.

Alongside her attention to those around her, the text often foregrounds the landscapes that catch her eye, her attentiveness to views from the train or car window. In doing so, it draws out how the environments around her, and how she moves within them, frame her view of the world and shape her perceptions, feelings and cognition. We gain an impression of the confusion, uncertainty and disorientation that comes from driving towards a line of pylons into the setting sun (1996: 12), the menace that derives from an underground car park (1996: 29), or the odd surges of desire for consumer goods that fall away as soon as she leaves the shopping centre (1996: 32). But we also learn of the pleasure she derives from seeing the agglomeration open up before her as she drives along the motorway:

> Un mouvement d'immense satisfaction m'envahit à reconnaître les signes de la banlieue parisienne. Le même que j'éprouve quand, en arrivant par l'autoroute A15 sur le viaduc de Gennevilliers, s'ouvre d'un seul coup un immense paysage d'usines et d'immeubles, de pavillons d'avant-guerre, avec en muraille de fond, la Défense de Paris. (Ernaux 1996: 106)

> [I am filled with a feeling of immense satisfaction when I see signs of the suburbs. I have a similar feeling when, driving over the Gennevilliers viaduct on the A15 motorway, a vast landscape of factories, apartment blocks and pre-war houses suddenly opens up, with La Défense in the distance as a backdrop.]

Like the evocative shot of the exit slip road in *Paris Match*'s brochure for Cergy-Pontoise in the early 1970s, the scene captures a sense of the speed, movement and energy channelled by large-scale infrastructure projects of civil engineering.

For the most part, Ernaux's Cergy is that of commuting and daily life: the RER, the Trois Fontaines shopping centre, the motorway. Unlike Rohmer in *L'Ami de mon amie*, her text does not take us to the banks of the Oise or the aquatic park in its meander, those spaces of leisure that Bernard Hirsch had envisioned as the centre of the new town. Rohmer's film, in turn, has little to do with the road or the RER. Through his use of waterside locations, Rohmer opens up another perspective on Cergy's manufactured landscapes. He articulates the integration of nature into the planned space of the new town and its repurposing as a leisure environment to enable, in the words of *Réflexions pour 1985*, 'the blossoming of the human subject' (Groupe 1985 1964: 79). Even as the wind blows across the open water of the old gravel pits and the trees sway in the breeze, the signs of a fabricated environment are hard to miss: the construction cranes on the belvedere, the jetties and the artificial beaches, the café terraces overlooking them (Fig. 4.4).

In a similar way, while its characters might have fled the alienating environments of the city for the restorative grandeur of the French Alps, *Buffet froid* plays itself out

FIG. 4.4. The fabricated landscape of Cergy-Pontoise in
Éric Rohmer's *L'Ami de mon amie* (1987).

FIG. 4.5. The domestication of nature in *Buffet froid* (1979).

in another highly engineered setting, the reservoir of a hydroelectric dam (Fig. 4.5).
In fact, nothing illustrates the reach of spatial planning more than an artificial lake
in the mountains, as the state finds ways to exploit the potential of its territory to
the full. By presenting the artifice of ostensibly natural environments, both films
capture how the production of space colonizes, domesticates and denatures nature.
Or, put another way, how it works constantly to incorporate France's natural and
undeveloped space ('le désert français', to recall Jean-François Gravier's phrase)

FIG. 4.6. A modernizer at work: Alexandre (François-Éric Gendron) on the phone in *L'Ami de mon amie* (1987).

more fully into the national territory, by bringing it under the purview of those whose mission is to improve it or make it better.

Rohmer's Cergy in *L'Ami de mon amie* presents an uncanny resemblance to the wish images assembled in *Paris Match*'s publicity brochure for the new town in 1971. More precisely, it suggests that Cergy had navigated the growing pains documented in *Enfance d'une ville* and was fulfilling its role as a place for France's modern, professional middle classes. The film explores the romantic intrigues of four central characters (two men, two women) who negotiate themselves into coupledom after various false starts, misrecognitions and misunderstandings. All four are in their twenties and thirties, white, educated and heterosexual. They are as yet without children, but that is likely a matter of finding the right combination of couples, which is where the film ends.

It is notable too how the film distributes social roles and attributes between the four characters. All of them reflect aspects of the modernizing dynamic, though while Blanche (Emmanuelle Chaulet) works in the cultural services department at Cergy Town Hall, her office bright and white, and Léa (Sophie Renoir) is an IT student, it is the male characters who most clearly embody civilizational advance as scientific knowledge or technical expertise: Fabien (Éric Viellard) works in a computing laboratory, and Alexandre (François-Éric Gendron), the most socially successful and professionally advanced of the four, is an engineer at the EDF electricity company in Cergy.[8] Alexandre in particular is representative not just

8   Rohmer roots the film in the reality of Cergy by making Alexandre a *cadre* at EDF. The company agreed in the early days of Cergy's development to establish a regional headquarters on a site near the prefecture. However, political and economic obstacles meant it was not until the early 1970s that building work got under way. See Hirsch (2000: 188–90).

of the kinds of middle-class professional who moved to the new town, but of France's modernizing avant-garde, in the lineage of the planning experts Rohmer had encountered in *Enfance d'une ville* (the first time we meet him, he is speaking commandingly down the phone to someone at the prefecture) (Fig. 4.6).

In many respects, the fact that three of the four have technical competence, and that Blanche's role can also be understood in terms of the technocratic machinery of governance, suggests the accomplishment of the 'scientific civilization' which the Groupe 1985 had identified as a prerequisite for progress (1964: 14). Concerted technical and scientific formation would create a population through whose actions modernization took shape on the ground and in reality. At once products of modernization through their education and training, Alexandre and the others are also its agents; and by situating agents of modernization within the new town — within their natural habitat, as it were — Rohmer reminds us again, as he did in *Enfance d'une ville*, that while infrastructure, landscapes and built environments are modernization's most visible signs, its motive force lies in the coordination of countless individual roles and actions through which a certain conception of scientific rationality is brought to bear on the world.[9]

The scientific civilization makes an intriguing appearance in another film of the period, Varda's *Sans toit ni loi*, which follows the vagabond Mona (Sandrine Bonnaire) on her journey around the south of France. At one point, she encounters a pair of agronomists working on a method of disease prevention in plane trees. The older of the two, university researcher Madame Landier (Macha Méril), takes Mona under her wing for a brief spell. However, Mona troubles Jean-Pierre (Stéphane Freiss), Madame Landier's research assistant, a younger man (the same generation as the protagonists of *L'Ami de mon amie*) for whom she seems to represent an affront to the moral and social order of things. After having encountered Mona by chance in a railway station towards the end of the film, he admits to his wife that 'she scares me because she disgusts me'. But about what is he so troubled?

Jean-Pierre's is one of a series of perspectives on Mona from different characters in the film, each of whom attempt to interpret, define or otherwise fathom an individual who nonetheless remains an enigma. Instead, as Susan Hayward (1990) and Alison Smith (1996) have argued, Mona becomes a screen on to which they project their own imaginings, desires, fixations and concerns. Jean-Pierre's attitude and dispositions are a reflection of his class and social position, but also of his social function, which he shares in particular with Alexandre in *L'Ami de mon amie*. As the human faces of a technocratic regime, the agronomist and the engineer are more domesticated than the sinister, lab-coated technicians running Godard's *Alphaville*, but they perform similar roles as regulators of space and territory.

Borrowing from Deleuze and Guattari in *Mille plateaux* (1980), we can see Alexandre and Jean-Pierre as agents of spatial striation. Their function is to regulate, organize, configure, hierarchize and otherwise 'fix' or 'institute' space as part of the machinery of the state (Deleuze & Guattari 1980: 592). They do all those

9   In *Les Nuits de la pleine lune*, released three years earlier, Rohmer had made the relationship even more explicit in the form of the character of Rémi, a town planner who lives and works in Marne-la-Vallée.

FIG. 4.7. Agents of spatial striation: managing plane tree disease in
Agnès Varda's *Sans toit ni loi* (1985).

things that transform space into territory and bring it under the state's purview
(1980: 479, 629). They enact gestures of territorialization and territorial command
in large and small ways, by maintaining electrical infrastructure or monitoring the
health of a plane tree (Fig. 4.7). They represent a certain form of human relationship
with the world (an attitude, to use Gaston Berger's term) that stands in contrast to
other forms of being and acting in it. One of the most striking of those forms of
being, to which theirs is diametrically opposed, is Mona's challenging disregard for
social norms and conventions, and in particular, as we shall see later, the disruptive
way in which she moves through space.

In Deleuze and Guattari's well-known formulation, striated space, which carries
the imprimatur of the state, is in constant tension and negotiation with smooth
space, 'l'espace lisse' (1980: 593). Archetypal examples of smooth space for them
are 'le désert, la steppe, la glace ou la mer' (1980: 615). They have in mind the
sand deserts and other 'empty quarters' which are home to nomadic populations.
At the same time, it is striking how the figure of the *désert* is a recurring trope in
the discourse of spatial planning and *aménagement*, expressed most obviously in the
title of Jean-François Gravier's polemic, *Paris et le désert français* (1947). More than a
way to characterize the developmental imbalance between Paris and the provinces,
the idea of a French desert seems to be a source of economic, social and even
moral anxiety, a cause for concern that becomes curiously over-determined, and is
manifested in a desire to regulate the territory as a whole and in its entirety.

Thus, in the ultimate gesture of spatial striation, *Réflexions pour 1985* predicts
that even 'zones désertiques' can be given a function within the national territory
through their conversion into national parks as spaces of leisure and (presumably
regulated) freedom:

Mais les zones désertiques ne devront pas être des terroirs vieillis où déclinent lentement des activités ancestrales et des populations aigries condamnées à une assistance permanente toujours insuffisante. Les déserts seront une rareté en Europe Occidentale: en tant que zones de loisirs et de liberté, ils seront donc recherchés si une discipline suffisante préserve leurs qualités. Leur conversion en parcs nationaux devra donc être organisée et éventuellement accélérée. (Groupe 1985 1964: 74)

[Empty zones should not be dying lands where traditional activities fade away and embittered populations are condemned to perpetual but always insufficient welfare. They will be a rarity in Western Europe: as a result, they will be sought out as zones of leisure and freedom, provided that their qualities have been preserved with sufficient discipline. Their conversion into national parks should therefore be organized and potentially accelerated.]

By the time of the 1980s, meanwhile, several films seemed preoccupied with the tandem of smoothness and striation, as if to confirm them as the defining spatial categories of the time. Not only did they show agents of spatial striation and regulation at work, but they often pointed to the possibility of smooth space as a promise or alternative, even if simultaneously they signalled its inherent elusiveness, impermanence or fluidity. At various points we see characters attempting to make a break for freedom or, to draw on the other key term in Deleuze and Guattari's analysis of spatial dynamics, open up lines of flight from the striated spaces of regulated life. This is certainly the sense we can ascribe to Franck's compulsive return to the same patch of *terrain vague* in *Série noire*, as if in frantic (but futile) search of the undefined potential and indeterminacy suggested by the term. The characters in *Buffet froid*, in contrast, remain enmeshed in the striated spaces of modernization from start to finish.

The gesture of escape is there in Besson's more optimistic staging of the parallel world lurking on the other side of the corridor walls in the Métro, and the way its periodic incursions into the Métro's regulated spaces undo or disrupt the work of territorialization being undertaken by the transport police. It is there too in a notable scene in Jean-Jacques Beineix's *37.2 degrés le matin* (1986) (in English, *Betty Blue*), which follows two young lovers, Zorg (Jean-Hugues Anglade) and Betty (Béatrice Dalle), on an episodic journey around France as their volatile relationship unfolds. Like *Subway*, the film is known for the playful referentiality and close attention to visual style, colour and surface appearance associated with the *cinéma du look*. The style might have irritated some, not least the critics at the *Cahiers du Cinéma*, for its affinities with music video and other 'low' visual forms (Austin 1996: 119). However, as Neil Archer (2012: 55) observes, the film's emphasis on feel and look means that (also like *Subway*) it shows itself attentive to the coexistence of different sorts of spaces, their phenomenological qualities, and their existential potentiality.

The lovers' journey begins on a beach by the Mediterranean at Gruissan-Plage, one of the resorts that emerged out of the DATAR's mission to develop the tourist industry along the Languedoc-Roussillon coast in the 1960s. It takes in the Parisian suburbs, before ending up back in the south at Marvejols in the Lozère. On Betty's

FIG. 4.8. The empty quarter as a space of freedom in
Jean-Jacques Beineix's *37.2 degrés le matin* (1986).

birthday, Zorg drives her out into the empty plateaux of the Cévennes to an
abandoned farmstead, and proposes it as a place of their own (Fig. 4.8). It seems
unlikely that Zorg has the means to buy it, and that its role is more symbolic. It
is an instance of the film's moves into spaces of the imagination, or what Archer
terms 'fantasy space' (2012: 56), posited as a place where their romance can escape
everyday constraints and fears. Nevertheless, what catches the eye is that the film
finds the objective correlative of the fantasy in one of France's *zones désertiques*, an
empty quarter abandoned and as yet unmodernized, and invites us to imagine it as
a place of liberty-to-be-defined.

Also important is the attention Betty and Zorg pay to what they see and hear:
the setting sun as it sinks behind a tree, the sound and feel of the breeze as it runs
down the hill, what we might describe as the sounds and signs of pure becoming.
Suddenly, in the middle of nowhere, in a film twenty years on from the projections
of the Groupe 1985, a moment opens up which suggests that progress and becoming,
mobility and liberty, are not necessarily the same — suggests indeed that, as
Deleuze and Guattari propose, 'peut-être faut-il dire que tout progrès se fait par
et dans l'espace strié, mais tout devenir est dans l'espace lisse' [it should perhaps be
said that all progress comes by and in striated space, but all becoming is in smooth
space] (1980: 607). Yet it is also the case that while becoming is the way of being
privileged by Deleuze and Guattari, and that it is in smooth space where becoming
can best flourish, they also acknowledge that becoming is not an easy way to be:
'voyager en lisse, c'est tout un devenir, et encore un devenir difficile, incertain' [to
travel in smooth space is all about becoming, but a becoming that is difficult and
uncertain] (1980: 602). Agnès Varda's Mona perhaps illustrates both of these things
more clearly than anyone.

Liberty, Progress and Becoming

Around the time that Delouvrier and his colleagues were looking back on the philosophy of the *Schéma directeur* and their efforts to engineer liberty through mobility (Hirsch 2003), Varda was undoubtedly at work on *Sans toit ni loi* (1985), a film that placed the nature of liberty at its core, and seemed to put liberty in dialogue precisely with spatial modernization and its effects. Just as Mona provokes fear and disgust in Jean-Pierre, the *ingénieur agronome*, so too she represents an ideal of freedom for the teenage girl who encounters her as she stops to draw water from a pump on the girl's family farm. At stake is why and how Mona embodies freedom, and why the particular form of freedom she embodies has resonance. Or, put another way, why the other characters in the film cannot help but register her presence, and why she cannot help but leave a disturbance on the surface of life.

Modernized landscapes emerge as a quiet but defining backdrop for Mona's journey. They tend only to be glimpsed, often obliquely, but nevertheless at significant moments. Right at the start, through the window of a truck that picks Mona up from the side of the road, the camera catches sight of one of the pyramidal apartment blocks in the resort of La Grande Motte, another manifestation of the tourist infrastructure created by the DATAR in Languedoc-Roussillon (Fig. 4.9). In the closing minutes of the film, as Mona stumbles towards the camera and the ditch in which we know she will die, she is caught between two horizontal lines. In the foreground is the drainage pipe over which she will trip and fall. In the background run the twin carriageways of a motorway, along which vehicles speed through the shot (Fig. 4.10).

At one level, these traces of infrastructure could be seen as little more than reality effects or accidents of location shooting, rather than anything meaningful. Nevertheless, by incorporating them, and in particular, by framing Mona's final movements between elements of spatial striation, the film is articulating a relationship between two ways of being in space and time. To a large extent, the closing scene reconfirms what the whole film has been about: the fact that Mona does not fit in, that she exists in, and opens up, spaces parallel to the regulated world of social normality. Mobilizing Foucault, Phil Powrie has theorized these as Varda's 'heterotopic' spaces (Powrie 2011). At the same time, Mona's presence and movement cannot but give meaning to the motorway and what it represents. From that point of view, through the presence and embodiment of different forms of modernization, the film is as much a portrait of a modernized France as it is about an alternative way of being within the country's modernized landscapes.

The way Mona moves through modernized French territory draws our attention to the nature of that territory, how life is regulated and channelled by different sorts of intervention in space, and how, through the figures of Jean-Pierre and Madame Landier, regulation is performed and produced by people on the ground. As such, parallels can be drawn between Mona's destabilizing presence in the spaces of southern France, and that of the homeless people in the Métro and RER, who disturb the flow of the traffic and whom Ernaux finds herself literally going out of her way to avoid. The tension Mona brings into the world is crystallized in the contrast between her and the agronomist, Jean-Pierre. Indeed, it is noticeable

FIG. 4.9. A glimpse of La Grande Motte in *Sans toit ni loi* (1985).

FIG. 4.10. The quiet presence of modernized landscapes in *Sans toit ni loi* (1985).

that the film gives a gendered dimension to the moral antagonism provoked by Mona. Madame Landier's attitude to Mona is curious and sympathetic, even if shot through with a self-confident sense of her own social superiority, whereas Jean-Pierre's is more unambiguously hostile.[10]

10   Smith 1996 analyses the ambiguity of Madame Landier's relationship with Mona, and how it involves a form of alternative self-image on Madame Landier's part, as well as the broader distribution of 'male' and 'female' patterns of response to Mona in the film.

However, Jean-Pierre is not simply the embodiment of the sort of middle-class moral anxiety that expresses itself in terms of fear and disgust, and whose strength is disproportionate to the actual threat represented by a marginal figure like Mona.[11] Rather, he represents a whole ethos of action in and on the world whose preoccupations include the sort of unregulated waywardness of figures such as Mona. His reaction recalls the alignment of planning with masculine order that we unearthed in de Gaulle's founding command to Delouvrier in Chapter 2. In many respects, he gives form to the figure of the engineer evoked by Foucault in his discussion with Deleuze and Guattari about infrastructure as a method of territorialization. While engineers enact what Foucault terms 'the power of normalization', their structural opposite is the vagabond, 'l'éternel agité [...] qui ne va nulle part' [constantly agitated, but going nowhere] (Chatelet & others 1973: 185). Jean-Pierre's presence and action as an *ingénieur agronome* materialize the contours and extent of the French territory as a managed space. Everything within that territory is a matter of concern and regulation for the state, including the plane trees and their health.

One of the first things we learn about Mona from the narrative voiceover, meanwhile, is that 'elle venait de la mer'. After the opening sequence where she is found dead in the ditch, the film loops back to an earlier stage of her story. Nestled in the dunes, the camera shows her emerging naked from the water in the morning light. She comes from beyond the edge of the territory, and proceeds to move through it in a disruptive way — a way that simultaneously comes and goes from sight, staged in particular through the structuring use of tracking shots, yet leaves a clear affective disturbance behind it, a ripple in the psychical fields of the people who encounter her. The series of tracking shots that catch Mona at different points on her journey are a formal solution to expressing both Mona's transversal movement through the territory and her relationship to it. In effect, they are the materialization in cinematographic form of movement as a line of flight. They create a space that opens up time as movement, figuring how Mona moves through space and evades spatial structures and constraints. In doing so, the space inscribed by the travelling shot 'contests and inverts other spaces', as Powrie argues (2011: 72); and, we might add, affords a perspective on other ways of being in space. While the camera sketches the flow of Mona's movement, her witnesses are captured in their stasis, interviewed using static shots as they construct narratives about Mona and attempt to give her meaning.

As expressions of Mona's way of being, however, the tracking shots are not clear cut. In each instance, the movement of the tracking shot exists before Mona, who is caught by the camera and accompanied by it for a minute or two. As Jean Decock observes in an interview with Varda, 'les travellings: vous commencez avant Mona, vous la rattrapez, vous la dépassez...' [the travelling shots start without Mona, they catch her up then overtake her] (Decock 1988: 381). The moment of parting is ambiguous: does Mona leave the space of the tracking shot, or does the tracking

---

11   And whose hypocrisy, furthermore, is brought to light when it emerges that Jean-Pierre is plotting to lay his hands on an elderly aunt's inheritance.

shot leave Mona behind? In response, Varda suggests that the tracking shots, into which Mona emerges then disappears, are a means of capturing at once the force of Mona's movement through the world, and the ephemerality of her presence within it: 'les travellings, c'est la marche de Mona, elle n'est qu'une chose dans un paysage qui existe toujours' [the travelling shots are Mona's walk, she is just a thing in a landscape that endures] (Decock 1988: 381).

Archer puts it well in proposing that 'the film's liberating possibility lies therefore in its efforts to depict liberty itself as a living force' (2012: 51). Yet like any form of energy, the nature of that force is to be in flux and transition, finding visible but momentary expression in Mona's shape and motion as a manifestation of being-in-time. Just as Zorg and Betty's visit to the empty quarter offers the pure sensation of becoming that can only ever be fleeting, so too Mona's existence, in its uncompromising alterity, offers an insight into the reality of being-in-time that is hard to recognize, accept and understand for those who encounter her. Meanwhile, notwithstanding the planners' own sense of life as flux, energy and circulation — a sense fundamental to their vision of *aménagement* — the fact that they translate it into infrastructure and other modernized forms as tangible expressions of progress is entirely in keeping with their societal function as agents of regulation and spatial striation. It is more visible to them, more prosaic (or impoverished, perhaps), but also more sustainable than the fleeting and mercurial expression of freedom as the pure force of becoming.

Mona's movement across the terrain of southern France affords a vision of a different way of being. In doing so, however, it also sharpens our awareness of the look, feel and organization of terrain as managed space and territory. Indeed, it is striking how frequently movement emerges as a form of knowledge or insight into French space during the 1980s and 90s. Sensitivity to contrasting spatial qualities, and a sense that awareness of those qualities comes through movement, are a mark of *Sans toit ni loi*, *37.2 degrés le matin* and the other French films I have discussed in this chapter. They show a common concern with staging how people navigate modernized spaces, how they might be contested or inverted (to use Powrie's terms), and how alternative forms of space might harbour different ways of being. As such, they perform a work of mediation of, and reckoning with, the transformations wrought by modernization that serves to re-present how its traces and legacies manifest themselves in different ways across the spectrum of lived experience.

Perhaps the clearest sign that some sort of collective reckoning with spatial planning was under way during the 1980s came when one of the state agencies most responsible for it decided to take stock of its actions. In 1983, twenty years after its creation, the DATAR commissioned a photographic survey from Bernard Latarjet, one of the agency's senior administrators, and the visual artist François Hers, to find out what had been happening on the ground. The DATAR's *mission photographique* mobilized twenty-nine photographers (including Hers himself) over a period of four years. Through their movement as they fanned out across the territory, they would draw out its varying material and phenomenological qualities, and the ways in which it had been shaped by state action. The survey produced around 16,000 contact sheets, subsequently archived in the Bibliothèque nationale de France along with a selection of original prints made by the participating photographers (Hers & Latarjet 1989: 18; Bertho 2013: 34). Two monumental photo-books were also published under the title *Paysages Photographies*, one on work in progress, the other at the end of the project (Hers & Latarjet 1985 and 1989, respectively).

The project's insistence on mobilizing a series of singular perspectives, twenty-nine embodied ways of seeing the territory, is significant. For the most part, it has been understood in art historical terms as an opportunity to assert documentary photography as a legitimate form of artistic expression within the French cultural field (Morel 2006, Bertho 2013). It is significant too in terms of foregrounding the presence in the landscape of a viewing subjectivity. Both moves are signalled in the titles of the photo-books, which operate a telling shift of language from the governmental and administrative (*territoire*) to the creative and aestheticizing (*paysage*), as if to challenge or interrogate the way of seeing of its sponsoring agency. In a way, the project forms a coda on a national scale to the hopes of Delouvrier and Hirsch, who had imagined the citizens of Cergy-Pontoise gazing out over the modernized landscapes of the new town from the belvedere at Gency. However, when the DATAR's photographers in turn cast their gaze over the scenes around them, as I have explored in more detail elsewhere (Welch 2019), they offered a picture that was simultaneously comprehensive and uncertain, in which signs of crisis were manifest.

At first glance, the second *Paysages Photographies* might give the impression that the work of French modernization is complete. The design of the cover jacket is clean and minimal (white background, spacious layout, Helvetica typeface), and the cover image by Holger Trülzsch looks like a scene from the leisure economy promised by the Groupe 1985 (Fig. 4.11). A figure lounging in the shade enjoys the view of the sea somewhere in Marseille, while an array of finished surfaces catches the sun and creates a luminous atmosphere. The perfection of French modernity is expressed simultaneously in the material qualities of its territory and the opportunities for leisure afforded to its citizens. Moreover, the seaboard location makes clear that perfection extends to the very limit of the territory. Yet just as Varda troubles French space by introducing Mona as an agent of disruption from the sea, so too *Paysages Photographies* disturbs our sense of French modernity when it takes us beyond the front cover, turns away from the coast, and moves inland.

The story it tells is of the reach, capacity and limits of the state's action on its territory. In part, it is a matter of the physical extremes and limits of territorial development. Sophie Ristelhueber's images of infrastructure in the Alps (power lines, roads, bridges) capture the astonishing ingenuity and ability with which an advanced civilization can imprint itself on the most daunting of mountain environments, while also indicating the fragility of those interventions in scenes of rock falls and bent crash barriers. Frequently, it is about a territory caught between the intentions of prospective planning on the one hand, and the developing realities of global economics on the other. Images by Gilbert Fastenaekens, on the decline of heavy industry in eastern France, and Christian Milovanoff, on the modern offices of the service industry in the south, articulate a shift underway within the French economy. Fastenaekens's images of industrial decline in particular signalled capital's

FIG. 4.11. A reflection on modernization: François Hers and Bernard Latarjet (eds), *Paysages Photographies: en France les années quatre-vingt* (1989). Author's personal collection.

challenge to the state as it asserted its right to circulate across borders, ebbing and flowing from one national space to another in the search for competitive advantage and opportunities for profit. They suggested that, however much it anticipated or predicted economic trends and patterns of growth (reasonably well in the case of the Groupe 1985, as Philippe Dubois had shown), the state's ability to control and manage those trends seemed less than secure.

Yet even as it sketches out the limits or challenges that state planning encounters, *Paysages Photographies* nevertheless reminds us of planning's inherent power, the sort of power that had enabled the creation of the new towns. With that power came the inevitable violence implicit within gestures of territorialization and spatial planning as change was imposed on the established order of things. Violence lurks beneath the surface in Raymond Depardon's contribution especially, which documents the impact on his family farm in Burgundy of the construction of the A6 motorway between Paris and Lyon during the 1970s. Alongside photos from the family archive of the farm and the land around it, Depardon records the encroaching presence of infrastructure (power lines crisscrossing the sky), signs of construction and improvement work in the fields (concrete drainage pipes), and the landscapes of production, circulation, flow and mobility brought in the wake of the motorway (light industrial units, warehouses, road junctions, road signs). The motorway itself remains invisible in the photographs. Instead, Depardon includes an extract from the map of the area by the Institut géographique national, France's cartographic agency. Bisected by the orange line that represents the motorway as it runs north-south, the map expresses its defining presence in the landscape and its influence on the built forms and environments observed by Depardon.

That the motorway is made visible only in symbolic form, as a line on a map, foregrounds not only the abstracting function of cartography as a technique of representation, but also the gap between those abstractions and the lived, material environments they stand for. Depardon's concern is with that gap and the spatial interventions it enables. It is also with the consequences entailed for those who live in what the map's white spaces imply are relatively empty quarters, but what his images show to be fertile and productive terrain. The unsaid drama of Depardon's project lies in the expropriation of his father's land by the government in order to build the motorway. Depardon spelt out its impact three decades later:

> J'étais en colère contre les grands travaux d'aménagement qui avaient démantelé la ferme de mon père en l'expropriant pour faire passer l'autoroute au milieu de ses terres, puis pour établir une zone industrielle et enfin une zone commerciale sur le reste de terres cultivables. Je n'avais qu'une envie, c'était de régler mes comptes avec ce désastre, ce grand chamboulement qui avait rendu mon père malade et l'avait précipité dans la dépression. (Depardon 2010: [9–10])

> [I was angry with the development works that had broken up my father's farm by expropriating his land to build the motorway, then an industrial estate and finally a shopping centre. My only desire was to settle my scores with this disaster, a great upset that had made my father ill and sent him into a depression.]

Depardon turns his project against the DATAR, interrogating the vertiginous collision between the power implicit within the cartographic view (which by extension is that of the planners at the DATAR) and the lived experience of *aménagement* on the ground. As he puts it, 'j'ai détourné cette commande publique [...] pour faire un travail personnel sur ce qu'il restait de la ferme et de son environnement' [I hijacked this public commission to do a personal project on what was left of the farm and its surroundings] (2010: [10]). Just as the market gardeners of Cergy-Pontoise were dispossessed in the name of progress through urban development, so too Depardon's father found himself sacrificing land for road building as a means of national advancement. Both encounters with prospective planning expose how it comes to be lived as loss not progress, and seems to produce the very affective and psychical problems (anger, depression and illness) that it had claimed to want to mitigate.

Shortly before Depardon set about settling his score with the DATAR through his contribution to its photographic survey, the motorway provoking his anger had been the catalyst for another interrogation of spatial modernization and its effects. In 1982, Julio Cortázar and Carol Dunlop would pass within striking distance of Depardon's family farm as they undertook a month-long journey down the motorway from Paris to Marseille in their campervan. Their trip, related in *Les Autonautes de la cosmoroute* (1983), was against the rules and norms of motorway travel. Rather than using it as the quickest means of movement between two points, they slowed and stretched their journey by visiting every rest area. They stayed within the precincts of the motorway for the duration of the trip, in contravention of the regulation limiting time spent on the motorway to forty-eight hours, as the toll tickets they 'lost' on the way made clear (Cortázar & Dunlop 1983: 265).

Their challenge to the regulations and the philosophy of the motorway can be seen as a form of resistance in the spirit of Michel de Certeau, an interrogation of the motorway's functional drive as speed space. However, taking their time is not simply or necessarily a gesture of defiance. What their slowness helps to do is accentuate the peculiarities of the space of the motorway and its odd relationship to the rest of the territory, most notably the *zones désertiques* through which it cuts, and which abut the fences lining its route. Slowness becomes a way of getting to know the space better, understanding how it works, and how it shapes our being. Like Varda in *Sans toit ni loi*, their interrogation of the motorway creates a sense that progress and becoming are not necessarily the same thing, nor that mobility and freedom are necessarily correlative. Cortázar and Dunlop were not alone in recognizing the spatial and phenomenological distinctiveness of the motorway, and it is via one of the most emblematic of post-war France's modernized landscapes that the chapter concludes.

How About a Spin on the Motorway?

In July 1972, after a spell at the Ministry of Education in Georges Pompidou's first government, Olivier Guichard was reshuffled into a more familiar portfolio. Under new prime minister Pierre Messmer, he became Ministre de l'Équipement et de l'Aménagement du Territoire. Shortly afterwards, the erstwhile director of the DATAR took to the wheel of his Citroën DS as part of *Les Liaisons moins dangereuses*, a promotional film by his new ministry about the 'vital necessity' of motorways for the country's development (Fig. 4.12). It was not so much that motorways were a new addition to the French territory: the Autoroute de l'Ouest, heading out from Paris towards Normandy and modelled on the German *autobahns*, had been built in the 1930s (Desportes 2005: 287–88). What mattered now was the role they had been given in driving forward French modernization.

Driving at speed down a long stretch of new tarmac, Guichard reported that the rhythm of motorway production was accelerating all the time. By the end of 1978, the rate of production would be 800km a year, 'in other words, almost the

FIG. 4.12. The need for speed: Olivier Guichard on the motorway in his Citroën DS in *Les Liaisons moins dangereuses* (1972).

distance between Paris and Marseille'.[12] In many ways, the quickening expansion of the motorway system seemed to make material the promise of spatial planning as a means of accelerating the country into the future. The motorway had a purity of function as speed space, shrinking the national territory by accelerating transit time across it. France's political and economic investment in the motorway network supported Virilio's analysis in *Vitesse et politique* that '*la vitesse est l'espérance de l'Occident*' [*speed is the hope of the West*] (1977: 54). Technical innovation in the domain of speed was the key to maintaining economic superiority and civilizational advance.

The film also concurred with Foucault's analysis of the centrality of road systems to *aménagement*, in terms of their territorializing function as catalysers and regulators of mobility, production and exchange (Chatelet & others 1973: 184–85). As traffic streams past industrial installations, the voiceover observes how motorways help to 'ravitailler des régions en perte de vitesse et de les intégrer dans le mouvement général de l'expansion' [revitalize those regions which are lagging behind and integrate them into the general movement of growth]. They do so not least, it notes (in a reminder of France's post-imperial shift of emphasis) by enabling integration into the European networks 'where the economic currents flow'. The film is alive with images of flow and circulation along wide bands of tarmac, while low-angle shots capture the impressive concrete infrastructure (bridges, flyovers, intersections) with which that movement is sustained. Nor was it shy about the technocratic

12   *Les Liaisons moins dangereuses* (Ministère de l'Équipement et de l'Aménagement du Territoire, 1972), available online as part of a French government archive of films by the Ministère de la Reconstruction et de l'Urbanisme and its successors <https://www.dailymotion.com/playlist/x34ije> [accessed 18 February 2021].

nature of motorway development. Shots of a control room with echoes of Godard's Alphaville show us engineers simulating the 'paysage autoroutier' [motorway landscape] on a mainframe computer, while the voiceover tells us that the work of simulation ensures the 'humanization' of the motorway and its role as an 'aesthetic element' of the landscape.

Far from being a disfigurement of the landscape, indeed, motorways had the capacity to enhance its beauty through their inscription within it: 'ces longs et larges rubans, symboles du futur, doivent être en somme [...] le mariage heureux des paysages naturels et artificiels, du passé et de l'avenir' [these long, wide ribbons, symbols of the future, should be the happy marriage of natural and manmade landscapes, of the past and the future]. They were a perfect expression of modernity in their blend of form and function. They enabled advancement towards the future in their role as speed space, while the forms they took enacted modernity in the landscape. Their beauty lay precisely in their manufactured quality, their ability to combine nature and artifice as they worked with and through the folds of the land and opened up perspectives over it.

When motorways percolate into French culture, they seem to encapsulate modernity as an epochal shift in perception, knowledge and sense of being, and provide a fitting environment for altered states of consciousness. Jean-Patrick Manchette's crime thriller, *Le Petit bleu de la côte ouest* (1976), is bookended by its protagonist, Georges Gerfaut, circulating Paris on the Boulevard Périphérique in his Mercedes as he listens to West Coast jazz. The ring road is empty, apart from a few lorries trundling along, and some cars going way beyond the speed limit. Several drivers are drunk, including Gerfaut, who has also taken barbiturates (Manchette 2005: 707). That he is doing so, the narrator tells us, is not connected with the drama of murder, kidnapping and pursuit with which he had recently been embroiled: 'ce qui arrive à présent arrivait parfois auparavant' [what is happening now has happened before] (2005: 708). Instead, it indicates simply that 'Georges est de son temps, et aussi de son espace' [Georges is of his time, and of his space] (2005: 794).

The idea that motorways might lurk on the edge of collective consciousness as a promise of escape and catalyser of excitement through the headiness of speed surfaces again in Beineix's *37.2 degrés le matin*. After a giddy evening of drink in the Parisian suburbs, Zorg and Betty's new friend, the restaurant-owning Eddy (Gérard Darmon), makes a sudden proposition: 'si je vous emmène faire un tour sur l'autoroute? 240!' [how about we went for a spin on the motorway? 240!] Eddy's car, a Citroën CX (successor to the DS and suggestive of his business success), had already been described by an admiring boy as 'une flèche', an arrow capable of 250kph. The conversation moves on and (wisely) the offer is not taken up; but the promise of the offer is on full display in the title sequence of Besson's *Subway*, through the noise and drama of the opening car chase.

Point-of-view shots from Fred's car position the spectator behind the windscreen and give wide-angled views of the arterial motorway channelling traffic towards Paris. Fred's ease at the wheel (he fiddles with music cassettes while barrelling past slower traffic) locates him as a child of the age of speed, used to handling

FIG. 4.13. At ease with speed: Fred (Christophe Lambert) on the motorway in *Subway* (1985).

the accelerated flow of events produced by speed, and the similarly accelerated judgements and actions it requires (Fig. 4.13). At the same time, the film suggests interestingly that his ease with speed has a traumatic origin. Later on, he tells the story of a childhood car accident which resulted from his father claiming he could drive his DS under a lorry, which left Fred spending five months in hospital and five years unable to speak. If Fred is a child of speed, it is not simply because he has adapted successfully to its requirements, but also because he was growing up at a time when France was learning and failing to handle the nature of speed and its consequences.

Moreover, as Cortázar and Dunlop suggest, motorways produce altered states as much as being a place where they find expression. In *Les Autonautes de la cosmoroute*, they home in on the motorway as a space engineered to produce certain effects and behaviours, by maximizing efficiency and reducing distraction. They are also alert to how it produces a new sort of consciousness in doing so. The long ribbon of asphalt they photograph from footbridges or rest areas appears as the essence of space-time as it unspools to the horizon, a material expression of time in space that enables the most rapid and efficient movement between point A and point B. It forms a total environment that absorbs and funnels everything into a vertiginous experience of pure speed and unencumbered becoming.[13] The sensation produced by motorway travel is not unpleasant, admits Dunlop, but potentially deadly. Only leaving the motorway can break the spell: 'pour ma part, il m'est arrivé de la quitter en raison même de ce vertige qui en fait aussi la charme afin de briser cette fuite en avant au moment où l'hypnose risque de devenir totale, fatale' [as for me, there are times when I have left the motorway precisely because of this dizziness which

13   One endorsed by the government, at least in the early days of the motorways. In *Les Liaisons moins dangereuses*, Guichard indicated that he was not in favour of a blanket speed limit: speed was of the essence. The state's position changed soon afterwards though, and by the time Eddy was proposing to try out the top speed of his Citroën CX, it had long taken the view that speed kills. A top speed of 120kph was introduced in December 1973, subsequently modified to 140kph then 130kph the following year.

is also its charm, in order to break the headlong rush at the point where it risks becoming complete and fatal] (Cortázar & Dunlop 1983: 23). The motorway is a place of absolutes, where death can come quickly. Perhaps this explains its lure for Manchette's drunken drivers as they circulate the Boulevard Périphérique like satellites round a planet.

At one level, we can see Cortázar and Dunlop's month-long journey down the motorway as a gesture of resistance against the hegemonic social and economic order it makes manifest. Going slowly on the motorway and visiting every rest area are ways of pushing against the rhythm of life it implies and imposes, where what matters is the headlong rush, the stimulation of flow and circulation, the need to prevent literal and figurative 'perte de vitesse'. On another, using the motorway against the grain is more a form of *détournement* through which other rhythms and temporalities can emerge. The motorway is the most highly developed form of automotive speed space, whose function is to reduce the time taken to cross space, and whose assertive confidence is most clearly shown (as Depardon suggests in his contribution to *Paysages Photographies*) by a bold line on a map. Yet by moving slowly down it, parcelling it out, staying in its rest areas and exploring its margins, Cortázar and Dunlop show it to be endlessly proliferating and almost unmappable. In Charles Forsdick's terms, they expose the fractal reality of a space that proposes and (crucially) understands itself to be Euclidian (Forsdick 2005b: 58).

As they do so, they can attempt to make it a space out of time, a distance that can never be completed: 'on pourrait faire un parking par jour, hors du monde, tu te rends compte, prendre ce monstre de vitesse et en faire une croisière de détente en toute liberté...' [do you realize, we could do one layby a day, out of the world, take this monster of speed and turn it into a relaxing cruise in complete freedom] (Cortázar & Dunlop 1983: 29). By using the motorway otherwise, it can be transformed into a line of flight, a route to freedom and 'total Happiness' (1983: 272). Their gesture gains weight and significance when we learn at the end of the book that Dunlop died a few months later. The journey becomes a way for both of them to try to escape time, even as they acknowledge that time cannot be beaten. The motorway, despite its appearance and function, initiates a sense of duration or becoming, but inevitably that sense can only be fleeting. Their arrival at Marseille after a month on the road means the return of 'la notion du temps' (1983: 268), a reinsertion into the externalities of what Henri Bergson called 'clock time', with its attendant regulation of social existence.

Their movements down the motorway draw out temporalities at once apparent (inscribed into and intended by its forms) and hidden (mobilized by using it against the grain). If they also articulate the motorway's distinctive spatial qualities, they do so not only by revealing its fractal nature — how it proliferates in unexpected ways beyond the bands of asphalt represented by the line on Depardon's map — but also by capturing how it coexists with the space through which it runs. Both things come to light in the motorway rest areas where, as they put it, 'l'autoroute commence à perdre consistance' [the motorway begins to lose consistency] (1983: 48). Yet while the mineral firmness of tarmac and concrete shades into a profusion of trees, bushes and other organic forms, the whole is bounded by a perimeter line, what Cortázar describes as 'cette interminable succession de huit cents kilomètres de grillages, talus, murs, haies agressives et autres murailles de Chine de fabrication française' [this interminable, 800-kilometre stretch of fencing, mounds, ways, aggressive hedges and other French-made Great Walls of China] (1983: 47). While the boundary is there for security, its role seems also symbolic, demarcating the space of the motorway and the specificities of temporality and consciousness it requires. That the travellers have absorbed the difference represented by the motorway becomes clear whenever they encounter gaps and breaches in its perimeter, shying away from the 'temptation' (1983: 46) to step beyond its limits, and preserving their own mental frontier between the durational time-space they have found on the motorway and the world beyond.

The spatio-temporal specificities they articulate also help to account for why the motorway's presence in the closing scene of *Sans toit ni loi* feels significant. In many respects, as I suggested earlier, it can stand for the regulated world and dominant modes of being from which Mona has removed herself (the world of 'les petits chefs de bureau', petty office managers, she calls it at one point). Yet to a degree, the last minutes of the film bring into dialogue two ways of being in time which are both, in their own way, strange and distinctive, and which are expressed in the differing forms of movement in the scene. If we notice the motorway as more than a dark grey line in the background, it is because of the horizontal rush of traffic along it, whose flowing speed contrasts with Mona's stumbling, foot-bound movement away from it, through the vines and towards the camera. The disjunction of the two captures the tension produced by the space-time of the motorway as it cuts through space, especially when that space is rural or agricultural, and moving at a different rhythm and pace. For all that the DATAR wanted motorways to hyphenate the present and the past as they flowed over the territory, the evidence was clear that they made manifest a break or rupture with the past as France entered a reconfigured socio-economic space-time with its own distinctive forms and qualities.

Such were the changes being observed by Depardon in the vicinity of his father's farm for the DATAR's photographic survey, as the A6 motorway made its presence felt in the landscape. The modular distribution sheds and warehouses he photographed on the periphery of the motorway were evidence of the burgeoning industry of logistics and distribution that accelerated with the increasing integration of France into the 'economic currents' of the European common market. They illustrated how the spatio-temporal requirements of commerce and capital spill beyond the speed space of the motorway to generate ancillary built forms in its environs. They also exemplified the sort of homogeneous landscapes that would increasingly define France's peri-urban environments (and indeed, the emergence of the 'peri-urban' itself as phenomenon and built form).[14]

In the early 1990s, the anthropologist Marc Augé found an enduring way to

14   As Depardon's camera showed, and others like the writer Jean Rolin would also begin to explore, spaces at the interface between the rural and the urban, or blending features of the two, were appearing in the French landscape well before urban geographers had settled on and theorized the notion of the 'peri-urban' as a way to analyse them. Adell 1999 offers an overview of the term and its emergence at a time when it was gaining conceptual traction.

describe the peculiarity of the spaces and locations that had caught the attention of Depardon, not to mention others like Ernaux, Cortázar and Dunlop, in what would become one of the defining French accounts of modernized space. He opened his account of what he termed 'supermodernity' by imagining the journey of a company executive as he leaves home, withdraws money from a cash machine, and takes the motorway round Paris to catch a flight from Roissy airport, leaving his car in an underground car park:

> Le trajet a été facile: la descente sur Paris par l'autoroute A11 ne pose pas de problème un dimanche matin. Il n'a pas eu à attendre à l'entrée, a payé avec sa carte bleue au péage de Dourdan, contourné Paris par le périphérique et rejoint Roissy par l'A1. (Augé 1992: 7)

> [The journey was easy: the drive down to Paris by the A11 motorway poses no problems on a Sunday morning. He didn't have to wait to get on, paid with his debit card at the Douran toll, circled Paris on the Périphérique, and reached Roissy via the A1.]

Augé captures a sense of the motorway not simply as an enormous system in itself, folded out over the territory, but as integrated with other elements of infrastructure to produce a gigantic, seamless machine of perpetual motion, circulation and fluidity. In doing so, he grasps the extent to which the planned world envisioned by the *Schéma directeur* and the DATAR had come to pass and framed daily life in France by the end of the twentieth century. As Augé also suggested in his critique of the bland, anonymous, homogeneous and endlessly reproducing locations he called *non-lieux* (non-places) — automated budget hotels, modular distribution sheds, motorway service stations, airport departure lounges — the costs of the vision were clear, not just aesthetically, but also in affective, emotional and psychical terms.

Augé's naming of *non-lieux* marked a significant moment in thinking about French space. It recognized and gave consistency to the sense that there was something qualitatively different about the nature of space in France at the end of the twentieth century. That sense had been finding different expressions in cultural form during the 1970s and 80s, as we have seen in this chapter, as French space underwent some substantial and radical transformations, and they in turn began to impinge on the collective consciousness. At the same time, manifestations of 'supermodernity' existed in ever starker contrast with France's marginalized urban peripheries, themselves a legacy of the country's modernizing urge, where time and space had appeared to stall. Those places, mapped by Maspero and Frantz in *Les Passagers du Roissy-Express* as they journeyed along the RER B, would loom increasingly large in the country's political and spatial imaginary as it struggled to navigate both the consequences of modernization and the increasingly unequal relationship between state and capital in a globalizing world. Chapter 5 explores the spatial dynamics playing out across French territory as the millennium turned. To do so, it tracks the life and career of the zone, one of the most persistent ways of talking about and enacting space in post-war France.

CHAPTER 5

❖

Zones (and Other Figures of Space)

CDG, DSQ, ZUP: Mapping the Spatial Tensions of Hexagonal France

Acceleration, as we saw in Chapter 1, drove the prospective view of progress in the 1960s. It was by embracing the principle of acceleration at work in human endeavour, argued Gaston Berger, that humanity could evolve ever more quickly in a virtuous circle of accelerating change. The more we progress, the more we invent, and the quicker our inventions enable us to progress into the future. The more quickly, too — as Pierre Massé made clear — we can leave the past behind. Acceleration found its material expression in the construction of speed spaces like the motorways, which could spear the nation into the future by accelerating the flow of traffic and compressing space through time gained. It found its human form in Olivier Guichard powering down the fast lane of the motorway in his Citroën DS in 1972.

Yet just as, in the 1980s, Agnès Varda would interrogate the assumptions about being and progress embedded in the motorway by placing it in dialogue with the foot-bound, wandering Mona, and the DATAR would commission a team of photographers to examine the effects of prospective planning on the French territory, so too the historical consequences of societal acceleration would come under close scrutiny. It was in a sense of the acceleration of history and its implications for collective memory where Pierre Nora anchored the multi-volume *Les Lieux de mémoire* [Realms of Memory], a project which had its origins in a reflection on 'la disparition rapide de notre mémoire nationale' (the rapid disappearance of our national memory) (Nora 1997: 15). The first of the three volumes was published in 1984, a year after the DATAR launched its *mission photographique*, and a year before the release of Varda's *Sans toit ni loi*.

Nora's introduction in the first volume diagnosed a crisis of memory born out of the 'acceleration of history' — the phrase stands boldly alone as the essay's opening words (Nora 1997: 23). Historical acceleration had provoked a rupture with the past and a fragmentation of collective, national memory whose signs were to be found in a growing interest in locations (physical, institutional and symbolic) where memory 'finds refuge' (1997: 23). In some respects, Nora's crisis of memory was just another sign of the broader sense of crisis that had been growing in France since the oil crises of the 1970s and the beginnings of neoliberal globalization had interrupted France's forward momentum. But the fact that Nora thinks the crisis through in spatial terms, as a question of where collective memory might be lodged, uncovered and recuperated, and sees it as having spatial manifestations in the first instance, foregrounds the extent to which space provided the figurative grounds for conceptualizing the nature of France's crisis and forms of response to it.

As a historiographical project, *Les Lieux de mémoire* was about mapping memory's places of refuge. Doing so also made it a restorative project, and therefore an activist or a political one. The act of mapping was a means of shoring up a sense of collective memory or identity. It brought a sort of historiographical emergency relief to the places where memory had taken refuge, and a way of compensating for the loss of the 'milieux de mémoire' which Nora identified as the wellspring of collective memory and cohesive identity (1997: 23, 28–29). Quintessential amongst these were the peasant cultures eroded by industrialization, urbanization and migration (that is to say, modernization *tout court*). On the other hand, the corollary of the project's will to recuperate was a tone of anxiety and melancholy, what Michael Rothberg calls a 'nostalgic plotting of loss' (2010: 6). Moreover, it seemed that Nora's nostalgia was structured by a fundamental and glaring amnesia. One of the things *Les Lieux de mémoire* precisely failed to plot, despite its self-evident significance in France's recent history, was how empire and its end shaped the French nation and national identity.

The absence of reflection on where memories of France's colonial history and decolonization might reside is considered one of the project's most problematic omissions (Tai 2001, Anderson 2004, Rothberg 2010, Achille, Forsdick & Moudileno 2020). Missing, in Perry Anderson's trenchant terms, is 'the entire imperial history of the country, from the Napoleonic conquests, through the plunder of Algeria under the July Monarchy, to the seizure of Indochina in the Second Empire and the vast African booty of the Third Republic' (2004: 10). What emerges instead is a noticeably hexagonal Frenchness that to any outside observer seems perversely negligent of France's imperial activities and its legacies. Indeed, it is hard not to imagine that there is something over-determined in its nostalgia for a time of national coherence through collective memory and that, as Stephen Legg suggests, such nostalgia might in fact be a displaced and disavowed melancholia for an imperial time of French power and influence in the world (Legg 2005: 490).

Yet in many respects, the project's occlusion of colonial history and decolonization (bar an article by Charles-Robert Ageron on the Colonial Exhibition of 1931 and a scattering of mentions elsewhere) is perhaps part of the point.[1] After all, Nora is unapologetic about its 'gallocentrisme' (1997: 21). For all its concern that the decay of collective memory lay in the acceleration of history, the project's bracketing off of empire and recuperation of a memory in hexagonal form was the logical historiographical outcome of the previous two decades or so of post-colonial nation-building through modernization. The whole point of that period had been about accelerating into the future and, to recall Kristin Ross's potent image, slamming

---

1   Étienne Achille (2021) has shown that while France's colonial past is not as absent from *Les Lieux de mémoire* as many critics have argued, traces of that past surface in spite rather than because of the historiographical nationalism of the project.

shut the door on the colonial past. As a means of shoring up the foundations for a hexagonal sense of national identity, one distributed across the physical and discursive space of the metropolitan territory, the post-colonial Gallocentrism of *Les Lieux de mémoire* made entire sense.

An impression of a project in search of hexagonal forms of identity emerges strikingly in Eugen Weber's essay on the hexagon as a figure of speech for metropolitan France, published in the second volume in 1986. The declarative simplicity of the title ('L'Hexagone') asserted the figure's ubiquity and self-evidence as a term for the country. No further gloss was required because its referent was clear enough. Yet Weber reveals early on that its ubiquity belied the novelty of its figurative usage: what looked like a commonplace was in fact an innovation (1997: 1171). Weber spends much of the essay discussing how he had been wrong in his assumption, shared with others, that the hexagon had a long history as a synonym for the country. In reality, it had gained currency only in the 1960s, as France was embarking on its post-colonial future.

Weber's account of the figurative birth of the hexagon serves almost as an allegory of the broader project of memorial consolidation and forgetting in post-colonial France in which *Les Lieux de mémoire* was itself implicated. Weber notes that there was a brief period of connotative instability when the hexagon was used pejoratively to describe a newly diminutive France, shorn of its colonial possessions, as more vestige than destiny (1997: 1187). However, those pejorative associations fell away quickly, neutralized by how the figure's self-contained, geometric precision could emblematize the country's advance through scientific and technical expertise. As Gaullist France entered its post-colonial era and worked to recalibrate its position in the world, the figure of the hexagon was at hand to help obscure memories of the lost expanse of empire.

We can see the hexagon's connotative shifts under way in the image on the cover of *Aménager l'hexagone* by planning administrator André Trintignac (Fig. 5.1). His survey of French spatial planning policy was published in 1964, barely two years after the country's return to its hexagonal frontiers. Superimposed on an outline of the metropolitan territory, itself isolated against a blue background, was a hexagonal shape in black containing signifiers of infrastructure (planes, buildings, tunnels, a grid of black lines suggesting roads). Meanwhile, Trintignac's systematic treatment of *aménagement* and its application across all levels and areas of the territory (urban, rural, regional, national) seemed to enact how French spatial planning envisaged simultaneously the total transformation of the territory and the transformation of the territory in its totality. No aspect of metropolitan France, urban or rural, would be left untouched. Such was the book's focus on the mainland that, with the exception of some brief discussions of Corsica, France's remaining overseas *départements* and *territoires* (the remnants of its colonial expansion) simply disappeared from sight.

It was as if the hexagonal grid on the cover of Trintignac's book was the mould giving post-colonial France the form and consistency it needed (and whose sense of identity *Les Lieux de mémoire* would later attempt to backfill). After centuries of

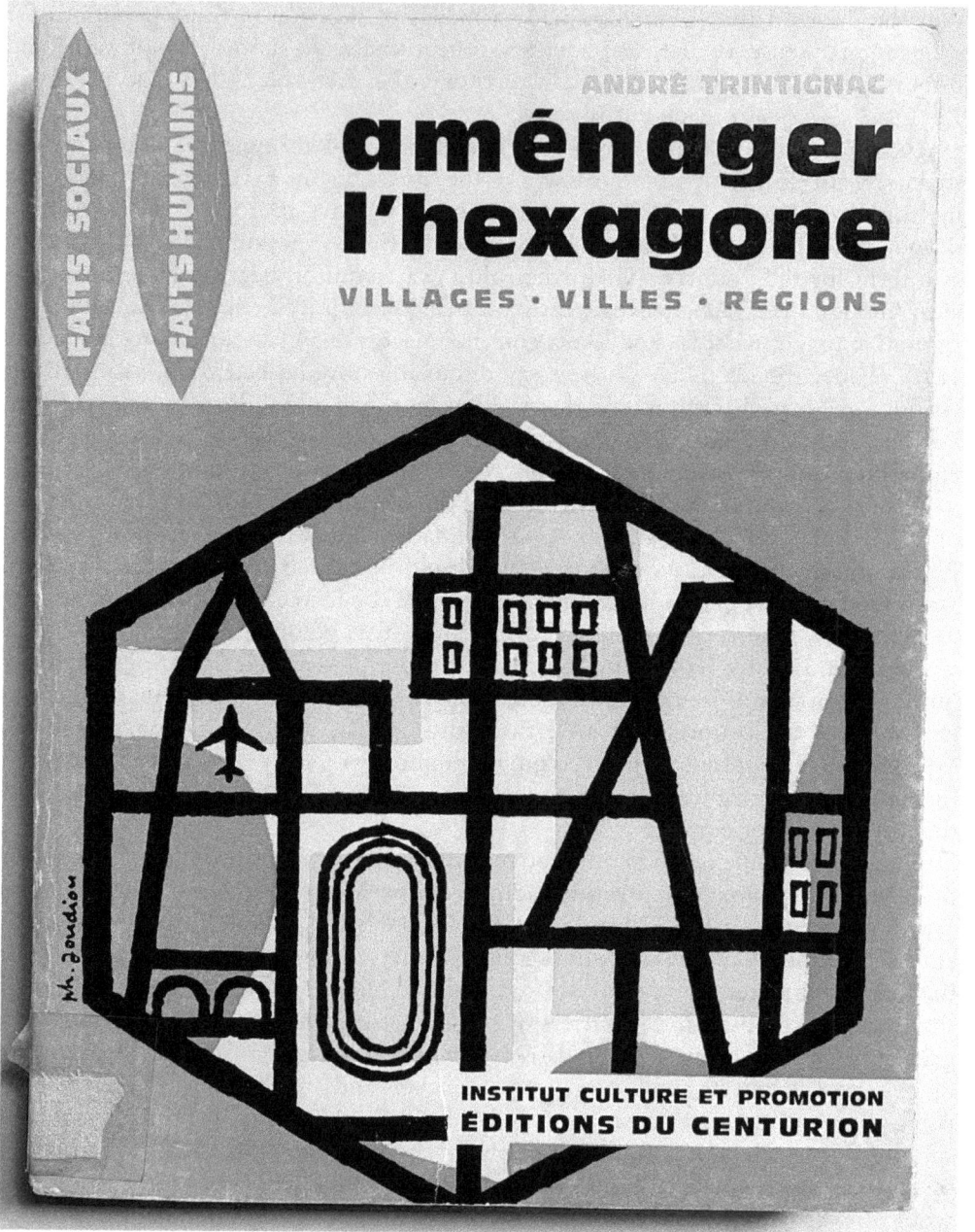

Fɪɢ. 5.1. The front cover of André Trintignac, *Aménager l'hexagone: villages, villes, régions* (1964). Author's personal collection.

colonial expansion, the country could finally turn its energy inwards and forge a strengthened territory ready to take its place at the vanguard of modernity. It would do so not least, as we have seen at various points, by bringing back home methods and techniques of territorial development honed in its colonial acquisitions. Trintignac's book never glosses the figure of speech it deploys in its title; to do so would undoubtedly have involved acknowledging the geopolitical crisis from which France had just emerged. Nevertheless, its demonstration of the scope and power of *aménagement* works elliptically to suggest that, borrowing Weber's terms, hexagonal France would prove to be more destiny than vestige. At the same time, even as the hexagon figured the nation's rupture with its colonial past and the shape of its post-colonial future, it nevertheless held within itself (hid in plain sight, it might be said) an insistent reminder that France was a country reshaped by decolonization, a reminder that would be deftly mobilized in due course.

Thirty years after Trintignac, Malik Chibane saw fit to appropriate the term for the title of his first feature film. Set on a housing estate in the suburbs to the north of Paris, *Hexagone* (1994) tells the story of members of the so-called *beur* generation of young adults, born (like Chibane) to Maghrebi parents who had emigrated to France during the *Trente glorieuses* and had been responsible for much of the physical labour of modernization. Chibane's film made clear that the reconfiguration of post-colonial France was at once territorial and demographic, but also that the demographic and social consequences of that reconfiguration were expressed in spatial terms especially. It was one of a cluster of films from the 1980s and 1990s that sought to make visible France's significant but marginalized ethnic minorities (Tarr 2005, Durmelat & Swamy 2011), and mapped out how the social problems they endured (unemployment, racial prejudice, police violence) were compounded by their spatial marginalization on the periphery of France's major cities. As Chibane put it in an interview the following year, 'voilà pourquoi *Hexagone* était un titre provocant: je ne prenais que des Beurs et disais l'Hexagone, c'est ça' [that's why *Hexagone* was a provocative title: I was showing only Beurs on screen and saying, that's what the Hexagon's about] (Marchais 1995).

While Chibane's gesture might have been provocative, it was also entirely accurate in its framing of France's new social and spatial configurations. In the first place, it foregrounded the everyday reality of a post-colonial, multi-ethnic France, along with the social, economic and political frustrations which defined it. That reality had begun to break through into public consciousness with urban unrest in the early 1980s, and then in more organized political form in the autumn of 1983 with the 'Marche pour l'égalité et contre le racisme' from Marseille to Paris, also known as the 'Marche des beurs' (Boubeker 2009: 73–74). Secondly, as Vinay Swamy puts it, the story told about characters living on a peripheral housing estate was 'also meant to be a *French* story' (Swamy 2011: 217).

By making them visible, locating them in the hexagon and asserting their metonymical connection to the nation ('je ne prenais que des Beurs et disais l'Hexagone, c'est ça'), Chibane's film reactivated the dormant post-colonial roots of a figure of speech which had by then acquired the unanchored, ahistorical quality

Fig. 5.2. The peri-urban landscape of modernized France in
Malik Chibane's *Hexagone* (1994).

of the commonplace. In doing so, it signalled that it was as much an exploration of post-colonial French space and territory as it was the demographic legacies of French colonialism and modernization. Or rather, the film was inviting its audiences to see that French modernization had produced spatial outcomes that had societal consequences, and that its societal consequences manifested themselves in spatial terms first and foremost.

Carrie Tarr notes that *Hexagone* begins with a 'striking establishing shot' that pans across open countryside until it settles on a large group of housing blocks caught by the sunlight in the middle distance (Fig. 5.2). Meanwhile the noise of low-flying jet aircraft builds in the soundtrack. For Tarr, the shot 'boldly displaces the cornfields and birdsong of *la France profonde*, placing the blocks of flats and the noise of planes at the centre, rather than the periphery, of the hexagon that is contemporary France' (2005: 54). Yet arguably what the shot is establishing is not so much the *displacement* of the rural by the urban in contemporary France as the profound *transformation* of the French territory as a whole during the post-war period — spatially, topographically and demographically. In what we see and hear, Chibane is presenting us with another of France's manufactured landscapes.

We are at Goussainville, an unassuming town around twenty kilometres to the north of Paris, yet whose recent history seemed to epitomize the profoundly transformative effects of French modernization on both the territory and its population. The *grands ensembles* picked out by Chibane's camera were constructed in the 1950s and 1960s as part of the state's response to the housing shortage in and around Paris. If jet aircraft are audible, and then glimpsed flying low over the town later in the opening sequence, it is because Goussainville is situated in the vicinity of Roissy-CDG airport, opened in 1974 as part of Delouvrier's *Schéma directeur* (Fig. 5.3).

FIG. 5.3. Under the flight path of Roissy-CDG in *Hexagone* (1994).

Indeed, in perhaps the most telling illustration and manifestation of French modernization as a form of erasure, the old village of Goussainville was notoriously abandoned by its residents shortly afterwards because it lay directly under the flight path of the new airport, a few hundred metres from the end of the runway.[2]

At one level, the camera's movement across the fringe of the Paris region can be read as presenting in spatial terms the diachronic process of modernization by which the rural increasingly gives way to (or is consumed by) the urban. Perhaps more significant is the synchronic reality it captures through sound and vision, a new reality of France's peri-urban space. We encounter a peculiar hybrid of the urban, rural, local and global, produced by the distinctive spatial policies of the post-war French state, and creating the specific social, political and cultural phenomenon of the *banlieue*.

The new spatial facts of French modernization, and the consequences deriving from them, are further revealed in the film's subsequent sequence. The camera takes us amongst the towers and blocks of Goussainville's *grands ensembles*, past children playing outside, before settling on a group of young men of Maghrebi descent hanging around outside the Maison du DSQ, a state-funded welfare and

2   Their fears about living in close proximity to Roissy had been exacerbated by an accident in June 1973, when the Soviet Union's supersonic rival to Concorde, the Tupolev Tu-144, crashed on Goussainville during a demonstration flight, killing all six crew and eight people on the ground. The abandoned village has developed a second life as a 'post-apocalyptic' 'ghost town' (Holt 2014) and alternative tourist attraction. At the very moment of its apotheosis, it seemed that French modernization could not help but create a dreamlike premonition of its own possible future as a ruined civilization. On the Goussainville crash, see the Bureau of Aircraft Accident Archives <https://www.baaa-acro.com/crash/crash-tupolev-tu-144s-goussainville-14-killed> [accessed 5 May 2021].

FIG. 5.4. Hanging around by the Maison du DSQ in *Hexagone* (1994).

advice bureau (Fig. 5.4). It is accompanied by a commentary later identified as the viewpoint of Slimane (Jalil Naciri), the film's male lead, who introduces the other characters and describes lives defined by unemployment, lack of opportunity, petty theft, clandestine activity, frustration and stasis ('il passe plus, le temps, il fuse' [time doesn't pass, it fizzles out]).

In its opening few minutes, by yoking Roissy-CDG together with the Maison du DSQ, *Hexagone* articulates some of the key contradictions inhabiting modernized France and shows how they express themselves in spatial terms. The two places are polar opposites in a number of ways. On the one hand, Roissy-CDG: one of the most important infrastructural legacies of Gaullist spatial planning. Emblematic of the Gaullist conception of modernization as a matter of flow, circulation, accelerating movement and productive dynamism, it is also representative of the sort of unanchored *non-lieux* identified by Marc Augé as both symptomatic of the spatial forms of advanced capitalism and fundamental to the channelling of its energies.

On the other hand, the Maison du DSQ and the cluster of people around it: a manifestation of how the French state was attempting to address the socio-economic problems of life in the *banlieue*, and more generally, how the *banlieue* had emerged as a key social and political problem in France by the early 1990s. Fundamental to the DSQ and subsequent policy measures though, as Sylvie Tissot (2007) has shown, was the discursive construction and designation by the state of *quartiers, zones* and other precisely defined locations, whose identity was predicated on being demarcated and differentiated (discursively, statistically and in policy terms) from those around them.

At stake in the co-presence of Roissy-CDG and the Maison du DSQ is more than a contrast between movement and stasis, freedom and circumscription. It is about the spatial logics at work on the French territory, the kinds of space they produce, and the consequences of those logics for the people caught up in them. It is about the tensions and contradictions inherent within the spatial and territorial imaginary of the French state, which themselves reflect and respond to the pressures on the territory with which the state must contend. The fact that these two types of place co-exist and, through cultural forms like *Hexagone*, are *seen* to coexist within the French territory is arguably central to why space became a social, political and cultural preoccupation in France during the 1980s and 90s. Their coexistence sets out the parameters of a social and economic crisis that was also (emerged most visibly as) a crisis of space. It signals too that the crisis of the *banlieues*, which entangled the social and the spatial and made clear how one was predicated on the other, was in turn a manifestation of the broader state of crisis (*la crise*) that had been precipitated by the economic crises of the mid-1970s, and their on-going repercussions.

The extent to which France's social crisis was simultaneously a spatial crisis is captured in the opening encounters of *La Misère du monde* [The Weight of the World], the epic collective investigation directed by Pierre Bourdieu into the 'social misery' that seemed to be endemic in France by the early 1990s, published a year before the release of *Hexagone*. In 'La Rue des jonquilles' [Daffodil Street], Bourdieu presents interviews with two working-class men, one French and one originally from Algeria. Both live in a housing development in post-industrial Lorraine:

> D'abord désigné par des initiales bureaucratiques, ZUP (Zone à urbaniser en priorité), puis rebaptisé 'Val Saint Martin', un de ces euphémismes par lesquels les responsables des 'opérations' de 'Développement social des quartiers' (DSQ) entendent 'changer l'image' des quartiers à rénover. (Bourdieu 1998: 19)

> [Initially designated by the bureaucratic initials ZUP, urbanization priority zone, then renamed 'Val Saint Martin', one of those euphemisms through which those in charge of the DSQ 'operations' hope to 'change the image' of neighbourhoods in need of renovation.]

Bourdieu's description is a lapidary telling of perhaps the most visible and consequential form of spatial production in post-war France. The seemingly anodyne shift from one acronym to another, from ZUP to DSQ, masks the drama of France's attempt to solve its post-war housing crisis in the 1950s and 60s by building large housing estates cheaply in often peripheral development zones, and how that attempt in turn provoked a series of problems — socio-economic, psychological, political — that would require further interventions from the state, of which the DSQ would be one. Moreover, those peripheral and often circumscribed locations, the *zones* and *quartiers* of the *banlieues*, would increasingly play a central and structuring role in the country's spatial, political and cultural imaginary.

What Bourdieu's scene-setting also helps to do is capture the different ways in which spaces are named by state administration, and how administrative discourse draws on the naming power of language, backed by the legal force of the state, to produce certain sorts and perceptions of space and exert the state's authority within them. As we will see later in more detail, ZUPs were legislated into existence in 1958, and enabled the state to acquire the land it needed for rapid urban development, including through expropriation where necessary. The Commission nationale pour le développement social des quartiers [National commission for neighbourhood social improvement] (CNDSQ), meanwhile, had been set up by the Mitterrand government in 1981 following disturbances that summer which had broken out on the housing estate of Les Minguettes on the outskirts of Lyon, before spreading to *grands ensembles* around other French cities such as Les 4,000 at La Courneuve. Both were included in a pilot DSQ programme established by the commission, which was led by Hubert Dubedout, the Socialist mayor of Grenoble. Following the publication in 1983 of Dubedout's report on the pilot, *Ensemble, refaire la ville* [Together, let's remake the city], the programme was expanded rapidly to include 148 *quartiers*, amongst which was Les Grandes-Bornes in Goussainville, where Chibane would film *Hexagone*.[3]

The urban unrest of 1981, fuelled by tensions between the police and local youths, many of whom were of North African heritage, had its roots in a converging set of circumstances. Chief amongst them were the rapid development of the *grands ensembles* as a response to France's post-war housing crisis; the demographic changes taking shape over the same period, as immigrant populations, particularly from North Africa, supplied the labour for French modernization; the rapid churn of populations in the *grands ensembles*, which saw higher-earning residents with aspirations to home ownership move out and replaced by those with lower and more unstable incomes; and the consequent concentration in the housing estates of poorer, less qualified populations who, because they were typically employed in low-skilled manual labour, were particularly exposed to the unemployment that was triggered by the economic restructuring of the 1970s and 80s, and was characterized by high levels of youth unemployment especially.

The unrest was one of the first domestic challenges for François Mitterrand's new Socialist government, though it also provided an opportunity to mark a break with its Gaullist and post-Gaullist predecessors. Dubedout did so neatly at the start of his report with a critique of the Giscard government's *Habitat et vie sociale* [Housing and social life] (HVS) programme, which had been launched in 1977 after several years in gestation. The HVS programme was an attempt to find a practical remedy to the growing political and social problems posed by the *grands ensembles*. Already in March 1973, Guichard had published a landmark *circulaire* proscribing the construction of *grands ensembles* in order to prevent 'the development of social segregation through housing' (*Journal officiel*, 3 April 1973: 3864). In some respects, Guichard's *circulaire* was legislation catching up with shifts in practice on the ground, such as the orientation towards new towns in the *Schéma directeur*. Nevertheless, it was a striking political acknowledgement of the social problems caused by ZUPs as a strategy of housing and spatial development. It also marked a point where the state began to articulate the problems of modernization through figures of spatial

---

3   On the creation of the CNDSQ, see Dikeç (2007: 48–56), Tellier 2013 and Tissot (2007: 51–63), who situates it in the context of the evolving identification, construction and administration of the *banlieue* as a social, spatial and policy problem during the 1980s.

discontinuity: the ZUPs had produced a rupture within the republican polity which saw some of its citizens segregated from the rest.

In the face of a rapidly decaying stock of *grands ensembles*, the consequence of cheap and quick construction in the previous decades, the focus of HVS was on improving quality of life through a programme of building renovation. However, argued Dubedout, the programme had been too preoccupied with physical renovation and not enough with the social and economic challenges faced by the residents (Dubedout 1983: 9–10).[4] The DSQ programme, in contrast, would involve a range of measures to tackle the problems of segregation that derived from spatial marginalization: improved transport links, community consultation and local democracy, employment opportunities through support for education and training, cultural initiatives (1983: 16–21). In effect, it was the culmination of a decade-long attempt to grapple with the social consequences of a spatial strategy, as well as a recognition that France found itself before a spatial problem that was a social problem, and vice versa.

Through their elliptical versions of this story, Chibane and Bourdieu draw out the coexistence of two spatial tendencies in post-war France and two ways in which space is apprehended by the state: one as system, network, movement and flow; the other in terms of boundaries, frontiers, delimitations and circumscriptions. The coexistence of the two signals that they are not mutually exclusive, but different manifestations of the same fundamental logic at work on French territory. That logic is governed by the imperatives of spatial production and territorial regulation, which take different forms at different moments, depending on specific economic, social and political circumstances (most obviously, periods of economic expansion versus periods of contraction and crisis), but manifest the same fundamental impetus of the state in terms of a will to spatial striation, organization and territorialization.

The insistent naming, definition and designation of space by the state, reflected in a corresponding accumulation of acronyms — from ZUP to DSQ via ZAD (*zone d'aménagement différé*) and ZAC (*zone d'aménagement concerté*) — are symptomatic of a persistent spatial reflex in France, where aspects of the social and the societal are repeatedly articulated by means of an array of spatial figures of speech: zones and hexagons, but also insertion and integration, segregation and fracturing. We can see such figures of speech as so many 'figures of space', expressions of how readily administrative, political, academic and cultural discourse in France turns to rhetorical figures and tropes deriving from the semantic fields of space; and how the French political, social and administrative imaginary is also a spatial imaginary, one whose reflex seems persistently and repeatedly to think things through in spatial terms.

At stake so far have been the more open forms taken by the French state's spatial reflex during the expansive phase of the *Trente glorieuses*, forms predicated on a belief

---

4   On the HVS programme and its origins, see Tellier (2010, 2015), whose accounts nuance Dubedout's politically motivated critique. As Tellier notes (2015: 13–14), one of the key figures behind the development of the programme was André Trintignac, author of *Aménager l'hexagone*, now confronted with some of the emerging problems of urban decay and social exclusion that post-war *aménagement* had begun to produce.

in *la prospective* and territorial modernization as accelerators of civilizational advance. While the locations and places to which they gave rise, places like Roissy-CDG and Cergy-Pontoise, were nevertheless influencing life on the ground, it was more closed forms of spatial reflex that gained purchase and visibility during the 1980s and 1990s. The proliferating designation of *quartiers* and other demarcated spaces was an indication of how the French crisis of recession and economic restructuring was manifesting itself in spatial terms, and how the pressures on French space and territory were becoming increasingly complex, varied and disruptive for the state to manage.

It was a sign of that spatial anxiety that by the mid-1990s, with the right-wing government of Édouard Balladur in power, DSQs would be displaced by *zones urbaines sensibles* [sensitive urban zones] (ZUS). Increasingly, as Mustafa Dikeç observes (2007: 94), the *banlieue* would be framed less as a social problem than as a problem of policing and security, and consequently, a threat to the very integrity of the French republic. It was no less telling that when Charles Pasqua introduced the reforms in February 1995 in his capacity as minister for *aménagement du territoire*, he also had the distinction of being minister of the Interior and, as such, in charge of national policing. Never before had the two portfolios most directly concerned with the management and regulation of national territory been held by a single individual. There was no clearer indication that spatial planning's disciplinary power had been acknowledged than its co-location in a minister also in command, to borrow from Louis Althusser (1970), of the repressive apparatus of the state.

The remainder of Chapter 5 sets out to investigate the coexisting spatial reflexes in play from the 1980s, the changing emphases between them as space (and those in it) becomes increasingly troublesome, and what is at stake in an administrative vocabulary of circumscription and delineation, of *quartiers* and *zones*. The latter term in particular is one of the most persistent and intriguing of French figures of space, not least because of its long history, fluid meanings and shifting uses between the administrative, the bureaucratic and the military, but also the poetic. Plotting its meanings, uses and contexts of use — most notably its long associations with militarized space — helps illuminate continuities and breaks between the state's differing spatial reflexes and practices as it seeks to maintain its authority over the national territory.

At the same time, I explore further the trend with which I began by way of introduction; namely, how the state's spatial anxieties find an echo in the noticeable preoccupation with space and place in French culture during the period, one which reverberates through to the present day. The body of films depicting life in France's marginalized suburbs is an obvious example (Tarr 2005). But across the field of cultural production, from writers like Jean Rolin to photographic projects like the DATAR's *mission photographique* or *France(s) territoire liquide*, the look and feel of contemporary French space emerges as a persistent theme and topos. Such work helps us grasp the multiple pressures at work on French territory, pressures which threaten to challenge, undo or resist the work of spatial regulation, and how they are bound up with the state's territorializing urge to delineate, define and police. Some of these pressures build from below: the pressures of delinquency, the opening up of lines of flight, the potentiality of the *terrain vague*, the traversal movement, the idea of liquid territory. Some are from beyond or outside, most notably the insatiable appetites of capital and its unstoppable, transformative power. Space is both locus and product of crisis, but it is also a place where life can be reimagined and reconfigured.

In the Zone: Space and/as Crisis

Around the time that the first volumes of *Les Lieux de mémoire* were coming out, another monumental historical study was reaching its conclusion. Appropriately enough, given Nora's preoccupation with how memory might seek refuge in spatial forms, its focus was on France's urban history. Edited by Marcel Roncayolo, *La Ville aujourd'hui* [The City Today] was published in 1985 as the fifth and final volume of Seuil's *Histoire de la France urbaine* [History of Urban France]. Where Nora took a sense of crisis as a given, Roncayolo struck a lightly sceptical tone as he opened his introduction to the volume. Talk of crisis was everywhere, he noted, and he was struck by how quickly it had 'devoured' memories of growth (Roncayolo 2001: 7). He observed instead, as one might expect of a historian aligned with Fernand Braudel and the Annales School, that economic fluctuations obscured longer term, more profound and ultimately more significant transformations (2001: 7).[5]

Nevertheless, the volume acknowledged the ambient mood of crisis in its subtitle ('urban change, decentralization and the crisis of the city dweller'). Moreover, Roncayolo's account of contemporary urban development suggested that the sense of historical dislocation identified by Nora had some striking spatial parallels. In his introduction, he drew out some of the spatial paradoxes that had arisen from post-war modernization, and were in turn contributing to how *la crise* was being lived in spatial and urban terms. On the one hand there were the 'new logics' of circulation and accessibility propelled by transportation, and the car especially (2001: 8), precisely the sort of logics embedded within the planning schemes of the DATAR and the District de Paris. On the other, the rapid expansion of urban space was characterized by discontinuity and fragmentation, which Roncayolo located in the use of 'le *zoning*' as an entrenched habit of spatial production (2001: 8–9). Spaces were designated, labelled and developed for specific functions (housing, industry, commerce) without giving proper attention to how they related to their surroundings.

For Roncayolo, one of the effects of urban expansion and the fragmented forms it took was to unsettle the frontiers between different sorts of space. His analysis confirmed Lefebvre's contention in *La Production de l'espace* that the rationalist organization of space ultimately leads to its opposite, the 'absurdity' of a fragmented reality (Lefebvre 1974: 366). People were 'multiterritorial', passing constantly from one sort of space to another, or living in hybrid spaces of rural and urban with no obvious distinction between the two: 'voici ce monde sans frontière fixe, ou vraisemblable' [here is a world without stable or apparent frontiers] (Roncayolo 2001: 9).

---

5   On Roncayolo's intellectual and institutional trajectory, see Paquot 2019.

Roncayolo might have been evoking the peculiar spatial hybridity captured at the start of *Hexagone* a decade later. Yet in many respects, his perspective on space — a sense both of spatial discontinuity and of uncertainty as to where certain types of space begin and end — was the perspective of those on the move and able to move, circulating within the territory and navigating its mosaic of zones. It was the perspective of the modernized citizen portrayed by Annie Ernaux in *Journal du dehors*. For it was also the case, simultaneously, that in certain parts of the territory, and for some people, some quite precisely defined and striking frontiers were emerging, many of them constituted by the state itself.

Two moments in 1983 crystallized the tensions being exerted on French space. Taken together, they formed a double commentary on the state of space in modern France, and the legacies and consequences of modernization. Both too were framed as 'missions', a common enough administrative term in France, but suggestive nevertheless of the state's sense of disquiet about what was happening on the ground, and its urgent need for illumination and resolution. That April, the Comité interministériel permanent pour les problèmes d'action régionale et d'aménagement du territoire [Interministerial council for the problems of regional action and spatial planning] (CIAT), which was attached to the prime minister's office and reviewed the work of the DATAR, approved the *mission photographique* marking its twenty years of spatial planning activity (Bertho 2013: 11).

The aims of the *mission*, as we saw in Chapter 4, were less celebratory than interrogative. Just as the creation of the DATAR expressed the confidence inherent in the prospective attitude, so too the photography project's terms of reference articulated a more general sense of doubt and uncertainty about what had happened to French space in the two decades since the DATAR had been at work. For Jacques Sallois, head of the DATAR at the time, writing in the first of the project's two photo-books, the *mission photographique* was concerned with 'la recherche d'une révélation des mouvements à l'œuvre dans notre société' [researching and revealing the movements at work in our society] (Sallois 1985: 13). Writing a few years later in the volume that marked the end of the project, Hers and Latarjet were more categorical about the nature of those trends. Like Roncayolo, what they observed was an odd mix of fragmentation and hybridity:

> Aux voisinages cohérents, si propices aux vues d'ensemble, succède un territoire de fragments et de vestiges. Champs clos, champs ouverts; habitats groupés ou dispersés; villes, bourgs et villages, centres et banlieues; milieux naturels ou transformés: les catégories anciennes de la géographie ne rendent plus compte de réalités hybrides qui n'ont même pas de nom. (Hers & Latarjet 1989: 15)

> [Places whose coherence is clear to see have been replaced by a territory of fragments and remnants. Open and closed fields; grouped or dispersed housing; towns, villages and hamlets, centres and suburbs; natural and manmade environments: the old categories of geography no longer apply to hybrid realities that don't even have a name.]

Many of the images portrayed the material forms manifesting the 'new logics' of modernization described by Roncayolo, but also the discontinuous and unfinished nature of the territory shaped by those logics. The evidence was there in Depardon's photos of the logistics sheds and drainage works accompanying the construction of the A6 motorway through Burgundy, in Holger Trülzsch's images of the urban infrastructure of Marseille and the vast *grands ensembles* of its *quartiers nord*, or in Lewis Baltz's shots of building sites and *terrains vagues* around the new petrochemical complexes of Fos-sur-Mer.

In January 1983, meanwhile, Hubert Dubedout had published *Ensemble, refaire la ville*, reporting on the work of the Commission nationale du DSQ, set up by Pierre Mauroy as prime minister in 1981 in response to the unrest in Les Minguettes and other *grands ensembles*. Dubedout's mission, set out in a letter from Mauroy in November 1981 (Dubedout 1983: 103–04), carried uncanny echoes of the arrangements which had initiated Gaullist *aménagement* two decades earlier: a delegate reporting directly to the prime minister and charged, as de Gaulle had put it at the time, of 'sorting out' the problem of the suburbs. The task of Dubedout's commission, in Mauroy's words, was to 'deal with the problem of social housing neighbourhoods' (1983: 103).

We saw earlier that Dubedout's report oriented the government towards a 'social' response to the problems made manifest by the riots. It recognized that social problems and policies had a spatial dimension, and could be thought through in spatial terms. One of the immediate steps was to undertake 'une mission opérationnelle dans seize zones considérées dans un état critique justifiant une intervention exceptionelle de l'État et un effort de solidarité nationale' [an operational mission in sixteen zones whose condition was serious enough to warrant special intervention by the State and an effort of national solidarity] (1983: 6). The 'zones' identified included Les Minguettes, as well as estates in Marseille's *quartiers nord* and Les 4,000 at La Courneuve (1983: 111). Within those zones, the focal point for action would be the 'développement social des quartiers'.

On the one hand, then, there was growing puzzlement and unease over the illegibility of French space. Meanwhile on the other came the discovery, through the spatial disturbance of civil unrest, of nodal points where the forces of crisis were concentrated. In a context of broader spatial anxiety, the emergence of such nodal points was a further challenge to the state's command over its territory. Its response, the one organized by Dubedout, was predicated on a logic of circumscription and discursive delineation as a means of legibility and a prelude to 'intervention'. As Sylvie Tissot shows, Dubedout's commission inaugurated a new domain of public policy which constructed the *quartier* as a space for administrative intervention through the work of an array of specialists. In doing so, it asserted the idea that 'la question sociale se traduit désormais spatialement' [social questions were henceforth expressed spatially] (2007: 97), an idea that gained substantial administrative, political, cultural and academic traction during the 1980s and 90s, and whose axiomatic formulation would be in terms of the 'problem' of the *banlieues*.

In Mustafa Dikeç's neat formulation, the work of the CNDSQ was an illustration of how urban policy is a 'place-making practice' (2007: 21). Just as the planners of the 1960s mobilized a representational apparatus of maps, texts, images and scale models to envision and produce France's modernized landscapes, so too modernization's legacies of socio-spatial crisis became visible through different practices of representation and types of expertise (commission reports, policy documents, population censuses, demographic profiling). But where the planners increasingly imagined space as a dynamic terrain of flow, networks, movement and circulation (articulated most clearly in the pivot from the PADOG to the *Schéma directeur*, as we saw in Chapter 2), the time now was of spatial demarcation and delimitation, the definition of problem areas, neighbourhoods and districts. The ground was prepared for interventions in zones of special operations as the state sought the best way to 'manage' (as Dubedout has it) its proliferating spatial, social and territorial challenges.

At one level, there was nothing surprising in the designation of sixteen zones being the administrative starting-point for the DSQ programme, nor in the appearance of the term in Dubedout's report. As Roncayolo observed, and the proliferation of acronyms during the period confirmed (ZUP, ZUS, ZAD, ZAC), the zone was a commonplace of spatial planning discourse and practice, and the term most frequently deployed to identify locations of territorial interest for the state. But like all commonplaces, it is a term worth dwelling on, because beneath its ubiquity lies a complex knot of uses and a multidimensional role in the designation of French space.

In particular, predating its emergence as an administrative category of spatial management and organization was a longer history of military usage, which the *Trésor de la Langue Française* and *Le Petit Robert* both date to the early nineteenth century. By the start of the twentieth century, according to the *Trésor, zone* had a settled meaning as 'une partie du territoire où s'exerce l'action de forces militaires' [part of the territory where military activity is exercised].[6] It is in the context of its military usage that the term becomes even more interesting as a figure of space. At the turn of the twentieth century, it acquired an additional dimension of meaning which arose precisely out of its military context, and saw it used to refer simultaneously to one form of occupation of space *and its very opposite.*

In the first instance, the term designated the *zone non aedificandi*, a cleared space some 250 metres wide beyond the military fortifications built around Paris during the 1840s. As James Cannon notes (2015: 2), the zone was governed by regulations which prevented constructions, plantations or other obstacles that would obscure a view of the approaching enemy. Nevertheless, while the land on which the fortifications were built was expropriated by the state, the zone in front of it remained in private hands, and its legal status was ambiguous (2015: 2–3). Over time, it became the location for informal allotments, squats and improvised housing, a marginal space where those on the social margins could gather. As such, *la zone* took shape in the cultural imaginary as an uncertain and unsettling place. Indeed, its unregulated nature was all the more noticeable for lying just beyond the clearest expression of territorialization by the state, like an unruly other or shadow self.[7]

6   *Trésor de la Langue Française informatisé*, ATILF-CNRS/Université de Lorraine <http://atilf.atilf.fr/tlf.htm> [accessed 19 May 2021].
7   On the cultural history of *la zone*, see Cannon 2015 and Beauchez & Zeneidi 2020.

This polarized but symbiotic tension between the regulated and the unregulated would inhabit the term and its derivations for the remainder of the century. According to *Le Petit Robert*, the verb *zoner*, which it dates to 1971, can refer to the administrative practice of zoning (*le zoning*), in the sense of organizing 'la répartition (d'un territoire) en zones et fixant, pour chacune d'elles, le genre et les conditions de l'utilisation du sol' [the division of a territory into zones that defines, for each of them, the type and conditions of land use]; but it can also refer to a way of life on the margins: 'mener une existence marginale, vivre en zone' [to lead a marginal existence]. The zone could be the catalyst for spatial production, an area of demarcation, regulation and spatial striation where the law lay down how space was to be used and by whom. It could also be a place beyond the laws of the state, what France's political right in the 1990s took to calling a 'zone de non-droit' [a lawless zone]. It was the realm of the *zonard*, the gang and the delinquent, or the 'badland' of the Republic, to use Dikeç's evocative phrase. When the language of zones was mobilized in such contexts, it inevitably came freighted with the legacy of its military uses; and that mattered when some of those uses had roots in the dying years of France's imperial activity. At the same time, the zone as badland or delinquent space would remain a nagging source of insecurity for the state, one made manifest in its constant recourse to the discourse and practice of zoning as a sign that its purchase on the territory was never quite complete.

The zone's circulation as term and concept between administrative and military discourse signals the proximity of the two fields of activity, a proximity we have seen emerge at various points. It is not quite that the administration of space and territory is in some sense always already militarized, but that the two fields are closely aligned in their habits of perception, thought and action — in their attitudes, we might say. They share the same sort of assumed agency and volition in relation to space as territory and domain of action of the state, something at once constituted by state power and constitutive of it. Their alignment lies in the French state's own strategic grasp of the relationship between defence and development of the territory, the first sign of which came in 1804, when Napoleon converted the École polytechnique, created by the Revolutionary government in 1794, into a military academy (a status it retains to this day). Meanwhile the ENPC, founded in 1747, many of whose graduates (such as Bernard Hirsch) were in charge of post-war spatial planning initiatives, had itself been made into an applied branch of the École polytechnique after the new academy had been established (Thœnig 1987, Desportes & Picon 1997).

If zoning was at once a method of territorial control and a sign of territorial anxiety, then it was no surprise to see the practice at work in both the military and administrative domains during the 1950s and 60s. The period saw significant innovations in relation to France's *politique foncière* [land ownership policy], as *aménagement* required the development of different zoning mechanisms through which land could be brought under the purview of the state and extracted from other hands. In August 1957, legislation was introduced which prepared the ground for the creation of *zones à urbaniser par priorité* [priority zones for urbanization]. ZUPs were areas earmarked for the construction of *grands ensembles*, the large-scale housing developments identified as the solution to France's increasingly acute housing problem. In many ways, the *loi-cadre* of 7 August 1957 was an emergency measure to respond to a state of crisis: its first article spelt out the target of 300,000 new housing units per year set by the third Plan (*Journal officiel*, 10 August 1957: 7906). The French state had to make sure it could lay hands quickly on the land it required, but it also needed the means to secure the land it might require in the future.

Both of those things were enabled by two further pieces of legislation a year later. In October 1958, the government published an *ordonnance* introducing new laws on expropriation by the state 'for reasons of public utility' (*Journal officiel*, 23 October 1958: 9694). On 31 December, it issued a decree authorizing the designation of ZUPs (by means of expropriation if need be) and through them, the construction of *grands ensembles* (*Journal officiel*, 4 January 1959: 269). In July 1962, signalling the growing momentum of *aménagement* as planned development (and fittingly enough, in the same month that Algeria acceded to independence), another law was introduced to enable the designation of zones for deferred development, or ZADs, giving the government a right of pre-emption (*droit de préemption*) of up to eight years (though far longer in reality) on land or property in the zone.

Our old friend André Trintignac was in no doubt about the significance of the planning reforms initiated by the *loi-cadre* of 1957 and the zoning mechanisms they introduced. They transformed planning from 'un instrument de sauvegarde' [a safeguarding instrument] into 'un instrument d'action' (Trintignac 1964: 54) by giving the French state the legislative and discursive tools it needed to pursue its policies of spatial development. In fact, the encoding of zones in law offered a compelling illustration of how the state can do and make things with words. It showed how the state can exploit its legislative and discursive power to name, control and produce space, and thereby create the conditions for a new reality. In being named a zone, space took on a special status, one neatly captured in the definition provided by the *Trésor de la langue française*: 'territoire qui répond à certaines normes ou qui est soumis à un règlement particulier, notamment en matière d'aménagement et d'urbanisme' [territory which meets certain norms or is subject to specific regulations, particularly in relation to urban and spatial planning].

Or, to borrow another of Trintignac's figures of speech, the set of land ownership laws introduced in the late 1950s and early 1960s were part and parcel of what he called the state's 'arsenal' of measures through which it could maintain control of land prices and ensure it had call on the land it required for spatial development (1964: 70). The ability to zone for deferred development in particular provided a way of strengthening the state against the inflationary threat of speculation and overcoming its historic weakness against private capital in this regard. In enhancing the state's ability to act in support of its strategic interests, the planning reforms demonstrated the alignment between spatial planning and national security, one further consolidated, as we saw in Chapter 2, by de Gaulle's *ordonnance* of January 1959, which made defence of the realm a matter for all areas of government activity.

At one level, of course, Trintignac's metaphor of the arsenal is simply that: an evocative way of characterizing the range of legislative measures the state had given itself. Yet if its military resonance catches the eye and (like all metaphors, as Jacques Derrida reminded us long ago) does more work of meaning than it intends, it is because the term reorients us towards the other context in which the state thought in terms of zones and used the power of naming at its disposal to transform space into a territory 'subject to specific regulations'. Laws, decrees, orders and other texts are precisely the instruments through which the state deploys its power, and with which it can mobilize and organize the other sorts of (more obvious) power at its disposal.

Around the time that the laws enabling ZUPs were being drawn up, the French military began to adapt its strategy in Algeria, where the challenge of suppressing the nationalist uprising was becoming increasingly fraught. In *A Savage War of Peace*, Alistair Horne notes that in 1956, General André Beaufre (who in later years would become a leading proponent of prospective thinking in relation to military strategy) was appointed to command the region east of Constantine. In a fresh attempt to contain the rebels, he divided his sector into three types of zone: *zones interdites* (forbidden zones, from where populations were resettled into *villages de regroupement*), *zones d'opérations* (operations zones, where the fighters of the Algerian Front de libération nationale were pursued by elite mobile troops), and *zones de pacification* (pacification zones, more populous areas where the focus was on economic development, education and propaganda) (Horne 1977: 166; see also Griffin 2010).

The coincidences of terminology between these two parallel developments are revealing of some notable continuities in the state's understanding and practice of space (or more accurately, on the part of the corporate bodies charged with doing the state's thinking and acting in relation to space and territory). At stake is not just the declamatory act of designating and naming spaces, and thereby creating new conditions within them (administrative, military and legal, and therefore also moral, ethical and political), but doing so through the introduction of a boundary differentiating the space of the zone from the space outside and beyond it. Zones demand borders and frontiers, divisions between inside and outside, a boundary beyond which the 'specific regulations' apply.

Moreover, as Trintignac intuits, and General Beaufre demonstrated, the creation of zones, whether administrative or military, is also a *defensive* strategy on the part of the state, a sign that it has perceived a threat to its security and stability. It is a gesture of reterritorialization against a disruptive and deterritorializing impulse. From that point of view, it was telling that the figure resurfaced in administrative and political discourse during the 1980s and 90s, beginning with Dubedout's report, as the *banlieues* became the locus of France's spatial crisis. The back cover of *Ensemble, refaire la ville* was prescient in assessing the challenge that lay ahead in relation to those on the spatial and social margins, and reached for another figure of space as it did so: 'réussir leur intégration sociale est sans doute "le défi" qui dominera les quinze prochaines années' [securing their social integration is without doubt the challenge that will dominate the next fifteen years]. Reintegration into a social and spatial whole was the solution to the segregation that had arisen from the spatial practices of modernization. Yet paradoxically, the first move in that process of reintegration seemed to involve the opposite, an administrative and discursive reassertion of spatial and social *division* through the designation of *zones* and *quartiers*.

Indeed, as the challenge ran on into the following decade, the political and administrative momentum lay with a logic of spatial division rather than reintegration. A key turning point came in March 1993 with the right's return to power under prime minister Édouard Balladur, in a second *cohabitation* with François Mitterrand. With it came the pivot towards framing the *banlieue* as a matter of security rather than social policy, and as such, a source of danger for the state and the republic. Doing so involved an eye-catching rhetorical manoeuvre, and the return of the administrative zone's unruly other. Politicians on the right began to evoke the presence of *zones de non-droit* in the *banlieue*, lawless places beyond the purview of the state where its authority had to be re-established.

The move was enabled by recent outbreaks of unrest, most notably the riots on the housing estates of Vaulx-en-Velin near Lyon in October 1990 (the area had joined the DSQ programme a few years earlier). The disturbances had been triggered by an incident during a police control in which a motorcyclist had been killed, an example of the proliferating number of *bavures policières* [police blunders] that signalled a more generalized mood of conflict between the police and the youths of the estates.[8] As both Patrick Champagne and Sylvie Tissot make clear, a sense of crisis was reinforced by an noticeable upsurge in national media coverage which presented the riots, and the places where they took place, as symptoms of an unresolved societal malaise (Champagne 1998; Tissot 2007: 19–29).

The media's response was also a sign of the growing momentum around the theme of *insécurité*, first mapped by sociologist Sebastian Roché (1993), that would dominate French political discourse over the following decade and beyond. There was debate over the extent to which a *sentiment d'insécurité* was grounded in the empirical realities of increased crime and violence, or was more a 'fantasmatic perception' (Alidières 2008: 211; see also Crenner 1996 and Bonelli 2010). (Roché for one was adamant that the former was the case.) Nonetheless, and perhaps more significantly, feelings of insecurity as an affective reality were reflected and further amplified by media debate and political discourse, particularly on the right, which lost no time in spotting that they could be exploited for political gain. A mood of insecurity, reinforced by the tactical designation of lawless zones of resistance to the state, required and justified expressions of force in the name of national security.

Thus, on 28 January 1993, the newspaper *Le Monde* reported a suggestion from right-wing politician Charles Pasqua, speaking as a former Interior minister, and no doubt burnishing his credentials as a hardliner ahead of an anticipated victory for the right in the forthcoming legislative elections, that recent police reforms risked 'l'édification de zones de non-droit où la sûreté personnelle n'est plus formellement assurée' [the creation of lawless zones where personal security

---

8   On *bavures policières* and their role in triggering urban unrest in France, see Minces & Tricaud 1989 and Jobard 2002.

can no longer be guaranteed]. The answer lay in mobilizing a 'national guard' of military conscripts 'pour assurer la protection des citoyens en banlieue' [to ensure the protection of citizens in the suburbs]. Following the right's victory two months later, during a statement to the National Assembly on his government's priorities in April 1993, Balladur observed that 'certains quartiers sont devenus des zones de non-droit' [certain neighbourhoods have become lawless zones]. Like Dubedout, he went on to evoke the solution through the spatial figure of incorporation: 'il faut réintégrer les banlieues déshéritées dans la communauté nationale afin que chacun puisse donner un sens à sa vie et croire en l'avenir' [we must reintegrate abandoned suburbs into the national community so that everyone can give meaning to their lives and believe in the future] (*Journal officiel*, 9 April 1993: 43). Notwithstanding Balladur's emphasis on an inter-ministerial approach to the urban problem, the tenor of subsequent discussions confirmed the shift in emphasis towards the *banlieue* as primarily a problem of security.

Towards the end of that month, Charles Pasqua addressed the National Assembly as a government minister during a debate on 'villes et banlieues' that followed Balladur's 'déclaration de politique générale' [outline of government policy]. Now holding the two key territorial portfolios of the Interior and *Aménagement du territoire*, Pasqua made clear that security and policing would be a key focus of his activity, giving notice of a range of measures designed to 'rétablir la sécurité des personnes et des biens' [re-establish the security of people and goods]: 'contrôles d'identité à caractère préventif' [identity spot checks], 'maîtriser les flux migatoires' [immigration controls], 'mieux ancrer la police dans la ville, afin de lutter contre le développement de la petite et moyenne délinquance' [better police presence in urban areas to fight the growth of delinquency] (*Journal officiel*, 29 April 1993: 242–43). While there was no sign of his earlier idea of a national guard for the *banlieue*, he nevertheless cast the government's objectives in martial terms:

> La bataille de la ville ne sera, en effet, gagnée que si nous mobilisons tous les acteurs au service de cette volonté. Elle ne sera une réussite que si nous nous donnons les moyens d'affirmer dans ces quartiers la présence et la permanence de nos institutions. (*Journal officiel*, 29 April 1993: 242)

> [The battle for the city will only be won if we mobilize all participants in the service of this aim. It will only be a success if we give ourselves the means to affirm in these neighbourhoods the presence and permanence of our institutions.]

At stake was reasserting the presence of the state and its institutions across the whole of the territory and re-establishing command in the *zones de non-droit*, not least by better controlling the flux and flow of people.

The government's approach reflected some long-standing spatial reflexes. It was oriented around its own set of 'priority zones', set out in Pasqua's law on territorial planning and organization in February 1995. Characterized by different forms of geographical, economic or social 'handicap', they included urban areas, now designated 'zones urbaines sensibles' (ZUS) or 'zones de redynamisation urbaine' (where tax incentives would be used to promote economic regeneration), as well as rural and other areas across the territory considered in need of development (*Journal officiel*, 5 February 1995: 1981). It was almost as if Pasqua had been reading his Deleuze and Guattari. Faced with indiscipline, riot or other threats to its authority, they suggest, 'le réplique de l'État, c'est de strier l'espace, contre tout ce qui risque de le déborder' [the State's response is to striate space against everything that threatens to overwhelm it] (Deleuze & Guattari 1980: 480). The administrative, legislative and discursive work of creating territorial categories, tools of spatial intervention, fiscal mechanisms and tax regimes is part of that process of spatial striation.

Just as the policy reforms of the late 1950s enabled the state to lay claim to territory through planning and expropriation, so too the law of 1995 looked for ways to gain purchase on space and consolidate territorial integrity. Balladur acknowledged as much in his opening remarks to the National Assembly at the start of the debate on the Pasqua law in July 1994: 'l'objectif qui est le nôtre est à la fois simple et ambitieux: retrouver davantage de cohésion nationale' [our objective is both simple and ambitious: to re-establish more national cohesion] (*Journal officiel*, 8 July 1994: 4216). It was axiomatic that the route to social (and therefore national) cohesion lay through spatial development: 'aménager le territoire, c'est faire de la géographie un élément positif dans la définition des politiques économiques et sociales' [territorial development means giving geography a positive role in the development of economic and social policy]. Yet as Deleuze and Guattari make clear, the effort of spatial striation bears witness to the continued pressures at work on the state, pressures which derived from the effects and consequences of French modernization.

The Pasqua law was a reterritorializing response to the deterritorializing threat perceived to reside in the *zones de non-droit* of the *banlieue*, zones whose challenge lay in the unruly, disruptive and (to use Pasqua's term) delinquent energies of their inhabitants. Meanwhile, the co-location of territorial security and territorial development in the single ministerial figure of Pasqua, along with his emphasis on policing and security ('mieux ancrer la police dans la ville'), asserted the disciplinary tendency always lurking within spatial production, regulation and other forms of state action on its territory. After all, as Foucault and Virilio had both argued in the 1970s, policing is a matter of societal organization, government and regulation of which the police as a corporate body is simply the most visible and specialized component (Virilio 1977, Foucault 2004).

From that point of view, we can see how Chibane's *Hexagone* is poised on the cusp of the state's switch of emphasis in its relationship to the *quartiers*. The presence in the film of the Maison du DSQ is a reminder of attempts during the previous decade to construct and resolve the urban problem as a social problem first and foremost — a problem of equality, education and inclusion. Much less obvious, as Tarr also notes (2005: 59), is the sense of the *quartier* as a place of crime and violence, a place where the state manifests itself as the police. When the police do appear on the estate, it is in the relatively low-key form of plain clothes officers in (failed) pursuit of Slimane's brother, one of Pasqua's 'petits délinquants'. A year later in Mathieu Kassovitz's *La Haine*, whose drama is bookended by real and fictional *bavures policières*, the police are present in force, in uniform and led by their commanding officers. As if to mirror the broader shifts in government discourse and policy, they make a show of arriving on the protagonists' estate, accompanied by the sound of helicopters overhead, to break up a rooftop barbeque and demonstrate their powers of spatial regulation in a *zone de non-droit*.

As a mode of response to the *zone de non-droit*, repression found its most acute form during the nationwide riots in the autumn of 2005. The riots began in Clichy-sous-Bois following the deaths of two teenage boys of Mauritanian and Tunisian heritage, who had hidden in an electrical substation after fleeing from a police control at the entrance to their housing estate. As the uprising spread across the country, the right-wing government of Dominique de Villepin declared a state of emergency across French territory, mobilizing legislation introduced in April 1955 during the Algerian War. The wording of the state of emergency, lifted from the law of 1955, is revealing. It allowed departmental prefects to 'instituer des zones de protection ou de sécurité dans lesquelles le séjour des personnes est réglementé' [establish regulated zones of protection or security] (*Journal officiel*, 9 November 2005: 11).

An annexe published with the state of emergency listed the zones where it applied. They included the whole of Paris and the surrounding *départements*, as well as Vénissieux and the other historically troublesome districts around Lyon. Responsibility for overseeing the implementation of the state of emergency lay in particular with Nicolas Sarkozy who, like his predecessor Pasqua, held the dual ministerial portfolio of the Interior and *Aménagement du territoire*. Equally keen to assert his credentials as a hardliner in matters of law and order, he had been quick to adopt Pasqua's favourite figure of space on taking up his post in 2002, suggesting in an interview with *Le Monde* that it was time to adopt a more offensive strategy against 'les délinquants et les mafias' [delinquents and gangs] and 'porter le fer dans les zones de non-droit' [get tough on lawless zones] (*Le Monde*, 30 May 2002).[9]

The government's move, in response to social unrest in areas with significant populations of African heritage, was an astonishing moment of neo-colonial territorial management. As Achille Mbembe made plain at the time, it was a re-enactment of the strategies of 'pacification' with which the French had attempted to subdue their colonial subjects (Mbembe 2005), strategies whose territorial forms were the sorts of zonal divisions implemented by André Beaufre in East Constantine during the Algerian War. In a blistering editorial for *Le Monde*, Philippe Bernard called the government's actions a 'colonial provocation' which could only antagonize those French citizens of North African origin for whom the memory of the Algerian War remained 'an open wound' (Bernard 2005).[10]

9   That Sarkozy could use the term *zone de non-droit* without further expansion was a sign of the right's success in making it a commonplace of political discourse by the early 2000s. Sebastian Roché observed that process under way in 1997 when, writing in *Le Monde*, he noted that 'plus que jamais, la question de l'insécurité urbaine est définie politiquement, autour de trois mots d'ordre: les "zones de non-droit", la délinquance, les incivilités' [more than ever, three key terms frame the discussion of urban insecurity in political discourse: 'lawless zones', delinquency and uncivilized behaviour] (Roché 1997). The quotation marks had disappeared by the time of *Le Monde*'s interview with Sarkozy five years later.

10   The provocation was all the more flagrant because it followed the controversy triggered by a law

Yet in other ways, the government's approach was entirely unsurprising. It was a reflection of the extent to which modernization and its aftermath drew on practices, reflexes and ways of seeing honed in France's colonies and brought back home after decolonization. Those reflexes emerge across the spectrum of administrative, political and military activity, as we have seen at various points, and never lie far beneath the surface, particularly under France's right-wing governments. Indeed, as Sylvie Thénault suggests, it is not unlikely that Villepin saw political advantage in mobilizing a law with such resonance in order to send a signal to voters feeling threatened by insecurity and scenes of civil disorder (Thénault 2007: 75). Certainly, the colonial modes of policing that broke cover in 2005 were lurking already in Pasqua's idea from 1993 of a 'national guard' to protect the law-abiding citizens of the *banlieue* from the denizens of the *zones de non-droit*.

Declaring a state of emergency across the metropolitan territory was also a logical end-point for the spatial dynamics in play since the end of the *Trente glorieuses*. To find it overseen by the minister in charge of territorial development captured something about the distance travelled over the three decades since the filming of Guichard at speed on the motorway. Gone was the confident sense of momentum that came with the prospective attitude, and was embodied in the image of Guichard in the fast lane. Instead, the various forms of crisis exerting pressure on the state, and its concomitant anxieties over territorial integrity, produced figural ways of talking which created a sense of spatial stasis, foregrounding space over time and highlighting states of spatial disjunction (zones, segregation and fractures, a need for spatial and therefore social cohesion). In policy terms, territorial anxiety manifested itself in expressions of security and containment as topoi of political discourse and strategies of territorial administration.

That anxiety also had a striking fetish object in the form of the *délinquant*. A decade apart, Pasqua and Sarkozy both fixed on delinquent behaviour as emblematic of the unruliness of the *zone de non-droit*. Yet what threat did delinquency pose to become such a feature of the political imagination? In his discussion of everyday life as praxis and resistance to the planned environments of modernization, Michel de Certeau proposes that narrative is a *delinquent* form. Where maps (the archetypal tool of the planner or military strategist) fix, differentiate and delimit, narratives traverse, disrupt and open up indeterminacies (1990: 189). The telling of space, its transformation from iconographic into narrative form, reconfigures and reconstitutes it by placing it in time. Narrative takes time. It orders observations, descriptions and ideas into a potentially limitless temporal sequence.[11] It is constantly

on France's 'overseas presence' brought forward in February 2005. The law's notorious fourth article called for 'le rôle positif de la présence française outre-mer, notamment en Afrique du Nord' [the positive role of the French presence overseas, and particularly in North Africa] to be taught in the secondary education curriculum (*Journal officiel*, 24 February 2005: 94). Driven by the right, holding a majority in the National Assembly, the law was widely interpreted as 'official revisionism' in relation to France's colonial history (Le Cour Grandmaison 2006: 128). The clause on the curriculum was ultimately dropped in 2006. On the law, alongside Le Cour Grandmaison, see Liauzu & Manceron 2006, Blanchard, Bancel & Lemaire 2006 and Bancel 2009.

11   As Georges Perec showed in *Tentative d'épuisement d'un lieu parisien* (1982), his attempt to describe a day in the Place Saint-Sulpice.

restless, mapping out contours and moving between the fixed points established by the map. It is about movement not stasis.

Likewise, suggests Certeau, social delinquency as a mode of being is restless, traversal and transgressive, not least because it is obliged to be so. It is the option left open to those who have to negotiate or somehow navigate the order imposed on the territory:

> La délinquance sociale consisterait à prendre le récit à la lettre, à en faire le principe de l'existence physique là où une société n'offre plus d'issus symboliques et d'expectations d'espaces à des sujets ou à des groupes, là où il n'y a plus d'autre alternative que le rangement disciplinaire et la dérive illégale, c'est-à-dire une forme ou l'autre de prison et l'errance au-dehors. (Certeau 1990: 190)

> [Social delinquency involves taking storytelling literally and making it the principle of physical existence in a situation where society no longer offers subjects or groups symbolic outcomes and expectations about spaces, and where there is no alternative between disciplinary compliance and illegal drift; in other words, a form of either imprisonment or vagrancy.]

For Certeau, delinquency as a social behaviour derives precisely from the disciplinary production of space, which seeks to eliminate the wriggle room of creativity and transversal movement in favour of regulated circulation. Delinquency becomes a mode of resistance in the very process of attempting to dodge and weave between the varying forms of striation (physical, institutional, disciplinary) that bring order to bear.

As such, it is fitting that *Hexagone* begins with a narrative voiceover telling the story of *banlieue* life from within. Along with the panning shot over the peripheral landscapes of Paris, it stages and establishes the place from which the inhabitants speak, the (lack of) room for manoeuvre they have, and the lines of flight they can attempt to open up within the space of the French hexagon. Slimane offers a delinquent tale of life as swerves, ruses and tricks, negotiations with the employment agency and other institutions of the state, and acts of petty crime, drug dealing and other forms of parallel economic activity. All are an inevitable outcome of the spaces, structures and social formations produced through territorial development. To live delinquently, the film suggests, is to see horizons of possibility but also the realities of containment, which more often than not turn movement into oscillation.

The 2005 riots seemed to fulfil the worst imaginings of France's political class. The *quartiers* were confirmed as wellsprings of insurrectionary energy whose tipping point had finally been reached. However, the fact remained that the imbalance of power between state and *quartier* was starkly visible in the ranks of police officers who could appear on the ground, or the state's administrative ability to control space and movement through zoning. As such, it is hard not to see the political preoccupation with delinquency as something over-determined: motivated by the search for political advantage amongst the parties of the right for sure, but also a displacement of other, more daunting challenges to the state's authority over its territory. If the visible focus of policy and policing was on the pressures from within the territory, also in play were the complexities of the relationship between state and capital.

Chief among these were the increasingly deregulated capital flows which were enabled by the neoliberal economic turn and were driving the energies of globalization. Édouard Balladur gestured towards them in his statement to the National Assembly in 1993: 'une fois résorbées les conséquences des deux chocs pétroliers, les années quatre-vingt ont vu le développement de mécanismes financiers qui perturbent gravement le système monétaire international et les perspectives d'une croissance saine et durable' [once the consequences of the two oil crises had been overcome, the 1980s saw the development of financial mechanisms which severely disrupted the international monetary system and the chances of healthy and durable economic growth] (*Journal officiel*, 9 April 1993: 34). It was a case of lurching from one crisis to the next, or perhaps more accurately, of the state finding itself in a permanent state of crisis in a globalizing world. In fact, while he did not draw a causal link between the two, Balladur went on to infer one a few lines later:

> En outre, notre pays connaît une crise de l'État. Celui-ci ne joue plus de façon satisfaisante son rôle de garant de l'ordre social et de la solidarité. Il a du mal à assumer ses responsabilités régaliennes essentielles dans les domaines de la justice et de la sécurité. (*Journal officiel*, 9 April 1993: 34)

> [Moreover, our country is going through a crisis of the State, which is no longer performing effectively its role as guarantor of the social order and solidarity. It is struggling to perform its essential sovereign functions in the domains of justice and security.]

Capital was exerting its own, yet more disruptive pressures on the territory even while it was the *quartiers* that felt the force of the state's efforts of control, regulation and territorialization.

The Delinquency of Capital

'Gaullist power wears a reforming and modernizing mask when in fact it wants simply to register and normalize capital's natural tendencies.' Jean-Luc Godard's conspiratorial whisper at the start of *2 ou 3 choses que je sais d'elle* exposed a truth that in reality was plain for all to see, if they looked hard enough. Gaullist modernization was predicated on the state seeking an accommodation with capital, enabling and ensuring a productive environment in which capital could thrive for their mutual benefit by operating various forms of spatial development through which its energies could be channelled. This was the dynamic driving the *Schéma directeur*, as we saw in Chapter 2, and the planners' preoccupation with flow and circulation as engines of freedom, mobility and prosperity. The economic crises and reconfigurations of the 1970s and 80s made clear how capital threatened the state's ability to maintain control over its territory and ensure its territorial integrity. As it was released from the social and political constraints defining the post-war settlement of 'embedded liberalism' (Harvey 2005: 11), capital asserted itself as the ultimate delinquent force, restless and nomadic, constantly in search of more productive climes.

Deleuze and Guattari noted the shift in 1980, at a point when the United States, soon joined by the United Kingdom, was beginning to pursue neoliberal policies of deregulation and privatization in order to free up capital mobility and accumulation. The capital flows of multinational corporations were becoming increasingly mobile, and increasingly at a remove from the state's powers of regulation and striation. Where state capitalism formed part of the armoury of territorialization, the multinational was becoming a potent agent of deterritorialization, opening up spaces where 'les points d'occupation comme les pôles d'échange deviennent très indépendants des voies classiques de striage' [points of occupation and poles of exchange increasingly act independently of the established modes of striation] (Deleuze & Guattari 1980: 614). Notwithstanding the French right's own embrace of privatization and other forms of market liberalization during the 1980s, it was precisely the consequences flowing from things like the 'financial mechanisms' of the neoliberal turn that made Balladur nervous a decade or so later, because of how they left the country exposed to capital's mercurial ebbs and flows.[12]

Signs of the changing dynamic between state and capital were also uncovered by the DATAR's team of photographers working on the *mission photographique*. Rather than modernization as a finished project, they were capturing the uncertain trajectory of space in transition, and how the territory was registering the different economic forces at work upon it (Welch 2019). There were the logistics sheds in the vicinity of the A6 motorway facilitating the circulation of commodities across France and an increasingly integrated Europe, the plate glass windows of modern offices where a tilt towards service industries was underway, but also abandoned and decaying heavy industrial plant in the eastern regions, evidence of capital flight and the effects of competition from cheaper producers overseas.

We can see their territorial investigations pursued by the writer Jean Rolin, whose work during the 1990s became increasingly preoccupied with the shifting qualities of French space and the ambiguities that constitute it. Rolin's sensitivity to those ambiguities is signalled in the very title of *Zones* (1995), which operates in the gap between the administrative and poetic senses of the term. The text takes the form of a journal recounting three trips around Paris and its near suburbs during 1994 on foot and public transport (bus, Métro, train, RER). The aims and logic of the trips remain opaque to the reader and apparently to the narrator, as Catherine Poisson observes (2000: 19); though as the narrator transports himself around the region, it becomes clear that what counts is not so much the destination, as the impressions he gleans through movement.[13] *Zones* joins Ernaux's *Journal du dehors*

---

12   France's uneasy relationship with neoliberalism is discussed by Prasad 2005, Amable 2017 and Masquelier 2020, among others. As Prasad argues, the influence of neoliberal thinking has been most evident in industrial policy (including a wave of privatizations in the 1980s and 1990s under governments of the right and left), while the most visible resistance to it has been in relation to state welfare policy, and particularly attempts at pension reform (such as the mass demonstrations that brought France to a standstill in the winter of 1995).

13   'Dans la soirée, après avoir bu deux ou trois poires en conclusion de mon dîner, dans un état,

in being a text about circulation, about how circulation has been engineered into people's lives by transport infrastructure, but also what circulation can reveal about the state of space in contemporary Paris.

In the first instance, the zones in question can thus be understood in terms of the transport authority's division of its network into concentric rings around the city, between which different journey tariffs apply. Yet if the narrator's travels through those zones exemplified the new logics of circulation described by Roncayolo a few years earlier, they also confirmed Roncayolo's analysis of contemporary space as simultaneously defined by fragmentation and discontinuity. Rolin's narrator is attentive to unexpected collisions and juxtapositions of different sorts of space, and in particular how infrastructures of circulation abut or overlay the space around them to produce marginal locations. He finds a striking example lodged beneath the Porte de la Chapelle on the Boulevard Périphérique, that sign of modernity-in-the-making filmed three decades earlier by Godard and Rohmer:

> Sous l'échangeur de la porte de la Chapelle, niché dans une étroite ouverture triangulaire entre les piliers du périphérique et ceux d'autres voies aériennes, se trouve un square, peut-être le plus saugrenu, le plus bruyant, le plus inaccessible et donc le moins fréquenté de tout Paris. (Rolin 1995: 180)

> [Beneath the interchange of the porte de la Chapelle, nestled in a narrow, triangular opening between pillars supporting the ring road and other overpasses, there is a square which is perhaps the most absurd, most noisy, most inaccessible and so least visited in the whole of Paris.]

In Sarcelles, he encounters the sort of spatial assemblage which, as it holds in relation different scales and qualities (local and global, generic and specific), epitomizes the odd combination of hybridity and fragmentation that characterizes modernized France. A group of generic chain hotels sit in a fenced compound next to a public park cut through by a line of pylons. While a cosmopolitan population gathers in the park, planes fly low overhead as they approach the runway at Roissy-CDG: 'vers dix-huit heures, sous les avions, au milieu des pylônes, le parc accueille une foule considérable et babélienne, majoritairement d'origine africaine ou antillaise' [around 6pm, beneath the planes and in the middle of the pylons, the park welcomes a substantial, babelian crowd, mostly of African or Caribbean origin] (1995: 90). Yet here as elsewhere, a defining feature of the scene is the boundaries and demarcations which emerge, both tangible (mesh and chain-link fencing) and intangible (different communities keep their distance).

The narrator's movements around the region happen within the regulated circuits of the transport system. Once back on foot, he is drawn to explore the sorts of unofficial, open or marginal spaces descended from the administrative zone's unruly other, the cleared land around the Parisian fortifications where alternative

---

donc, de légère ébriété, je suis descendu vers la gare Saint-Lazare en ruminant la lancinante question de ce que je pourrais bien faire, en "voyage" à Paris, qui ne soit pas du journalisme pittoresque ou de la sociologie de comptoir' [That evening, have drunk two or three pear liqueurs to round off my dinner, and thus in a state of light drunkenness, I headed down towards the Saint-Lazare station while pondering the nagging question of what exactly my 'travels' in Paris might involve other than some sort of colourful journalism or barroom sociology] (Rolin 1995: 40).

ways of being were more or less tolerated. The expansiveness of the public park at La Villette on the northern edge of Paris opens up an alternative sense of being in time: 'comme une lande, ou un marais, ou un bord de mer, il permet d'embrasser une étendue de ciel assez vaste pour qu'on y sente le temps passer, la vie s'écouler, les saisons se succéder' [like a heath, or a marsh, or the edge of the sea, it opens up a perspective on the sky large enough to feel time passing, life flowing, the seasons succeeding one another] (1995: 63). Meanwhile, *terrains vagues* offer seclusion and refuge for those on the margins.

During his third trip, the narrator ducks through a hole in the perimeter fence around the site earmarked for development as the Stade de France near St Denis, where he finds a collection of people living tucked away and out of sight (1995: 147). Yet just as the sense of becoming afforded by the park is only fleeting, so too is the sanctuary of the *terrain vague*. The narrator shows us a space in transition, caught between two phases of use, as the government (like those in other western economies) attempted to manage the consequences of deindustrialization by pivoting the area towards leisure, media and other forms of service industry. From that point of view, *Zones* becomes a *lieu de mémoire*, a repository for memories of a landscape and community lost to the passage of space through time, and its repurposing for the benefits of the economy.

Over subsequent texts at the turn of the millennium, Rolin develops his investigation into the dynamics and forces in play across the French territory. Central to it are his narrator's own traversal movements, which draw out those forces through the connections they make.[14] In *Traverses* (1999), whose title confirms the method of enquiry as much as it describes the text, the narrator spends time in the former industrial heartlands of eastern France. The steel-making town of Longwy illustrates the region's difficult negotiations with deindustrialization, globalization and the flows of capital: the decline of the steel industry through foreign competition in the 1970s, reorientation towards the production of consumer goods through inward investment from Japanese and South Korean multinationals in the 1980s, but then the sudden disappearance of those factories in the 1990s as the Asian economies entered recession and the firms retreated (Rolin 1999: 42–43). Meanwhile, the narrator grasps how the industry has shaped the landscape, but also how its influence is destined to fade away as space cycles through different phases of economic life: 'non seulement les usines — de plus en plus clairsemées et de plus en plus économes de main-d'œuvre — mais aussi tout ce qui avait essaimé autour d'elles, et qui était de la même façon voué à disparaître' [not only the factories — more and more scattered and needing smaller and smaller workforces — but also everything that swarmed around them, and which was likewise destined to disappear] (1999: 49).

Increasingly we get a sense not just of the mosaic quality of French space, but also how many spatial fragments themselves have a traversal quality. Their orientation and function are defined as much by their role in a global system of movement, trade and circulation as by their position within French territory. In *La Clôture* (2002),

14   Ari J. Blatt (2017) situates Rolin's traversal texts as part of a broader trend of topographic writing in France which takes shape during the 1990s and 2000s.

which homes in on the Boulevard Ney on the northern edge of Paris, a scruffy *terrain vague* located by a slip road on to the Boulevard Périphérique takes shape as a staging-post where cars and other goods pause on their way to the African continent:

> Le principe est simple: Golden Shipping reçoit d'un peu partout les véhicules à bout de souffle — d'où sa situation au bord du périphérique — , et dès qu'ils sont au nombre de huit on les place sur un camion qui les achemine à Anvers, d'où ils embarquent sur un navire roulier à destination de la côte africaine. (Rolin 2002: 170–71)

> [It's a simple concept: Golden Shipping receives old bangers from all over — hence its location next to the ring road — and as soon as there are eight of them, they are loaded on to a transporter that takes them to Antwerp, from where they are put on a roll-on/roll-off ship destined for the African coast.]

The pavements of the boulevard, on the other hand, are the workplace of sex workers arriving from Africa and Eastern Europe. The recent murder in the vicinity of one of them, Ginka Trifonova, illuminates how the trafficking of women shadows the movement and commerce of goods.

Likewise, the narrator encounters asylum-seekers and clandestine migrants whose journeys bring them along the boulevard. Some, like Lito, an army officer from Zaïre, are caught in stasis while they await processing by the asylum office. Others are merely glimpsed on their way elsewhere. Viewed from the narrator's perspective on the Boulevard Ney, French territory comes to resemble a constellation of nodes or fistulae where waste ground, street corners and import-export offices connect with an array of places around the globe, and open up to the more or less legal flows of people and goods.[15] As the hovering presence of the police at various moments in the text suggests, they are also points where the state's control over its territory begins to look uncertain.

In *Terminal frigo* (2005), the scale and view shift, from scraps of rough ground to the maritime edges of the territory, where international port zones form the nation's most obvious interface with the rest of the world, and where circulation and exchange take on their most tangible physical form. Ports also make plain the consequences flowing from increasingly deregulated and globalized trade, and in particular the rapid expansion of container traffic. Its scale and sophistication are reflected in the vast container handling zones, where automation has reduced the volume of human labour to a minimum, as well as in an insatiable demand for space. Visiting the port zone at Le Havre, the narrator notes how the efficiencies of time and labour that containers create seem inversely proportional to the vast amount of space they require for handling and storage (Rolin 2005: 186). Meanwhile, in the port's race to keep up with the expanding volume of container movements as global trade grows, and because it is caught in a logic of competition with other northern European container ports, it cannot stop consuming space, encroaching on surrounding neighbourhoods like a rising tide (2005: 196).

---

15   Rolin's narrator traces a path through that constellation in *L'Explosion de la durite* [The Explosion of the Radiator Hose] (2007), accompanying a used car through import-export channels via Antwerp to the DRC, where the plan is to use it as a taxi.

If the revolution in maritime transport represents a technical advance, it also has inevitable social and human costs. On a visit to Dunkerque, the narrator describes the decline of organized port labour in the town, and how in the face of legislative reforms to 'improve competitiveness' and 'modernize' working practices (that is to say, break the power of the trade union), fissures began to emerge in the community of dock workers (2005: 114). Indeed, it is quickly apparent that while everything is done to smooth the flow of global commerce, the fortunes of people are much less of a concern.[16]

In common with other regulated zones, and for all they are part of a worldwide machine of circulation, ports appear in the landscape as demarcated spaces, separated from their surroundings by barriers, chain-link fencing and entry protocols. Gravitating round them are precarious populations of refugees and clandestine migrants, like those glimpsed passing through Paris in *La Clôture*, shadowing the commodities they hope to follow across the Channel; but also like the people stuck on the Boulevard Ney — like Slimane and his friends in *Hexagone*, in fact — they become caught in a perpetual time of waiting, dodging the attention of the police, before occasionally getting lucky and being reported by their peers as having 'managed to get across' (2005: 168).

The pressures and flows traced by Rolin during the 1990s and 2000s found appropriate figural form in the notion of 'liquid territory' which frames the photography project *France(s) territoire liquide*. The project was initiated in 2011 by Jérôme Brezillon, Frédéric Delangle, Cédric Delsaux and Patrick Messina, who approached the British photography curator Paul Wombell to be its artistic director (Wombell 2014: 149–50) and assembled, in Ari Blatt's nice formulation, a 'loose federation' of forty-three photographers working on landscape and territory (Blatt 2019: 198). The group aligned itself explicitly with the DATAR's *mission photographique* in its desire to interrogate French territory; and while it was keen to assert its artistic independence (the project website describes it as a 'self-produced and independent photographic mission on the French landscape'), the backing it went on to receive from the DATAR was a clear endorsement of *France(s) territoire liquide* as the spiritual successor to the planning agency's own *mission*.[17]

Likewise, just as the DATAR project revealed French modernization to be something approaching an unfinishable project, so too *France(s) territoire liquide* emphasizes the centrifugal and transversal forces rippling across the surface of the territory. Already, its title posed a subtle challenge to the idea and possibility of the singular territory, 'one and indivisible', willed by the French republican state. Instead, it offered what Raphaële Bertho ([n.d.]) terms a 'kaleidoscopic' vision of the territory lived as celebration or promise rather than threat. In his discussion of

16   A glimpse of this inverted hierarchy comes in Ari Kaurismäki's *Le Havre* (2011), where the container becomes the means by which a group of clandestine migrants from Africa are smuggled into the country before being discovered on the dockside by customs officials.

17   The lineage was also reflected in the project's material forms, and most notably the photo-book published by Seuil, whose large, square format and cover design carry echoes of the second *Paysages Photographies* volume published by Hazan for the DATAR in 1989. For more on the place of *France(s) territoire liquide* in the tradition of French photographic missions, see Blatt (2022: 93–95).

the project, Wombell takes as a given what Rolin and others had encountered on the ground, namely that the state's purchase on its territory was being challenged by technological change and capital flows, even as it sought to maintain (the illusion of) control:

> Comment une nation se définit-elle lors d'une période de changement technologique rapide au cours de laquelle les frontières sont définies par les ondes électromagnétiques plutôt que par les murs et une période au cours de laquelle les décisions voyagent de parlements en salles de conseil d'administration? (Wombell [n.d.])

> [How does a nation define itself during a period of rapid technological change during which frontiers are defined by electromagnetic waves rather than walls, and when decisions are made in boardrooms rather than parliaments?]

The figure of 'liquid territory', as Wombell observes (2014: 146, n. 2), invokes Zygmunt Bauman's characterization of 'liquid modernity' as fundamentally shifting, provisional and uncertain in ways which are both destabilizing but also (for those with the necessary forms of capital at their disposal at least) potentially creative and enabling of self-fashioning (Bauman 2000).

Liquid territory is similarly shifting and mutable, 'the object of constant metamorphoses', as Bernard Comment puts it in his preface to the *France(s) territoire liquide* photo-book (Comment 2014: 4). A recurring preoccupation with France's physical and administrative borders in the book reflects how the very sense of French territory has been reshaped by the geopolitics of European integration. Albin Millot goes looking for the traces of a frontier that has dissolved into the landscape, enabling fluidity of movement across the supranational space of the European Union, albeit for those with the right credentials. The flux of goods and people is caught in Beatrix von Conta's images of ports, road bridges and the heavy goods vehicles whose movements they shape, and in Marion Gambin's portrait of life on the motorways and service stations connecting Paris, Calais and Le Havre.

But a few pages later come Julien Chapsal's images of the coast around Calais, where clandestine migrants end up 'half way between the territory of departure and the territory of arrival' (Comment 2014: 283). For them, borders and frontiers persist which are as tangible as ever, and much is done to halt rather than sustain movement. Chain-link fencing defines the limits of fluidity for those without the necessary credentials. Yet Chapsal's images also show what he calls 'signs and traces of territorial appropriation' (2014: 283), evidence of occupation and lines of flight. A hole in the fence and scuffed earth around it reveal the restless movements of those who are attempting to navigate the barriers before them and sometimes managing, in the words of Rolin's narrator, 'to get across'.

In many ways, a feeling of territory's being-in-time, forever reshaped by forces of change, is one *France(s) territoire liquide* shares with the prospective planners of the Gaullist era. Much less visible in what the photographers see, however, is the expression of agency inherent within the prospective attitude, the sense that territorial metamorphosis was in the hands of the planners, and that territorial becoming had a linear directional flow, like a motorway cutting across country.

FIG. 5.5. a & b. François Deladerrière's investigation of interstitial space in *France(s) territoire liquide* (2014). Images reproduced by kind permission of the photographer.

Instead comes the impression, as Wombell suggests, that motive agency lies elsewhere, in unpredictable and obscure places, displaced from parliaments to corporate board rooms or server farms.

The epistemic shift between the two is captured nicely in Michel Bousquet's contribution on Jean Bertin's *aérotrain*, developed in the 1960s with the backing of the DATAR as an advanced form of high-speed land transport (amongst other things, as we saw in Chapter 3, it was initially expected to connect Cergy-Pontoise with La Défense). While the project was abandoned in the 1970s, the test tracks built for the prototypes remain, spearing through the countryside south of Paris only to end abruptly and peculiarly in the middle of a field, making manifest its arrested development. In Bousquet's images, they take on an inevitably elegiac quality, like monumental vestiges of a lost civilization, or memories of a prospective dream. As an 'old project for the future' (2014: 247), viewed from a future that is now the present, the remnants of Bertin's *aérotrain* serve as another reminder of how, when visions of futurity find expression in material forms, they become reified as relics or fossils of a bygone era.

From that point of view, it is notable that the *France(s) territoire liquide* photo-book concludes with images by François Deladerrière which focus on *terrains vagues*, *friches* and other forms of waste or leftover space, what he terms 'les zones oubliées du paysage' (2014: 389), the forgotten zones of the landscape. He shows us the sorts of interstitial places to which Rolin's narrator would gravitate: the weathering and graffitied underside of a flyover, the shrub land bordering a container transit park, old tyres dumped in a quarry (Figs 5.5a, 5.5b). Like Rolin's narrator, Deladerrière also finds evidence of the persistent resistance and adaptability of life, hanging on and making space for itself in the 'folds' of the landscape, as he calls them. They are 'endroits où la vie est possible, il y a là une forme d'état sauvage' [places where life is possible, where there is a sort of wild state of being] (2014: 389). Thus, the evocation of liquid territory takes a final turn via the shadow or poetic sense of the zone as unkempt margin, and as such, a place where the unruly energies of potentiality can be found.

For *France(s) territoire liquide* to come to rest in scruffy edgelands, and suggest as it does that the *friche* and *terrain vague* in some sense best capture the idea of liquid territory, sums up all that is complex, unstable and indeterminate about French territory and its journey since the age of prospective planning. It suggests as well that indeterminacy and instability are the defining condition of space as it moves through time. Indeed, in the final analysis, we can perhaps see French modernization as a heroic attempt precisely to manage the potentiality and potential disruptiveness of space-in-time. Certainly, indeterminacy emerges as a persistent source of concern in the work of spatial planning. It is there in its preoccupation with the unproductive empty quarters of the *désert français*, in its urge to zone, regulate and spatially striate, and in its disquiet over the unruly quarters it discovers on the urban margins. Yet indeterminacy is in turn produced by those same actions, as zoning strategies create the urge for lines of flight as delinquent movement, or planned space becomes space left behind but living on as relic or dream memory.

Deladerrière's images capture something of planning's inherent tensions in the way they hold disciplined and undisciplined space together in the frame. Vehicles speed across the flyover, their tail lights streaking red in the long exposure like parallel lines of electrical wire, while signs of resistance and appropriation accumulate on the supporting pillars beneath. Containers marking a pause in their endless journey round the globe abut the vegetation that reclaims leftover space, proliferates and brings life as soon as an opportunity presents itself.

The tensions and pressures playing out on post-war French territory find visible form in spatial configurations like the peripheral housing estate, the port zone, the *friche industrielle* or the *terrain vague*. But they also emerge in different forms of movement through, across and beyond it — the regulated flow of people and goods, the cosmopolitan blending of identities, but also the darker and more shadowy movements of clandestine migration, human trafficking and terrorist networks. We have come a long way from the time-travelling, teleological confidence of Gaston Berger and the prospective attitude. Where French space and territory now find themselves, and what their horizons might be, are questions I explore in my concluding discussion.

CODA

❖

A Space Oddity

Olivier Guichard has emerged as an unlikely but perceptive philosopher of planning and time over the course of *Making Space in Post-war France*, thanks in no small part to his understanding of *aménagement* as action for and in the future. To recall Guichard's time-travelling formulation, 'l'aménagement ne vit pas dans l'époque présente; il doit toujours la devancer' [spatial planning doesn't live in the future; it must always be one step ahead of it] (1965: 26). We have also seen how Guichard, Massé, Delouvrier and their colleagues deployed the legislative, political, administrative and bureaucratic resources of the French state as they built machinery to translate such philosophical insights into material outcomes on the ground and enact the state's power and desire to make space.

Part of that bureaucratic 'arsenal', remembering André Trintignac's metaphor (and its various associations), was the ZAD. Introduced into law in July 1962, the *zone d'aménagement différé*, or deferred development zone, provided the administrative means for enabling *aménagement* as anticipated future. Declaring a ZAD gave state agencies the right to acquire land that might be required for future projects, for example by buying up farmland on the outskirts of urban areas as it became available. ZADs also froze land prices, neutralizing the inflationary danger of property speculation. Delouvrier used ZADs to ensure the District de Paris could lay its hands on the space needed to implement the *Schéma directeur*, and in particular, build the new towns (Murard & Fourquet 2004: 146). ZADs were also deployed around the provincial cities whose development was essential for the DATAR's strategy of distributing economic growth across the national territory.

One of those *métropoles d'équilibre* was Nantes, situated on the Loire in western France. As a largely rural and agricultural region, the west was considered by Guichard and the DATAR to be most in need of a strong dose of modernization (that Guichard had his electoral base in the region undoubtedly fed his enthusiasm for the idea). The predominance of smallholdings meant inefficiencies of land use and, as Guichard puts it in *Aménager la France*, 'an inherent lack of technology' (1965: 68). Industrial activity was similarly haphazard, made up largely of small businesses and lacking a robust cohort of 'technical managers' to inject some dynamism into proceedings. The function of a provincial city like Nantes was to be a 'home for innovation and culture' (1965: 68), from where enlightenment and education could radiate into the darker corners of the provinces. At the same time, connecting it more effectively to the flows and currents of the national territory would galvanize the area as a whole. Building a motorway between Lyon and the Atlantic seaboard, suggests Guichard, would 'innerver une vaste partie relativement abandonné du territoire français' [invigorate a vast but relatively forgotten part of the French territory] (1965: 130). A regional airport could perform a similar function, connecting the west to the rest of France and the world.

In 1965, work began on the regional development plan for the Loire region, which included the scoping of possible locations for a new regional airport to serve Nantes and nearby Saint-Nazaire, as well as Brittany further north. When the development plan was approved in 1970, it contained a proposal to build a new airport twenty kilometres to the north of Nantes near the village of Notre-Dame-des-Landes. In January 1974, during Guichard's second stint as minister for *aménagement*, and a couple of months before he attended the inauguration of Roissy-CDG, the prefect of Loire-Atlantique published a decree announcing a ZAD at Notre-Dame-des-Landes, where 1,225 hectares of farming and rural land were earmarked as the site for the future airport. Guichard would probably not have anticipated quite how much deferral of the development there would be. He certainly would not have anticipated the ZAD's ultimate fate some four decades later.

In January 2018, after numerous false starts and long-running opposition from protestors occupying the site, the French government finally called time on plans for an airport at Notre-Dame-des-Landes. Meanwhile, in the hands of those protestors, the ZAD had morphed into a *zad*, or *zone à défendre* [zone to defend], and a new spatial consciousness had emerged within the metropolitan territory, driven by resistance to infrastructure and the assumptions it expressed.

The saga of Notre-Dame-des-Landes is another story of the French state's unending negotiation with capital in the space of its territory and how, more often than not, that negotiation produces territorial reforms. The economic crises of the 1970s and 80s put the airport project into abeyance for over two decades. It regained momentum during the 2000s and 2010s with renewed efforts to boost regional growth through the development of metropolitan areas. Fundamentally, the policy pursued during the first two decades of the twenty-first century was a continuation of the DATAR's regional development plan in the 1960s. However, in a sign of France's accommodation with neoliberal orthodoxy, *métropoles d'équilibre* were reframed as engines of 'competitiveness'. Key to territorial development in the neoliberal age was less the redistributive agency of the state, than the entrepreneurial spirit of competition between regional cities, destined to succeed or fail within the domestic and international marketplace of urban centres. Infrastructure had its part to play as catalyst and driver of those energies by sustaining networks, enabling creative flows and improving, as the French government's website has it, the country's 'attractiveness'.[1]

The ideological inflection from state to market found legislative expression in the Sarkozy government's 2010 laws on territorial reform, which instituted the *métropole* as a new administrative and democratic entity by grouping together the *communes*

---

1   'Les Métropoles' <https://www.gouvernement.fr/action/les-metropoles> [accessed 23 August 2021].

within a conurbation. The government press release announcing the proposed legislation in October 2009 captured the essence of the reforms:

> Afin d'assurer une meilleure prise en compte du fait urbain et de renforcer la capacité des plus grandes agglomérations françaises à soutenir la compétition avec leurs homologues européennes ou internationales, le projet de loi propose un nouveau cadre institutionnel: la 'métropole'.[2]

> [To ensure the realities of urban life are better accounted for, and to reinforce the ability of France's largest conurbations to compete with their European and international counterparts, the bill proposes a new institutional framework, the 'metropole'.]

The role of the *métropole* as a locus of competition was enshrined in the law passed a year later, which exhorted the participating *communes* to develop their new territory 'in order to improve their cohesion and competitiveness' (*Journal officiel*, 17 December 2010: 15).

The emphasis on regional conurbations was an assertion of the increasingly urban character of twenty-first century France ('le fait urbain'), and a reassertion of the idea that cities were the principal drivers of economic growth and development. It was also a pragmatic response to the economic realities of the age, shaped by the accelerated flows of capital and data under globalization and the four fundamental freedoms of the single market (free movement of goods, capital, services and people) within the European Union. The pursuit of those territorial reforms by the centre-left government of Socialist president François Hollande (2012–17) showed the extent to which the orthodoxy of progress through (market-driven) competition had been absorbed by the political mainstream in France. In January 2014, the Hollande government passed legislation that 'affirmed' the strategic centrality of *métropoles* and provided the legal framework for the Grand Paris metropolitan region, a project initiated by Sarkozy in 2007 (*Journal officiel*, 28 January 2014).[3]

Local political leaders, many of whom were from the Socialist party, were already making the renewed case for an airport at Notre-Dame-des-Landes in terms of the competitive health of the region. Writing in *Le Monde* in February 2011, five of them, including Jean-Marc Ayrault, mayor of Nantes and president of the new Nantes *métropole*, and Jean-Yves Le Drian, president of the Brittany region (subsequently prime and defence ministers respectively under Hollande), attacked the 'partisans of immobility' whose opposition to the airport would put a break on the region's dynamism: 'pour accueillir des entreprises, lutter contre le chômage, nous devons mettre tous les atouts de notre côté' [we need as many assets as possible if we are to welcome businesses and fight unemployment]. Economic

---

2   'Réforme des collectivités territoriales', Conseil des ministres du 21 octobre 2009 <http://archives.gouvernement.fr/fillon_version2/gouvernement/reforme-des-collectivites-territoriales-0.html> [accessed 23 August 2021].
3   On the alignment of contemporary urban policy in France with neoliberal orthodoxy, see Theresa Enright (2016, 2017). She argues that Sarkozy's Grand Paris initiative can be seen in part as a response to the national outbreak of urban unrest in 2005 in the way it set out 'to quell unrest and to turn working class and immigrant suburbs into profitable, highly specialized nodes of post-industrial production' (2017: 566).

expansion needed movement, flow and mobility, to which the key (of course) was infrastructure: 'l'accessibilité aérienne est un facteur majeur de développement économique' [accessibility by air is a major factor in economic development] (Auxiette & others 2011).

By the time Ayrault and the others came to write their article in *Le Monde*, 'les partisans de l'immobilisme' were well entrenched on the ZAD. Not only that, but the *zadistes*, as they became known, would have agreed entirely with how the politicians described them. To disrupt the building of the airport, for them, was to strike at the assumptions made manifest and sustained by infrastructure. They were assumptions about the nature of progress, that progress would only come through movement and circulation, that civilizational advance was driven by 'the flux of the well-connected, the networked and the developers' (Mauvaise Troupe 2018: 116).

After a lengthy period of public consultation beginning in 2002, a Declaration of Public Utility had been published in 2008, formally authorizing the process of tendering and construction. Not long afterwards, protestors began to occupy the site, creating informal communal settlements and building alliances with the farmers who were still working the agricultural land within the ZAD.[4] Once again, to recall Paul Virilio's remarks about May 1968, inhabiting had become an offensive revolutionary act. The stage was set for a protracted battle with the French government over the following decade, which saw it attempt to seize control of the ZAD at various points through forced eviction and demolition.

The battle was both predicated on and crystallized the territorial dynamics in play during France's post-war period. At its heart was a fundamental irony. Having used its naming power to create the special territorial regime of the ZAD, the state found it had been displaced from it. Deferring space had given others time to lay claim to it. Once more, a *zone de non-droit*, a space beyond the reach of the state, was opening up within the territory. And as the *zadistes* astutely observed, the state 'does not passively accept that the perimeter of its territory be put into question' (Mauvaise Troupe 2018: 176). Hence the turn to its repressive arm, most frequently in the early 2010s, once the construction contract had been awarded (to building conglomerate Vinci) and attempts were made to get work on the site underway.

Moreover, the protestors, armed with a theoretical sophistication that provided some compensation for the otherwise unequal balance of power between the two sides, were busy transforming the ZAD into an entirely new thing, a consciously different sort of place, 'a strange territory' (Mauvaise Troupe 2018: 150), a space oddity. In recognition of the performative power acquired by language in the hands of the state, as the protestors occupied the site, they also made sure to occupy — to 'hijack', in their words (2018: 135) — the term which had brought it to life. The *zone d'aménagement différé* became a *zone à défendre*. To signal that its substance had changed, the acronym's capital letters morphed into the lower-case letters of a noun,

4   A useful chronology of the airport project is provided in Chéreau, Brévan & Kbaier (2013), one of three reports produced after a public consultation during 2012, as tensions around the project were at their height. The *zadistes* provide their own account writing as the Mauvaise Troupe collective together with the NoTAV activists in Italy's Susa valley protesting against a proposed new rail line between Lyon and Turin (Mauvaise Troupe 2018).

and the ZAD was turned into a *zad*. In a similar way, the protestors took over the phrase that, as we have seen, had become a commonplace of political discourse as the state confronted its delinquent suburbs. They conceived of the *zad* precisely as a *zone de non-droit*, a 'lawless zone' that allowed them 'the leisure of experimenting with new existences' (2018: 126).

In operating the shift from ZAD to *zad*, the collective kept in play the ambiguities inhabiting the zone as both the unruly space of the popular imagination, a place of 'dark corners and secret zones' (2018: 127), and an administrative construct, a tool for producing territory. They set out to think the *zad* through in territorial terms as a space to be conceptualized, organized and defended. The key question, the group acknowledged, would be 'what it was that was being "defended" in the "zone"' (2018: 136).

Even more interesting was the answer they found. It lay in the sorts of locations where *France(s) territoire liquide* came to rest as it offered its closing view of space in contemporary France: the *terrains vagues* and other uncertain spaces we have seen sought out and populated by people at various points. In usurping an infrastructure of managed circulation, the *zadistes* posed the future of Notre-Dame-des-Landes as a place of potential and indeterminacy, a place where 'a certain instability or insecurity opens up the possibility for the unimagined to transpire' (2018: 143). The chance of the *zad* lay in creating the conditions for the *terrain vague* to persist and thrive, and for its fleeting forms of alternative life to find a more sustainable home. Thus it was, for example, that space was made in the *zad* to accommodate migrants and asylum seekers from the camps around Calais (2018: 145).

The French government's final capitulation in January 2018, as it threw in the towel and announced the abandonment of the airport, was a stunning moment. It marked a defeat for a certain understanding of spatial planning, one whose momentum we have tracked through the post-war period, which equated progress and development with infrastructure and built form. That understanding had been vanquished by an alternative vision of how space might be made, in those two senses of organizing territory and giving room.

Yet even at the moment of its defeat, it seemed the state could not help but express itself through force, once again attempting evictions of the *zad* in April and May 2018. As the police made violent incursions into the zone, it was hard to avoid the feeling that, in the aftermath of a humiliating defeat, revenge was being taken after the fact. Nevertheless, with the *zadistes* remaining on the site into the 2020s, and indeed having begun their own accommodations with the law by signing occupation agreements with the prefecture, there are clear signs that a future, in all its instability and insecurity, still remains for the *zad* to create.

Making Space in Post-war France began at an airport which expressed the triumphant realization of France's modernizing dream. It ends at a place where that dream showed both its persistence and its vulnerability. If Notre-Dame-des-Landes is a fitting location for our journey to conclude, it is because the story of the *zad* sums up the territorial dynamics at work in post-war France and the persistence of the French state's spatial reflexes: its conception of territory as the management of flux and flow, and more specifically, in Guichard's terms, as the organization of 'flux rationnels' (1965: 88); its performative ability to produce space through discourse; its response to threats posed to its hold on territory; its ineluctable need to find accommodation with capital.

In hijacking the ZAD, transforming it into a *zad*, and maintaining the *zad* within and apart from French territory, the *zadistes* of Notre-Dame-des-Landes displayed a grasp of France's spatial logics that also served to expose their limits. But such is the power of those logics that even in a sharpening context of climate crisis, and however much they are framed in terms of 'sustainable development' or 'environmental quality', their limits and dangers seem fated (and the French state is by no means alone in this) to be occluded and ignored. Embodied and displayed as they are in the *zad* at Notre-Dame-des-Landes, alternatives appear, at the moment at least, to be in some sense unthinkable. The future may well reside in the French state learning to live with unregulated space, space which is out of the time of planning. But all the evidence suggests that its impulse to make territory — to make space its own — is too strong; that France cannot resist the desire to create a reality from its dreams and imaginings, and exploit its power to do so.

REFERENCES

❖

Bibliography

ACHILLE, ÉTIENNE. 2021. 'Playing Devil's Advocate: Digging up the Colonial Past in Pierre Nora's *Les Lieux de mémoire*', *Francosphères*, 10.1: 9–25

ACHILLE, ÉTIENNE, CHARLES FORSDICK and LYDIE MOULIENO (eds). 2020. *Postcolonial Realms of Memory: Sites and Symbols in Modern France* (Liverpool: Liverpool University Press)

ADELL, GERMÁN. 1999. *Theories and Models of the Peri-urban Interface: A Changing Conceptual Landscape*, Peri-urban Research Project Team, Development Planning Unit, UCL

ALIDIÈRES, BERNARD. 2008. 'Du *Sentiment d'insécurité* au *Frisson de l'émeute*: Sébastian Roché face aux représentations dominantes en France', *Hérodote*, 130: 209–21

ALTHUSSER, LOUIS. 1970. 'Idéologie et appareils idéologiques d'État', *La Pensée*, 151: 3–38

ALVERGNE, CHRISTEL, and PIERRE MUSSO. 2003. *Les Grands Textes de l'aménagement du territoire et de la décentralisation* (Paris: La Documentation française)

AMABLE, BRUNO. 2017. *Structural Crisis and Institutional Change in Modern Capitalism: French Capitalism in Transition* (Oxford: Oxford University Press)

ANDERSON, BENEDICT. 1984. *Imagined Communities: Reflections on the Origin and Spread of Nationalism* (London: Verso)

ANDERSON, PERRY. 2004. 'Union sucrée', *London Review of Books*, 23 September, 10–16

ANDERSSON, JENNY. 2018. *The Future of the World: Futurology, Futurists, and the Struggle for the Post-Cold War Imagination* (Oxford: Oxford University Press)

ARCHER, NEIL. 2012. *The French Road Movie: Space, Mobility, Identity* (Oxford: Berghahn)

AUGÉ, MARC. 1992. *Non-lieux: introduction à une anthropologie de la surmodernité* (Paris: Seuil)

AUSTIN, GUY. 1996. *Contemporary French Cinema: An Introduction* (Manchester: Manchester University Press)

AUXIETTE, JACQUES, and OTHERS. 2011. 'Déménager l'aéroport de Nantes: "un choix raisonné et responsible", *Le Monde*, 14 February 2011 <https://www.lemonde.fr/idees/article/2011/02/14/demenager-l-aeroport-de-nantes-un-choix-de-raison_1479881_3232.html> [accessed 23 August 2021]

BANCEL, NICOLAS. 2009. 'The Law of February 23, 2005: The Uses Made of the Revival of France's "Colonial Grandeur" ', in *Frenchness and the African Diaspora: Identity and Uprising in Contemporary France*, ed. by Charles Tshimanga, Didier Gondola and Peter J. Bloom (Bloomington: Indiana University Press), pp. 167–83

BARTHES, ROLAND. 1972. *Mythologies* (Paris: Seuil/'Points')

BASDEVANT, DENISE, CATHERINE CHATIN, and PATRICE MILLERON. 1979. *Les Villes nouvelles en Île-de-France* (Paris: Hachette/GCVN/'Guides bleus')

BAUCHET, PIERRE. 1966. *La Planification française: vingt ans d'expérience* (Paris: Seuil)

BAUMAN, ZYGMUNT. 2000. *Liquid Modernity* (Oxford: Blackwell)

BEAUCHEZ, JÉRÔME, and DJEMILA ZENEIDI. 2020. '*Sur la Zone*: A Critical Sociology of the Parisian Dangerous Classes (1871–1973)', *Critical Sociology*, 46.4–5: 693–710

BENJAMIN, WALTER. 1999. *The Arcades Project*, trans. by Howard Eiland and Kevin McLaughlin (Cambridge, MA: Belknap Press)

BERGER, GASTON. 1964. *Phénoménologie du temps et prospective* (Paris: Presses universitaires de France)

BERNARD, PHILIPPE. 2005. 'Banlieues: la provocation coloniale', *Le Monde*, 18 November <https://www.lemonde.fr/idees/article/2005/11/18/banlieues-la-provocation-coloniale-par-philippe-bernard_711625_3232.html> [accessed 6 August 2021]

BERTHO, RAPHAËLE. 2013. *La Mission photographique de la DATAR: un laboratoire du paysage contemporain* (Paris: La Documentation française)

——[N.D.]. 'FTL par Raphaële Bertho' <http://www.francesterritoireliquide.fr/ftl-par-raphaele-bertho> [accessed 6 August 2021]

BITOUN, PIERRE. 1988. *Les Hommes d'Uriage* (Paris: La Découverte)

BLANCHARD, PASCAL, NICOLAS BANCEL and SANDRINE LEMAIRE (eds). 2006. *La Fracture coloniale: la société française au prisme de l'héritage colonial* (Paris: La Découverte)

BLATT, ARI J. 2017. 'Traversing the *territoire*', *Romanic Review*, 108: 277–92

——2019. 'Picturing a Nation of Local Places in the *Observatoire photographique du paysage* and *France(s) territoire liquide*', in *France in Flux: Space, Territory and Contemporary Culture*, ed. by Ari J. Blatt and Edward Welch (Liverpool: Liverpool University Press), pp. 186–215

——2022. *The Topographic Imaginary: Attending to Place in Contemporary French Photography* (Liverpool: Liverpool University Press)

BOLTANSKI, LUC. 1982. *Les Cadres: la formation d'un groupe social* (Paris: Minuit)

BONELLI, LAURENT. 2010. *La France a peur: une histoire sociale de 'l'insécurité'* (Paris: La Découverte)

BOSCHETTI, ANNA. 1985. *Sartre et 'Les Temps Modernes': une entreprise intellectuelle* (Paris: Minuit)

BOUBEKER, AHMED. 2009. 'Outsiders in the French Melting Pot: The Public Construction of Invisibility for Visible Minorities', in *Frenchness and the African Diaspora: Identity and Uprising in Contemporary France*, ed. by Charles Tshimanga, Didier Gondola and Peter J. Bloom (Bloomington: Indiana University Press), pp. 70–88

BOURDIEU, PIERRE (ed.). 1998. *La Misère du monde* (Paris: Seuil/'Points')

BOURDIEU, PIERRE, and LUC BOLTANSKI. 1976. 'La Production de l'idéologie dominante', *Actes de la recherche en sciences sociales*, 2.2–3: 3–73

BOURDIEU, PIERRE, and MONIQUE DE SAINT MARTIN. 1978. 'Le Patronat', *Actes de la recherche en sciences sociales*, 20–21: 3–82

BRAUDEL, FERNAND. 1961. 'Gaston Berger (1896–1960)', *Annales: Histoire, Sciences Sociales*, 16.1: 210–11

BUCK-MORSS, SUSAN. 2000. *Dreamworld and Catastrophe: The Passing of Mass Utopia in East and West* (Cambridge, MA: MIT Press)

BUGAT, STÉPHANE. 1979. 'Caméra sur Cergy', *Cergy magazine*, 4–5: 30–33

BUSBEA, LARRY. 2007. *Topologies: The Urban Utopia in France, 1960–1970* (Cambridge, MA: MIT Press)

CANNON, JAMES. 2015. *The Paris Zone: A Cultural History* (London: Routledge)

CARDINAL, MARIE. 1976. 'Une femme dans la ville', *Cergy magazine*, 1: 32–37

CARPENTER, JULIET, and CHRISTINA HORVATH (eds). 2015. *Regards croisés sur la banlieue* (Oxford: Peter Lang)

CERTEAU, MICHEL DE. 1990. *L'Invention du quotidien*, 2 vols (Paris: Gallimard/'Folio-essais'), I (*Arts de faire*)

CHAMPAGNE, PATRICK. 1998. 'La Vision médiatique', in *La Misère du monde*, ed. by Pierre Bourdieu (Paris: Seuil/'Points'), pp. 95–123

CHATELET, GILLES, and OTHERS. 1973. *Les Équipements du pouvoir: villes, territoires et équipements collectifs* (Paris: Recherches)

CHENU, ROSALYNE. 1994. *Paul Delouvrier, ou la passion d'agir* (Paris: Seuil)

CHÉREAU, CLAUDE, CLAUDE BRÉVAN and ROUCHDY KBAIER. 2013. 'Transfert de l'aéroport de Nantes-Atlantique: rapport de la commission du dialogue', 63 pp. <https://www.vie-publique.fr/sites/default/files/rapport/pdf/134000221.pdf> [accessed 20 August 2021]

CLARKE, JACKIE. 2011. *France in the Age of Organization: Factory, Home and Nation from the 1920s to Vichy* (Oxford: Berghahn)

CLAUDIUS-PETIT, EUGÈNE. 2003. 'Pour un plan national d'aménagement du territoire', in *Les Grandes Textes de l'aménagement du territoire et de la décentralisation*, ed. by Christel Alvergne and Pierre Musso (Paris: La Documentation française), pp. 130–34

COMMENT, BERNARD (ed.). 2014. *France(s) territoire liquide* (Paris: Seuil)

CONLEY, VERENA ANDERMATT. 2012. *Spatial Ecologies: Urban Sites, State and World-Space in French Cultural Theory* (Liverpool: Liverpool University Press)

CORTÁZAR, JULIO, and CAROL DUNLOP. 1983. *Les Autonautes de la cosmoroute* (Paris: Gallimard/'Du monde entier')

CRENNER, EMMANUELLE. 1996. 'Insécurité et sentiment d'insécurité', *INSEE Première*, 501 (December): 1–4

CUPERS, KENNY. 2014. *The Social Project: Housing Postwar France* (Minneapolis: University of Minnesota Press)

DAVIS, MURIAM HALEH. 2010. 'Restaging *Mise en Valeur*: "Postwar Imperialism" and The Plan de Constantine', *Review of Middle East Studies*, 44.2: 176–86

DEBARBIEUX, BERNARD, and SYLVIE LARDON (eds). 2003. *Les Figures du projet territorial* (La Tour d'Aiges: Éditions de l'Aube/DATAR)

DECOCK, JEAN. 1988. 'Entretien avec Varda sur *Sans toit ni loi*', *The French Review*, 61.3: 377–85

DELEUZE, GILLES, and FÉLIX GUATTARI. 1972. *Capitalisme et schizophrénie 1: L'Anti-Œdipe* (Paris: Minuit)

——— 1980. *Capitalisme et schizophrénie 2: Mille plateaux* (Paris: Minuit)

DELOUVRIER, PAUL. 1967. *La Région parisienne face à son avenir* (Paris: Tendances)

——— 1989. 'Discours des ambassadeurs', in *25 ans de villes nouvelles en France*, ed. by Jean-Eudes Roullier (Paris: Economica), pp. 27–53

DEPARDON, RAYMOND. 2010. *La France de Raymond Depardon* (Paris: Seuil/Bibliothèque nationale de France)

DESPORTES, MARC. 2005. *Paysages en mouvement: transports et perceptions de l'espace, XVIIIe–XXe siècles* (Paris: Gallimard)

———, and ANTOINE PICON. 1997. *De l'espace au territoire: l'aménagement en France, XVIe–XXe siècles* (Paris: Presses de l'École nationale des ponts et chaussées)

DEVAUD, EMMANUEL. 1965. 'Le Plan français: mythe et technique', *Critique*, 214 (March), 275–84

DGRP (Délégation générale au District de la région de Paris). 1965. *Schéma directeur d'aménagement et d'urbanisme de la région de Paris* (Paris: La Documentation française)

DIKEÇ, MUSTAFA. 2007. *Badlands of the Republic: Space, Politics and Urban Policy* (Oxford: Blackwell)

DOBSON, JULIA. 2017. 'Dis-locations: Mapping the Banlieue', in *Filmurbia: Screening the Suburbs*, ed. by David Forrest, Graeme Harper and Jonathan Rayner (Basingstoke: Palgrave), pp. 29–48

DUBEDOUT, HUBERT. 1983. *Ensemble, refaire la ville* (Paris: La Documentation française)

DUBOIS, PHILIPPE. 1985. 'Vingt ans après: les projections 1985 confrontées à la réalité', *Economie et statistique*, 177: 3–10

DULONG, DELPHINE. 1997. *Moderniser la politique: aux origines de la Cinquième République* (Paris: L'Harmattan)

DURANCE, PHILIPPE. 2007. 'Genèse de la prospective territoriale' (Paris: CNAM/Lipsor) <http://www.intelliterwal.net/Documents/2007–08_Durance-Philippe_Genese-Prospective-territoriale.pdf> [accessed 30 October 2022]

DURMELAT, SYLVIE, and VINAY SWAMY (eds). 2011. *Screening Integration: Recasting Maghrebi Immigration in Contemporary France* (Lincoln: University of Nebraska Press)

EFFOSSE, SABINE. 2002. 'Entretien de Jean-Eudes Roullier', 10 July, première campagne d'archives orales 'Acteurs et mémoires de villes nouvelles' réalisée pour le compte du Programme interministériel Histoire et Evaluation des villes nouvelles

ELDEN, STUART. 2016. *Foucault's Last Decade* (Cambridge: Polity Press)

ENGRAND, LIONEL, and OLIVIER MILLOT (eds). 2015. *Cergy-Pontoise: formes et fictions d'une ville nouvelle* (Paris: Pavillon de l'Arsenal)

ENRIGHT, THERESA. 2016. *The Making of Grand Paris: Metropolitan Urbanism in the Twenty-First Century* (Cambridge, MA: MIT Press)

——2017. 'The Political Topology of Urban Uprisings', *Urban Geography*, 38.4: 557–77

ERNAUX, ANNIE. 1996. *Journal du dehors* (Paris, Gallimard/'Folio')

——2000. *La Vie extérieure* (Paris: Gallimard)

FARMER, SARAH. 2020. *Rural Inventions: The French Countryside After 1945* (Oxford: Oxford University Press)

FELSKI, RITA. 2011. 'Suspicious Minds', *Poetics Today*, 32.2: 215–34

FORSDICK, CHARLES. 2005A. *Travel in Twentieth-Century French and Francophone Cultures: The Persistence of Diversity* (Oxford: Oxford University Press)

——2005B. 'Projected Journeys: Exploring the Limits of Travel', in *The Art of the Project: Projects and Experiments in Modern French Culture*, ed. by Johnnie Gratton and Michael Sheringham (Oxford: Berghahn), pp. 51–65

FOUCAULT, MICHEL. 1976. *Histoire de la sexualité 1. La Volonté de savoir* (Paris: Gallimard/'Tel')

——1994. 'Le Jeu de Michel Foucault', in *Dits et Écrits*, 4 vols (Paris: Gallimard/'Sciences Humaines'), III (1976–79), 298–329

——2004. *Sécurité, territoire, population: cours au Collège de France, 1977–1978* (Paris: Seuil/Gallimard)

FOURASTIÉ, JEAN. 1965. *Les 40,000 heures* (Paris: Laffont-Gonthier)

——1979. *Les Trente glorieuses, ou la Révolution invisible de 1946 à 1975* (Paris: Fayard)

FOURQUET, FRANÇOIS. 1982. 'L'Accumulation du pouvoir ou le désir d'État: synthèse des recherches du Cerfi de 1970 à 1981', *Recherches*, 46: 9–85

——1993. 'L'Espace/temps de la prospective', *Espaces et sociétés*, 71: 165–87

FREDENUCCI, JEAN-CHARLES. 2003. 'L'Entregent colonial des ingénieurs des ponts et chaussées dans l'urbanisme des années 1950–1970', *Vingtième Siècle: revue d'histoire*, 79: 79–91

GAÏTI, BRIGITTE. 2002. 'Les Modernisateurs dans l'administration d'après-guerre: l'écriture d'une histoire héroïque', *Revue française d'administration publique*, 102: 295–306

GIARD, LUCE. 1990. 'Histoire d'une recherche', in Michel de Certeau, *L'Invention du quotidien*, 2 vols (Paris: Gallimard/'Folio-essais'), I, i–xxx.

GIRARDON, JEAN. 2006. *Politiques d'aménagement du territoire* (Paris: Ellipses)

GODARD, JEAN-LUC. 1971. *2 ou 3 choses que je sais d'elle: découpage intégral* (Paris: Seuil/'Points-Films')

GOZLAN, ANNIE. 1976. 'Cergy de 0 à 3 ans', *Cergy magazine*, 1: 20–21

GRAVIER, JEAN-FRANÇOIS. 1947. *Paris et le désert français* (Paris: Le Portulan)

GRIÈRE, EVELYNE, and OTHERS. 1974. 'Habiter une ville nouvelle: représentations, expressions de besoins, informations' (unpublished report for the Compagnie française d'économistes et de psychosociologues)

GRIFFIN, CHRISTOPHER. 2010. 'Major Combat Operations and Counterinsurgency Warfare: Plan Challe in Algeria, 1959–1960', *Security Studies*, 19.3: 555–89

GRITTI, JULES. 1967. 'Les Contenus culturels du *Guide bleu*: monuments et sites "à voir"', *Communications*, 10: 51–64

GROUPE 1985. 1964. *Réflexions pour 1985* (Paris: La Documentation française)

GROS, ANDRÉ. 1957. *Les Conseillers de synthèse* (Paris: Société internationale des conseillers de synthèse)

GUIADER, VINCENT. 2008. 'Socio-histoire de la prospective: la transformation d'une entreprise réformatrice en expertise d'Etat' (unpublished doctoral thesis, Université Paris-Dauphine)

GUICHARD, OLIVIER. 1965. *Aménager la France* (Paris: Laffont-Gonthier)

GUIGUENO, VINCENT. 2003. 'L'Aménagement du territoire en action', *Vingtième Siecle: Revue d'histoire*, 79: 37–41

——2008. 'Building a High-speed Society: France and the Aérotrain, 1962–1974', *Technology and Culture*, 49.1: 21–40

HAFFNER, JEANNE. 2013. *The View from Above: The Science of Social Space* (Cambridge, MA: MIT Press)

HAINGE, GREG. 2008. 'Three Non-places of Supermodernity in the History of French Cinema: 1967, 1985, 2000', *Australian Journal of French Studies*, 45.3: 197–211

HALL, PETER. 1988. *Cities of Tomorrow: An Intellectual History of Urban Planning and Design in the Twentieth Century* (Oxford: Blackwell)

HARGREAVES, ALEC G. 1995. *Immigration, 'Race' and Ethnicity in Contemporary France* (London: Routledge)

——1997. *Immigration and Identity in Beur Fiction: Voices from the North African Immigrant Community in France* (Oxford: Berg)

——2011. 'From "Ghettos" to Globalizations: Situating Maghrebi-French Filmmakers', in *Screening Integration: Recasting Maghrebi Immigration in Contemporary France*, ed. by Sylvie Durmelat and Vinay Swamy (Lincoln: University of Nebraska Press), pp. 25–40

HARVEY, DAVID. 1985. *Consciousness and the Urban Experience* (Oxford: Blackwell)

——1989. *The Condition of Postmodernity* (Oxford: Blackwell)

——2005. *A Brief History of Neoliberalism* (Oxford: Oxford University Press)

HAYWARD, SUSAN. 1990. 'Beyond the Gaze and into *femme-filmécriture*', in *French Film: Texts and Contexts*, ed. by Susan Hayward and Ginette Vincendeau (London: Routledge), pp. 285–94

——2014. 'French Noir 1947–79: From Grunge-Noir to Noir-hilism', in *International Noir*, ed. by Homer B. Pettey and R. Barton Palmer (Edinburgh: Edinburgh University Press), pp. 36–60

HECHT, GABRIELLE. 1998. *The Radiance of France: Nuclear Power and National Identity after World War II* (Cambridge, MA: MIT Press)

HEIMER, MARC. 1967. 'Paris dans 20 ans', *Paris Match*, 1 July: 41–56

HELLMAN, JOHN. 1993. *Knight-monks of Vichy France: Uriage, 1940–1945* (Montreal: McGill-Queen's University Press)

HERS, FRANÇOIS, and BERNARD LATARJET (eds). 1985. *Paysages Photographies: travaux en cours, 1984–1985* (Paris: Hazan)

——1989. *Paysages Photographies: en France les années quatre-vingt* (Paris: Hazan)

HEWITT, NICHOLAS. 1991. 'The Birth of the Glossy Magazines: The Case of *Paris Match*', in *France and the Mass Media*, ed. by Brian Rigby and Nicholas Hewitt (Basingstoke: Macmillan), pp. 111–28

HIRSCH, BERNARD. 2000. *Oublier Cergy... L'Invention d'une ville nouvelle: Cergy-Pontoise, 1965–1975* (Paris: Presses de l'École nationale des ponts et chaussées)

HIRSCH, BERNARD (ed.). 2003. *L'Aménagement de la région parisienne* (Paris: Presses de l'École nationale des ponts et chaussées)

HOLT, OLIVIA. 2014. '40 Years of Vacancy in the Eerie Paris Ghost Town of Goussainville', *Atlas Obscura*, 15 August <https://www.atlasobscura.com/articles/ghost-town-goussainvile-vieux-pays> [accessed 5 May 2021]

HOOPER, BARBARA. 1992. '"Split as the Roots": A Critique of the Philosophical and Political Sources of Modern Planning Doctrine', *Frontiers*, 8.1: 45–80

—— 1998. 'The Poem of Male Desires: Female Bodies, Modernity and "Paris, Capital of the Nineteenth Century"', in *Making the Invisible Visible: A Multicultural Planning History*, ed. by Leonie Sandercock (Berkeley: University of California Press), pp. 227–54

HORNE, ALISTAIR. 1977. *A Savage War of Peace: Algeria 1954–1962* (Basingstoke: Macmillan)

IAURP (Institut d'aménagement et d'urbanisme de la Région parisienne). 1968. *Pontoise-Cergy ville nouvelle* (Paris)

JOBARD, FABIEN. 2002. *Bavures policières? La force publique et ses usages* (Paris: La Découverte)

JOSSE, RAYMOND. 1966. 'L'École des cadres d'Uriage (1940–1942)', *Revue d'histoire de la Deuxième Guerre mondiale*, 61: 49–74

JOUSSE, THIERRY. 1995. 'Le Banlieue-film existe-t-il?', *Cahiers du Cinéma*, 492 (June): 37–39

KING, RUSSELL. 1993. 'Help Yourselves at Bertrand Blier's *Buffet froid*', *Nottingham French Studies*, 32.1: 99–108

KUISEL, RICHARD. 1981. *Capitalism and the State in Modern France* (Cambridge: Cambridge University Press)

LATOUR, BRUNO. 2005. 'From Realpolitik to Dingpolitik, or How to Make Things Public', in *Making Things Public: Atmospheres of Democracy*, ed. by Bruno Latour and Peter Weibel (Cambridge, MA: MIT Press), pp. 14–41

LE COUR GRANDMAISON, OLIVIER. 2006. 'Sur la réhabilitation du passé colonial en France', in *La Fracture coloniale: la société française au prisme de l'héritage colonial*, ed. by Pascal Blanchard, Nicolas Bancel and Sandrine Lemaire (Paris: La Découverte), pp. 125–32

LEFEBVRE, HENRI. 1970. 'Réflexions sur la politique de l'espace', *Espaces et sociétés*, 1: 3–12

—— 1974. *La Production de l'espace* (Paris: Anthropos)

LEFEBVRE, HENRI, and OTHERS. 1983. 'Henri Lefebvre répond à V. E. P.', *Villes en parallèle*, 7: 51–63

LEGG, STEPHEN. 2005. 'Contesting and Surviving Memory: Space, Nation, and Nostalgia in *Les Lieux de mémoire*', *Environment and Planning D: Society and Space*, 23: 481–504

LEVINE, ALISON J. 2008. 'Mapping *Beur* Cinema in the New Millennium', *Journal of Film and Video*, 60.3–4: 42–59

—— 2019. 'Depth of Field: Farmland and Farm Life in Contemporary French Documentary', in *France in Flux: Space, Territory and Contemporary Culture*, ed. by Ari J. Blatt and Edward Welch (Liverpool: Liverpool University Press), pp. 63–91

LIAUZU, CLAUDE, and GILLES MANCERON. 2006. *La Colonisation, la loi et l'histoire* (Paris: Syllepses)

LYOTARD, FRANÇOIS. 1979. *La Condition postmoderne: rapport sur le savoir* (Paris: Minuit)

MANCHETTE, JEAN-PATRICK. 2005. *Romans noirs* (Paris: Gallimard/'Quarto')

MARCHAIS, DOMINIQUE. 1995. 'Malik Chibane', *Les Inrockuptibles*, 22 November <https://www.lesinrocks.com/cinema/malik-chibane-99380-22-11-1995/> [accessed 27 April 2021]

MARCHAND, BERNARD. 1993. *Paris, histoire d'une ville: XIXe-XXe siècle* (Paris: Seuil/'Points')

MARGULIES, IVONE. 2014. 'The Changing Landscape and Rohmer's Temptation of Architecture', in *The Films of Éric Rohmer*, ed. by Leah Anderst (Basingstoke: Palgrave Macmillan), pp. 161–75

MARTIN, OLIVIER, and PATRICIA VANNIER. 2002. 'La Sociologie française après 1945: places et rôles des méthodes issues de la psychologie', *Revue d'Histoire des Sciences Humaines*, 6.1: 95–122

MASPERO, FRANÇOIS. 1990. *Les Passagers du Roissy-Express* (Paris: Seuil/'Points')

MASQUELIER, CHARLES. 2020. 'Theorising French Neoliberalism: The Technocratic Elite, Decentralised Collective Bargaining and France's "Passive Neoliberal Revolution"', *European Journal of Social Theory*, 24.1: 65–85

MASSÉ, PIERRE. 1965. *Le Plan, ou l'anti-hasard* (Paris: Gallimard/'Idées')

—— 1967A. 'Prévision et prospective' [1959], in *Étapes de la prospective* (Paris: Presses universitaires de France), pp. 99–131

—— 1967B. 'Les Attitudes envers l'avenir et leur influence sur le présent' [1966], in *Étapes de la prospective* (Paris: Presses universitaires de France), pp. 335–44

MAUVAISE TROUPE. 2018. *The ZAD and NoTAV: Territorial Struggles and the Making of a New Political Intelligence*, ed. and trans. by Kristin Ross (London: Verso)

MBEMBE, ACHILLE. 2005. 'La République et sa Bête: à propos des émeutes dans les banlieues de France', *Africultures*, 65: 176–81

MERLIN, PIERRE. 2002. *L'Aménagement du territoire* (Paris: Presses universitaires de France)

MET, PHILIPPE, and DEREK SCHILLING (eds). 2018. *Screening the Paris Suburbs: From the Silent Era to the 1990s* (Manchester: Manchester University Press)

MEYNAUD, HÉLÈNE. 2009. 'Actualité de Guy Palmade, pionnier en France des sciences humaines en entreprise: commentaires sur les débats de la journée du cirfip du 23 mars 2007', *Nouvelle revue de psychosociologie*, 5.1: 89–95

MILNE, ANNA-LOUISE. 2006. 'From Third-worldism to Fourth-world *Flânerie*? François Maspero's Recent Journeys', *French Studies*, 60.4: 489–502

MINCES, JULIETTE, and DOMINIQUE TRICAUD. 1989. 'Les Bavures policières sont-elles inéluctables?', *Hommes et Migrations*, 1127: 25–31

MIRIMANOFF, ANNE. 1976. 'Éditorial', *Cergy magazine*, 1: 7

MONOD, JÉRÔME, and PHILIPPE CASTELBAJAC. 2021. *L'Aménagement du territoire* (Paris: Presses universitaires de France/'Que sais-je?')

MOREL, GAËLLE. 2006. *Le Photoreportage d'auteur: l'institution culturelle de la photographie en France depuis les années 1970* (Paris: CNRS)

MORREY, DOUGLAS. 2005. 'The Noise of Thoughts: The Turbulent (Sound-)Worlds of Jean-Luc Godard', *Culture, Theory and Critique*, 46.1: 61–74

MOZÈRE, LIANE. 2004. 'Foucault et le CERFI: instantanés et actualité', *Le Portique*, 13–14: 1–10

MURARD, LIONEL, and FRANÇOIS FOURQUET (eds). 2004. *La Naissance des villes nouvelles: anatomie d'une décision (1961–1969)* (Paris: Presses de l'École nationale des ponts et chaussées)

NEWSOME, BRIAN. 2009. *French Urban Planning 1940–1968: The Construction and Deconstruction of an Authoritarian System* (Oxford: Peter Lang)

NORA, PIERRE (ed.). 1997. *Les Lieux de mémoire*, 3 vols (Paris: Gallimard/'Quarto'), I (*La République, La Nation*)

OLSON, KORY. 2018. *The Cartographic Capital: Mapping Third Republic Paris* (Liverpool: Liverpool University Press)

ORME, MARK. 2006. 'Imprisoned Freedoms: Space and Identity in *Subway* and *Nikita*', in *The Films of Luc Besson: Master of Spectacle*, ed. by Susan Hayward and Phil Powrie (Manchester: Manchester University Press), pp. 121–34

OSTROWETSKY, SYLVIA. 1983. *L'Imaginaire bâtisseur: les villes nouvelles françaises* (Paris: Librairie des Méridiens)

PAGÈS, MAX. 2008. 'Le Rôle précurseur de Guy Palmade et l'institutionnalisation de la psychosociologie', *Nouvelle revue de psychosociologie*, 5.1: 69–77

PAQUOT, THIERRY. 2019. 'Marcel Roncayolo (1926–2018): le piéton de Marseille', *Hermès*, 83: 282–87

Paris Match. 1971. *Cergy-Pontoise: naissance d'une ville*, 11 December

PASKINS, JACOB. 2016. *Paris Under Construction: Building Sites and Urban Transformation in the 1960s* (London: Routledge)

PEEPLES, JENNIFER. 2011. 'Toxic Sublime: Imaging Contaminated Landscapes', *Environmental Communication*, 5.4: 373–92

PEREC, GEORGES. 1965. *Les Choses: une histoire des années soixante* (Paris: Julliard)

—— 1982. *Tentative d'épuisement d'un lieu parisien* (Paris: Bourgois)

PERROUX, FRANÇOIS. 1962. *La Quatrième Plan française* (Paris: Presses universitaires de France/'Que sais-je?')

POISSON, CATHERINE. 2000. 'Terrain vague: *Zones* de Jean Rolin', *Nottingham French Studies*, 39.1: 17–24

POUVREAU, BENOÎT. 2003. 'La Politique d'aménagement du territoire d'Eugène Claudius-Petit', *Vingtième Siècle: revue d'histoire*, 79: 43–52

POWRIE, PHIL. 2011. 'Heterotopic Spaces and Nomadic Gazes in Varda: From *Cléo de 5 à 7* to *Les Glaneurs et la glaneuse*', *L'Esprit créateur*, 51.1: 68–82

PRASAD, MONICA. 2005. 'Why Is France So French? Culture, Institutions, and Neoliberalism, 1974–1981', *American Journal of Sociology*, 111.2: 357–407

RABINOW, PAUL. 1989. *French Modern: Norms and Forms of the Social Environment* (Chicago: University of Chicago Press)

RÉMOND, RENÉ. 2005. 'Introduction: Paul Delouvrier, un grand commis de l'État', in *Paul Delouvrier: un grand commis de l'État*, ed. by Sébastien Laurent and Jean-Eudes Roullier (Paris: Presses de Sciences Po), pp. 9–10

RICE, CHARLES, and KENNY CUPERS. 2017. 'Éric Rohmer in Cergy-Pontoise', *AA Files*, 14: 112–22

RICŒUR, PAUL. 1966. 'Prévision économique et choix éthique', *Esprit*, February, 178–93

RIDON, JEAN-XAVIER. 2000. 'Un barbare en banlieue', *Nottingham French Studies*, 39.1: 25–38

ROCHÉ, SEBASTIAN. 1993. *Le Sentiment d'insécurité en France* (Paris: Presses universitaires de France)

—— 1997. 'Citoyenneté, civilité et sécurité', *Le Monde*, 26 November <https://www.lemonde.fr/archives/article/1997/11/26/citoyennete-civilite-et-securite_3807863_1819218.html> [accessed 6 August 2021]

ROLIN, JEAN. 1995. *Zones* (Paris: Gallimard)

—— 1999. *Traverses* (Paris: Nil)

—— 2002. *La Clôture* (Paris: P.O.L.)

—— 2005. *Terminal frigo* (Paris: P.O.L.)

—— 2007. *L'Explosion de la durite* (Paris: P.O.L.)

RONCAYOLO, MARCEL. 2001. *La Ville aujourd'hui: mutations urbaines, décentralisation et crise du citadin* (Paris: Seuil/'Points')

ROSELLO, MIREILLE. 2001. *Postcolonial Hospitality: The Immigrant as Guest* (Stanford, CA: Stanford University Press)

ROSS, KRISTIN. 1995. *Fast Cars, Clean Bodies: Decolonization and the Re-ordering of French Culture* (Cambridge, MA: MIT Press)

ROTHBERG, MICHAEL. 2010. 'Between Memory and Memory: from *Lieux de mémoire* to *Nœuds de mémoire*', *Yale French Studies*, 118–19: 3–12

RUIDIAZ, ANNE-CHARLOTTE DE. 2003. 'Le Projet 3M France de Cergy-Pontoise: du "tas de rouille" à l'édifice patrimonial', *Ethnologie française*, 33: 31–39

SAINT-PIERRE, CAROLINE DE. 2002. *La Fabrication plurielle de la ville: décideurs et citadins à Cergy-Pontoise, 1990–2000* (Paris: Créaphis)

SALLOIS, JACQUES. 1985. 'Introduction', in *Paysages Photographies: travaux en cours, 1984–1985*, ed. by François Hers and Bernard Latarjet (Paris: Hazan), pp. 12–13

SANDERCOCK, LEONIE. 1998. 'Introduction: Framing Insurgent Histories for Planning', in *Making the Invisible Visible: A Multicultural Planning History*, ed. by Leonie Sandercock (Berkeley: University of California Press), pp. 1–33

—— 2003. 'Out of the Closet: The Importance of Stories and Storytelling in Planning Practice', *Planning Theory & Practice*, 4.1: 11–28

SCHILLING, DEREK. 2018. 'Screening France's New Towns After 1968', in *Screening the Paris Suburbs: From the Silent Era to the 1990s*, ed. by Phillipe Met and Derek Schilling (Manchester: Manchester University Press), pp. 170–88

SCHMID, MARION. 2015. 'Between Classicism and Modernity: Éric Rohmer on Urban Change', *French Studies*, 69.3: 345–62

SCOTT, JAMES C. 1998. *Seeing Like a State: How Certain Schemes to Improve the Human Condition Have Failed* (New Haven, CT: Yale University Press)

SEC (Société d'Étude et de Coopération). 1978. 'Vivre à Cergy-Pontoise, ville nouvelle' (unpublished report)

SHEPARD, TODD. 2006. *The Invention of Decolonization: The Algerian War and the Remaking of France* (Ithaca, NY: Cornell University Press)

SILVERMAN, MAX. 1999. *Facing Postmodernity: Contemporary French Thought on Culture and Society* (London: Routledge)

SMITH, ALISON. 1996. 'Strategies of Representation in *Sans toit ni loi*', *Nottingham French Studies*, 35.2: 84–96

SMITH, NATHANIEL. 1969. 'The Idea of the French Hexagon', *French Historical Review*, 6.2, 139–55

SOJA, EDWARD. 1989. *Postmodern Geographies: The Reassertion of Space in Critical Social Theory* (London: Verso)

SOUTOU, GEORGES-HENRI, and ALAIN BELTRAN (eds). 1995. *Pierre Guillaumat: la passion des grands projets industriels* (Paris, Institut d'histoire de l'industrie-Rive Droite)

SUDLOW, BRIAN. 2017. '*Réflexions pour 1985*: A Study in the Vernacular of Progressive Compliance', *Interventions*, 19.5: 692–705

SWAMY, VINAY. 2011. 'Repackaging the *Banlieue*: Malik Chibane's *La Trilogie urbaine*', in *Screening Integration: Recasting Maghrebi Immigration in Contemporary France*, ed. by Sylvie Durmelat and Vinay Swamy (Lincoln: University of Nebraska Press), pp. 211–27

TAI, HUE-TAM HO. 2001. 'Remembered Realms: Pierre Nora and French National Memory', *American Historical Review*, 106.3: 906–22

TARR, CARRIE. 2005. *Reframing Difference: 'Beur' and 'Banlieue' Filmmaking in France* (Manchester: Manchester University Press)

TEILHARD DE CHARDIN, PIERRE. 1955. *Le Phénomène humain* (Paris: Seuil)

—— 1959. *L'Avenir de l'homme* (Paris: Seuil)

TELLIER, THIBAULT. 2010. 'Aux origines de la politique de la ville: les opérations HVS', *Recherche Sociale*, 95: 20–38

—— 2013. ' "Ensemble, refaire la ville": l'enjeu de la citoyenneté urbaine dans les prémices de la politique de la ville (1973–1983)', *Migrances*, 41: 135–45.

—— 2014. 'L'Invention de la politique de la ville en France: la fin de l'expertise urbaine d'inspiration chrétienne?', *Chrétiens et Sociétés*, 21: 33–49

—— 2015. 'Habitat et vie sociale ou la contribution de la FORS à la naissance de la politique de la ville', *Recherche Sociale*, 214: 12–24

THÉNAULT, SYLVIE. 2007. 'L'État d'urgence (1955–2005). De l'Algérie coloniale à la France contemporaine: destin d'une loi', *Le Mouvement Social*, 218: 63–78

THŒNIG, JEAN-CLAUDE. 1987. *L'Ère des technocrates* (Paris: L'Harmattan)

THORNTON, EDWARD. 2017. 'The Rise of the Machines: Deleuze's Flight from Structuralism', *The Southern Journal of Philosophy*, 55.4: 454–74

THROGMORTON, JAMES. 1996. *Planning as Persuasive Storytelling: The Rhetorical Construction of Chicago's Electric Future* (Chicago: University of Chicago Press)

TISSOT, SYLVIE. 2007. *L'État et les quartiers: genèse d'une catégorie de l'action publique* (Paris: Seuil)

TOBIN, YANN. 1995. 'État des (ban)lieues', *Positif*, 415 (September): 28–30

TRINTIGNAC, ANDRÉ. 1964. *Aménager l'hexagone: villages, villes, régions* (Paris: Centurion)

VADELORGE, LOÏC. 2005. 'Mémoire et histoire: les villes nouvelles françaises', *Les Annales de la recherche urbaine*, 98: 7–13

—— 2014. *Retour sur les villes nouvelles: une histoire urbaine du XXe siècle* (Paris: Créaphis)

VIRILIO, PAUL. 1976. *Essai sur l'insécurité du territoire* (Paris: Stock)

—— 1977. *Vitesse et politique: essai de dromologie* (Paris: Galilée)

WAKEMAN, ROSEMARY. 2009. *The Heroic City: Paris 1945–1958* (Chicago: University of Chicago Press)

—— 2016. *Practicing Utopia: An Intellectual History of the New Town Movement* (Chicago: University of Chicago Press)

WEBER, EUGEN. 1997. 'L'Hexagone', in *Les Lieux de mémoire*, ed. by Pierre Nora, 3 vols (Paris: Gallimard/'Quarto'), I (*La République, La Nation*), 1171–90

WELCH, EDWARD. 2005. 'Experimenting with Identity: People, Place and Urban Change in Contemporary French Photography', in *The Art of the Project: Projects and Experiments in Modern French Culture*, ed. by Johnnie Gratton and Michael Sheringham (Oxford: Berghahn), pp. 156–71

—— 2018. 'Objects of Dispute: Planning, Discourse, and State Power in Post-war France', *French Politics, Culture & Society*, 36.2: 103–25

—— 2019. 'Angels of History: Looking Back at Spatial Planning in the Mission photographique de la DATAR', in *France in Flux: Space, Territory and Contemporary Culture*, ed. by Ari J. Blatt and Edward Welch (Liverpool: Liverpool University Press), pp. 13–34

—— 2020. '"*Match* nous a raconté une histoire": Thinking with Roland Barthes about Photography, Publics and the Exercise of Power in Post-war France', in *Photography and Its Publics*, ed. by Melissa Miles and Edward Welch (London: Bloomsbury), pp. 63–77

—— 2021. 'Build the Imaginary: Urban Futures and New Towns in Post-war French Spatial Planning', *Journal of Urban Cultural Studies*, 8.2: 167–86

WINOCK, MICHEL. 1999. *Le Siècle des intellectuels* (Paris: Seuil/'Points')

WOMBELL, PAUL. 2014. 'Des territoires liquides', in *La Mission photographique de la DATAR: nouvelles perspectives critiques*, ed. by Marie-Caroline Bonnet-Galzy (Paris: La Documentation française), pp. 145–57

—— [N.D.]. 'FTL par Paul Wombell' <http://www.francesterritoireliquide.fr/ftl-par-paul-wombell.html> [accessed 6 August 2021]

Filmography

Alphaville, dir. by Jean-Luc Godard (Athos Films, 1965)

L'Ami de mon amie, dir. by Éric Rohmer (Les Films du Losange, 1987)

Buffet froid, dir. by Bertrand Blier (Sara Films/Antenne 2, 1979)

Le Cercle rouge, dir. by Jean-Pierre Melville (Les Films Corona/Selenia, 1970)

Le Couple témoin, dir. by William Klein (Artco-Films, 1977)

2 ou 3 choses que je sais d'elle, dir. by Jean-Luc Godard (Argos Films, 1967)

Enfance d'une ville, dir. by Éric Rohmer (ORTF, 1975)

La Haine, dir. by Mathieu Kassovitz (Les Productions Lazennec, 1995)

Le Havre, dir. by Aki Kaurismäki (Pandora/Pyramide Productions/Sputnik, 2011)

Hexagone, dir. by Malik Chibane (Alhambra, 1994)

I... comme Icare, dir. by Henri Verneuil (Antenne 2/V Films, 1979)

Les Liaisons moins dangereuses (Ministère de l'Équipement et de l'Aménagement du Territoire, 1972)

Métamorphoses du paysage, dir. by Éric Rohmer (Institut pédagogique national, 1964)

Naissance des pieuvres, dir. by Céline Sciamma (Lilies Films, 2007)

Sans toit ni loi, dir. by Agnès Varda (Ciné Tamaris/Antenne 2, 1985)

Série noire, dir. by Alain Corneau (Prospectacle/Gaumont, 1979)

Subway, dir. by Luc Besson (Les Films du Loup/Gaumont, 1985)

Trente hectares de bonne terre, dir. by Jean-Pierre Gallo (France Régions 3, 1981)

37,2 degrés le matin, dir. by Jean-Jacques Beineix (Cargo Films, 1986)

INDEX

❖

www.ingramcontent.com/pod-product-compliance
Lightning Source LLC
Chambersburg PA
CBHW080542090426
42734CB00016B/3178